Withdrawn
Outdated Material

BEST ENTRY-LEVEL JOBS

The Princeton Review

BEST ENTRY-LEVEL JOBS

RON LIEBER AND TOM MELTZER

Random House, Inc.
New York
www.PrincetonReview.com

Princeton Review Publishing, L. L. C.
2315 Broadway
New York, NY 10024
Email: bookeditor@review.com

ISBN 0-375-76414-3
ISSN 1017-1381

Editorial Director: Robert Franek
Editors: Erik Olson and Spencer Foxworth
Designer: Scott Harris
Production Editor: Vivian Gomez
Production Coordinator: Scott Harris

Manufactured in the United States of America.

9 8 7 6 5 4 3 2 1

ACKNOWLEDGMENTS

I had three first jobs. My day job was writing for *Lawyers Weekly USA*. At night and on weekends, I was a stringer for the Associated Press (turn to page 44 to read why it's valuable training for aspiring reporters). The third job was writing *Taking Time Off* with Colin Hall, who's still my all-time favorite coworker.

Taking Time Off would not have endured without the team at The Princeton Review. I remain indebted to John Katzman for hooking me up with Rob Franek and Erik Olson. They're not only accomplished idea men but also were exceptionally flexible coconspirators. I'm also grateful to Jeanne Krier, who makes publicity magic wherever she goes, and Tom Russell at Random House, for agreeing to take on both this book and *Taking Time Off*. Meanwhile, much of the credit for this particular enterprise ought to go to Tom Meltzer and Spencer Foxworth, who did almost all of the heavy lifting throughout this process.

The idea for this book came to me in 1998, as my brother, David, and sister, Stephanie, were trying to make the best out of their first jobs. I tried to exorcise their particular demons in the form of a 1999 story for *Fast Company*. I'm grateful to Bill Taylor and Alan Webber for providing that forum. Although I'm not on the career beat full-time anymore, I'm so much better at everything I do thanks to intensive attention from the likes of Edward Felsenthal, Jesse Pesta, Neal Templin, and Eben Shapiro at the *Wall Street Journal*.

Finally, thanks go out to Liebers, Bramsons, Krimstons, and Kantors everywhere. Jodi, as much as I've tried (and failed) to cut down on the number of jobs I've taken on over the years, this new husband gig suits me pretty well, I think. I can't wait to see what new projects spring from it.

—Ron Lieber

I would like to thank my editors, Erik Olson and Spencer Foxworth, my coauthor, Ron, and of course my wife, Lisa.

—Tom Meltzer

CONTENTS

INTRODUCTION

SO WHAT DO YOU WANT TO BE WHEN YOU GROW UP?

If you're about to graduate from college, the best way to answer this question is also the most honest one: I don't know because I'm not a grown-up yet.

Somewhere along the way, people got it into their heads that 22-year-olds should finish school with a clear idea of what they want to do for a living. And nowadays, most parents are worried sick if their children graduate and don't immediately find jobs, find jobs that aren't lucrative, or find jobs that don't sound impressive when they tell other parents about them at cocktail parties.

But how on earth can you possibly know what you want to do with your life when all you've ever done is go to school? Sure, summer jobs help. Internships give you a sense of what the real world is like. But the vast majority of internships aren't substantive and don't last long enough to give you a true feel of what it would be like to work for that company or in that industry for years, decades, or through to retirement.

And consider this: In all likelihood, your first job will have little to do with your last job. Taking a job is not an irreversible trip down a one-way career path. In fact, for many 22-year-olds, the function of a first job is merely to help them figure out what they don't want to do. It's an experiment, almost like picking a major, but in some ways less important. After all, you have much longer than four years to figure out what you want to be when you grow up.

Now, about being a grown-up. You hear the word "adolescent" thrown around a lot when you're in high school. But most specialists in human development believe that adolescence extends long past the time when you're done growing into your own body. You're not truly a grown-up until you're done growing into your own head. And that can't possibly happen until you've been on your own for a while, living in your own place, fending for yourself financially, and working for a living.

So we've established that you have every reason in the world not to know what you want to be when you grow up when you're only 22 years old. It turns out that college curriculum designers understand this. Many college graduates wrap up their undergraduate educations each year having majored in English, history, economics, and other courses of study that point to no obvious single first job. This is a perfectly good thing for students because they should be looking to shape their minds and not trying to scribble the first draft of their resumes during their college years. Trade school can come later; after all, that's all law school and medical school really are—just fancier-sounding forms of trade school.

But for all of the college seniors who haven't gotten into medical school and don't have a spot waiting for them in the family business, the impending graduation date is a paralyzing black mark on their calendars. Being clueless as to what you want to do is perfectly fine. In fact, we're more likely to be worried about people who think they know exactly what they want than about people who have no idea at all. There should probably be half the number of law schools there are today, given that half of all lawyers end up leaving law or wishing that they could but can't because they have saddled themselves with enormous student loans. Certainly, no law schools should be letting 22-year-olds anywhere near their classrooms without having them work in close proximity to lawyers for a few years to see what it's actually like.

There is a big difference, however, in not knowing what you want to do and having nothing to do at all. This is the fate that befell many college seniors during the economic doldrums of 2001 to 2003. Unemployed college graduates living at home with their families have become cliché by now.

Who's responsible for this development? It's easy enough to point the finger at vague economic forces larger than all of us. After all, unemployment grew much higher in the first few years of this century than it had in the latter part of the 1990s. The burden of resposibility, however, falls on the politicians who cut the budgets that led tuition at state universities to rise at a rate much higher than that of inflation. As a result, people left school—with and without degrees—in increasing numbers with five-figure student loan debts. Not even the most lucrative entry-level jobs will support servicing that debt while you are simultaneously paying rent on a first apartment. And if you don't have a four-year degree, good luck finding a job.

Still, there were jobs out there, even though the usual suspects who show up on college campuses to recruit each year weren't hiring as many people as they normally do. Students just had to figure out what industries the remaining jobs were in and what companies were still growing enough to take in entry-level hires. Many students think it's the college career office's job to present these opportunities to them on a silver platter and simply allow them to select. When the selection is limited, these students throw up their hands and say that the career counselors can't help anyone who doesn't want to work for a big company.

These criticisms are mostly unfair. Like everyone else at universities (including students who sometimes struggle to get into the classes they need to graduate on time), the career placement office is stretched thin. It only makes sense for the advisors to spend the most amount of time courting the smallest number of companies that can hire the largest number of graduates. Anything else is inefficient. The best most offices can do is provide a bookshelf full of do-it-yourself guides for people interested in smaller companies or underpublicized industries and a list of faculty members who are well-connected in specific fields. Another valuable and horribly underutilized resource they offer is a list and the contact information of alumni in various lines of work or a back issue of alumni magazines so students can read up on who's doing what where.

At the end of the day, it is you who is responsible for finding your way into the world, which is as it should be. Through absolutely no fault of your own, however, you probably lack some sense about what's possible beyond what older friends and parents' friends do all day. Even if you treat your trips to the career placement office as if it were an academic course, you still may not find the real-world stories and nitty-gritty details that tell you where the best first jobs are and, more importantly, what makes a first job great.

So that's where we come in. Some time ago, we came to the sad conclusion that most first jobs actually aren't very good and usually aren't fulfilling by design. The idea of the first job as a right of passage is nothing new. In the old days, you had to apprentice yourself to a tradesman and work free in return for an education in how to perform a set of tasks. Needless to say, the most grueling and menial tasks always fell to the apprentice.

In fact, a similar form of indentured servitude still exists today, except the ending isn't always nearly as happy. In academia, for instance, graduate students often teach the large survey courses that offer little stimulation for instructors. In return, they get a below-poverty-level wage and the opportunity to study for their PhD in between teaching classes. This goes on for six or seven years, and then these graduate students discover that the professor jobs they've been gunning for all along have hundreds of applicants for each available position.

Another example of indentured servitude is entry-level work in medicine. It's been determined that the best way to turn medical school graduates with six figures of student loan debt into doctors is to have them stay up all night working in hospitals for a tiny bit more than minimum wage. In the medical field, there are jobs for most of the people who want them. But when practicing medicine these days, individuals feel constantly compromised by limits imposed by insurance companies, harassed by know-it-all patients, or ignored by patients who disappear after seeing them a few times. The job has become more like any other job, which makes many people wonder whether it's worth all of the pain and suffering.

Run-of-the-mill first jobs for 22-year-olds in private companies, government offices, or nonprofit organizations aren't lousy in such dramatic ways. But in some respects, their unpleasantness is that much more annoying because it seems as if it could be so easy to make them better.

So most first jobs are built around a philosophy of making workers pay their dues. This isn't bad in theory. Materials must be procured, goods must be counted, numbers must be crunched, facts must be checked, and research must be compiled. There are plenty of mind-numbing details within each of these tasks that are nevertheless vital to the functioning of any organization. During your first year, your mind may be numb most of the time. But it's important to know where the details come from. The problems start when you don't get to see the impact of those details. All too often in first jobs, you don't get to play a role in creating the report that contains your work, go to the meeting where it's discussed, or meet with the customer who ends up using it. Your work has no sense of context.

Consider this, too: Bruce Tulgan, the preeminent consultant to companies who want to figure out how to best treat younger workers, notes that the whole culture of paying dues is partly based on the idea that there's a club you get to join once you're done shelling out. A generation or so ago, that club was the job-for-life club—the one where you worked for forty years at one company and got a gold watch and a great pension at the end.

But nowadays few people want to work at the same company for their entire career. Any number of conditions keeps this from happening: their closest colleagues move on, their spouse gets a job elsewhere, they get a new boss, they want to change careers, or a recruiter comes after them with a great offer. Many potential employers are suspicious of people who stay in one place too long. (Do they lack ambition? Can they hack it outside the warm embrace of their current position? Have they gone soft after so many years?) New management that shows up at your place of work may also be suspicious of you if you were part of the old regime for too long. And there's the possibility that you'll eventually be laid off if you stick around one place for several decades.

The point of all this is only to state what's now plainly obvious to employees but never seems to get through to employers: What's the point of making people pay their dues if there isn't any club for them to join? A lousy first year or two in the workplace shouldn't be the price of admission for people who simply want to earn a living. All that's certain these days is that you, your boss, and your company are likely to be around for the next year or so. Beyond that, who can say? So in that time, you ought to have a right to come watch a few meetings, go to a conference, meet a few customers, tag along with your boss on a business trip, learn how to sell something, or learn how to create an Excel spreadsheet. Getting left in a silo somewhere to do the same thing every day is unacceptable, yet it happens to 22-year-olds all the time. If you're the kind of person who does his or her homework before taking any risks—and you are if you are reading this book—you deserve better.

The irony here is that all of us are told we're on top of the world when we graduate, only to find that we've hit rock bottom on our first day of work. Even good first jobs rarely offer the same stimulation and sense of camaraderie that college did. And colleges just make things worse by throwing lavish graduation ceremonies that raise expectation levels to unreasonable heights. "Extremely sobering" is how Richard D. Thau, author of *Get It Together by 30: And Be Set for the Rest of Your Life,* described his first job-hunting experience after graduating from Haverford College: "On Sunday, the commencement speaker said I was one of the smartest people in America. Then, on Monday, I had to take a typing test."

Seeing the pure absurdity of this, a growing number of college graduates in the 1990s finished school and then "dropped out." Having seen their parents get fired or come home (after dinner was already over) exhausted from the effort necessary to merely survive in the workplace, they opted not to go to work for large companies. Instead of paying their dues for somebody else, they made up their own jobs by starting their own companies. These days, this movement is dismissed with a wave of a hand since most purported career experts assume that most of this start-up wave was made up of get-rich-quick Internet scam artists who ended up out of business within a few years.

It's true that the initial Web boom was fueled by people in their twenties, like the founders of Yahoo! and Netscape, since they were often the only ones with the combination of ideas, technical know-how, and courage to take advantage of an entirely new medium. But once ambitious people in their thirties on Wall Street started to take interest, greedy people in their forties and fifties started piling in as well, and the opportunities couldn't keep up with the expectations that anybody who wanted to could make a million bucks off the Internet. People in their twenties had little to do with those expectations, except for the fact that many of them happened to be wildly successful early on.

Now that we're done with that brief defense of young Internet entrepreneurs, we should note that the desire to start and run companies is only getting stronger among people who have recently graduated from college. In addition to the fact that young people are dissatisfied with old ways of entering the workforce, they can't help but notice that there are plenty of others like them with very little experience who've created successful businesses that have nothing to do with the Internet. Nantucket Nectars, Magnetic Poetry, Chipotle Mexican Grill, and Kate Spade are just a few of the household names that grew from the scratched-out business plans of people who now serve as role models for scores of students who want to create similar ventures. When the power of youth is unleashed, the results are tantalizing.

Consider this sobering observation that comes from Glen T. Meakem, one such Internet entrepreneur who is also a Gulf War veteran: "We've won two wars while the current crop of graduates was in college. Both of those were won by platoons of 18- to 22-year-olds on the ground being led by commanders who were often just a few years older. If we're capable of defending our country, isn't it insulting that we're shunted as a matter of course in most corporations to some isolated corner to do grunt work for a few years?"

It's ridiculous, of course, but nobody said you had to go work for the companies that treat young people this way, either. You may have noticed by now that we haven't yet mentioned the name of a single good place to work. That's because in some ways, making sure the building blocks of a great first job are present in any position is just as important as who the company is that offers it and what the company does. So it's crucial to understand the current you're fighting against first: the tendency of most entry-level jobs to revert to mediocrity or worse.

Therefore, before we start naming the employers who actually get it, we'd like to isolate all of the different ways in which many employers fail their entry-level hires. We're doing this for a couple of reasons. First, we hope that employers will read this book, too, and that some of them will get the hint that they're just not cutting it. But we also want you to use this list as an evaluation guide. Some of these things may be crucial for you depending on what you want to do, while others could be irrelevant for any number of reasons. For instance, advancement doesn't matter much for most investment bank analysts, since relatively few of them stay longer than two or three years at one place. And if you don't have any student loans, salary may not be that important if you're working for Newell Rubbermaid, since you're likely to be stationed in areas where the cost of living is relatively low. They better have a good expense reimbursement system, however, if you're going to be driving to stores all of the time. Still, if you're lucky enough to get a few job offers, you'll want to at least consider your opportunities and the people and places they're coming from by using many of the following standards:

- Are you entering a program or merely taking on a job? Many big companies have turned the first job into something resembling a degree-granting institution. There's an admissions committee, fellow class members, course work, a dean who keeps track of all the new arrivals, and other such accoutrements. You may like structure like this, or you may find it stifling. Washington Mutual's PACE Program and GE's Corporate Leadership Development Programs, for example, prepare new hires for the challenges ahead with tons of formal training.

- Will you be doing work that makes you excited or makes other people excited when they hear that you're doing it? As a general rule, you have to like what you're doing all day if you expect to be truly successful. How will it sound when you explain it to others? Will you be proud of what you do? Occasionally, you may pull weeks of late nights because you know it will be worth it once a particular project gets done; you'll be able to say you worked on something so cool even though you may not have gotten paid. Entry-level positions with the League of American Theatres and Producers, the Peace Corps, and NPR may fall into this category for you.

- How much responsibility will you have? Some companies don't let 22-year-olds near the big customers—or even the boss's boss. Will they trust you to take trips on your own or to send emails without having them vetted? One of the best feelings of all as a young person in the workforce is to feel that you have a little piece of the business that belongs to you—a set of results that you're responsible for and actually have some control over. Will they trust you with something like this? They should. Teach for America, Newell Rubbermaid, and Boston Beer have entry-level positions that grant first jobbers an enormous amount of independence and shoulder them with a great deal of responsibility.

- Who will your mentors be? This is a tricky one, since you can't always figure this out in advance. In many companies, they'll try to assign someone to look after you before you even arrive. While the thought is nice, these relationships can sometimes feel forced. It's probably better for you to forge these relationships on your own after you arrive by approaching people who have something in common with you (say, an alma mater) or are in a part of the organization where you'd like to be someday. While evaluating potential jobs, it's important to find out whether everyone who's already in an entry-level position has someone like this. As you'll note in their profiles, Ogilvy and KPMG both value mentor/coach relationships.

- How will you get your feedback? Who will you get it from and how often? Are the bosses themselves evaluated on the basis of how well they give feedback to the people who work for them? The feedback process is a bit like being graded in college in that there will probably be some grading system to give you a sense of where you stand in comparison with your colleagues and against the expectations they have for you. Good feedback is given more than once a year. It happens every day or as often as possible, either on schedule or on demand, and it's thorough enough to cover every aspect of what you do and how you do it. Newbies at Katz Media and Wells Fargo learn as much (or more) through feedback from their seniors as they do through formalized training.

- How good are the bosses? How well they give feedback is only one small part of what makes them effective. Are these people who have volunteered to help younger people along, or are they doing it because they have to? Once you enter the workforce, you'll probably recognize the unique psychological makeup of an entry-level employee in yourself. You have super-high expectations for this first job that you've been preparing for all of your life. You don't want to be disappointed. Yet in many ways, you have no earthly idea what you're doing or supposed to be doing. Who's signed up for the privilege of keeping track of you and why? Did they start at this company themselves? Goldman Sachs' Big Buddy program, for example, pairs a new analyst with an experienced associate who helps him or her negotiate the new, sometimes alien, landscape that a high pressure workplace presents to a new college graduate.

- Who will your peers be? How many people tend to get hired each year, and where do they come from? Is it like college all over again, with happy hours and weekend get-togethers? Or is it not a particularly social enterprise? These are crucial and often overlooked questions for recent graduates, since it can be extremely difficult to move to a new city without knowing anyone. So what does the company do to ease the transition? Once you've started, these people will become your colleagues, and if you stay at the organization or in that line of work, they'll become your network. So what kind of people does the place draw? Will you fit in? In Newell Rubbermaid's Phoenix Program it won't matter; you won't see your peers on a day-to-day basis once you've completed your initial training since you're out on the road. And if you don't like happy hours, figuring out how to build a network at Booz Allen Hamilton is going to take some creative thinking.

- How much will you learn about how the company works? Some of the worst organizations put people like you to work without ever bothering to explain to you what they do and how it all happens. Other good organizations take weeks to teach you everything. Entry-level jobs like those in Home Depot's Business Leadership Program teach you the different aspects of how the total enterprise functions before you finally settle into one position within the business. This is to acknowledge an obvious fact that most first jobbers ignore: Most people graduate from college and have no idea whether they belong in sales or marketing or whether they best function as an editor or a Web developer. You wouldn't buy a car without test driving it first, so why do so many places make 22-year-olds pick their very first job without showing them what it's like?

- Some of the best companies to work for will continue to give you exposure outside of your own area. This may happen through weekly lunch meetings for first jobbers where different executives talk about what their group does or through field trips to see other teams in action. If this sort of thing doesn't seem to go on at a place you're thinking about working for, ask if you can put it together yourself. That shows initiative and curiosity, two traits all hiring managers look for. Members of the Green Corps spend two months out on their own in the field organizing campaigns and events, but every two months or so, corps members come together to debrief each other on their most recent events, get more training, and prepare for their next campaigns out in the field.

- How much money do you want to make? How much money do you need to make? These are two different, but equally important, questions. There's no shame in wanting to make a lot of money as fast as possible. If you're a trader or a really good salesman, you can make a lot of money fast (and lose it just as fast as you make it). Moreover, big bucks often require long hours, which lead to those supposedly high-paying jobs that actually pay less per hour than other jobs where the annual salary is much lower. Engineers do well, as you'll see in the profiles for Raytheon and Schlumberger; bankers also do well, as the numbers for Goldman Sachs show. However, one job requires you to be out on an oil rig far from friends and family, while the other job will keep you in the office until past midnight on some nights. Are you prepared to give up weeknights out and weekends away to make your desired salary? For many, it's the "need to make" part they have to reckon with before facing down their inner materialists. Though interest rates are still low, the average student loan balance just keeps going up, so you may be facing a payment of several hundred dollars a month. Combine that with a job in a low-paying creative industry in a big expensive city, and you could be looking at an impossible financial situation. Will your family help you out the first year? You should be calculating your loan payments and talking to your family before you even begin to look for work. Places like Random House don't pay starting salaries commensurate with big technology companies and investment banks; but if you stick around for a while and show some aptitude for and commitment to the publishing industry and score a few big wins, you could become one of those legendary publishers in a corner office working with the great authors of our age. Know this before you sign on.

- Perks are out there. Northrop Grumman offers employees pet insurance, Electronic Arts gives its video gaming geeks $100 toward a gaming console, and the League of American Theatres and Producers gives the president's assistant free tickets to just about every show on (and off) Broadway. While you may not be worried about child care benefits and health care right now, you should pay careful attention to the retirement plan, which may seem like it should be the last thing on your mind. The fact is, the more you put away in your first couple of years on the job, the better off you'll be at age sixty-five. That's because the sooner you set money aside, the more time it has to earn interest. If you care at all about retiring comfortably, do not scrimp on this now. And ask tough questions of some of the companies that don't let you participate in their 401(k) plans right away and instead make you wait a year before putting money aside. What kind of welcome message does that send?

- Advancement. You may not want to stick around for a long time at a company. Some entry-level workers at Deloitte want to get a few years of experience and then leave to work for a client company or to go back to business school. Then again, you may be like those rare people who like their entry-level jobs so much they won't want to leave for a long time. In that case, talk to people who started working straight out of college and have been at the same company for years. Have there been enough opportunities for change and advancement to keep them interested and engaged? It's good to keep in mind that the chairman and chief executive officer of Caterpillar started as an entry-level trainee with the company more than thirty years ago; today, he runs an enterprise valued at more than $26 billion.

- Industry leaders: Many organizations have reputations as not only great places to work but also as great places to have worked for. In many respects, it's like having gone to a really good college. Not having gone there won't shut you out from later success in life, but it'll be easier to get your foot in the door if you're coming from the right place. If you want to build a career as an accountant, for example, experience with KPMG is simply going to get you further than experience with a smaller, lesser-known firm. Try to figure out where alumni of the first jobs you're considering end up. If it's a program that ends after two years, where did last year's "graduates" go next? What kinds of jobs did they get? What graduate schools did they get into?

We had few rules for choosing the jobs that we feature in this book. There were no minimum salaries or geographical requirements or quotas. Our goal was to profile jobs both in the for-profit and nonprofit sectors and across numerous industries. We wanted to find places where people were happy, engaged with their work, nicely compensated, well positioned for advancement, getting great preparation for graduate school, doing really interesting stuff, or any combination of these things. To profile these organizations, we interviewed not only their official representatives, but also, and more importantly, hundreds of the people who were currently holding (or formerly held) the positions we describe. They're the ones who know best what having one of these jobs is like, so we contacted as many of them as we could. In a few cases, the organizations themselves refused to help us contact their workers, but through other means we were able to contact and interview a sufficient number of their entry-level employees to write accurate and balanced profiles of their jobs.

We consider this list a beginning. We plan to do another edition of this book soon, in which we'll add new companies and drop any jobs where the quality of the experience has declined. You may have worked at a place you think is even better than the places we've profiled here. If so, drop us a line at bookeditor@review.com and let us know about it.

How This Book Is Organized

The main body of this book is separated into two sections: "Jobs Within Organizations" and "Jobs Without Organizations." The primary difference is that jobs in the former (and larger) chapter are offered by specific companies or nonprofit organizations, while jobs in the latter section are either widely available at many companies and organizations or freelance/independent in nature. The jobs in the first chapter appear in alphabetical order according to the name of the company or nonprofit organization. The jobs in the second chapter appear in alphabetical order according to the job title.

Each of the jobs listed in this book has its own profile. To make it easier to find information about the jobs in which you are interested, we have used the same format for each job.

At the beginning of each profile is the name of the organization, followed by the name of the position(s) or program(s) described. (For the jobs in the "Jobs Without Organizations" chapter, the name of an organization will obviously not appear.) The body of the profile comprises ten possible fields of information. Not every field will appear for every job, as the information driving that field may not have been reported to us, or the information may not be applicable to a particular job. Some companies and nonprofits, for example, do not have data on how many entry-level employees are still with the company after three, five, and ten years simply because they haven't been operating for that long; therefore, that field would not appear. In a profile that has complete information, however, you can expect to see the following:

THE BIG PICTURE

This is a short description of what the company or nonprofit organization does, and, if appropriate, how entry-level employees fit into the picture.

STATS

This section is a snapshot of the facts that most job seekers want to know right away: where the job is located; how many applications are received each year and the number of job openings; the titles of the available position(s) and the average number of hours currently worked each week by the people holding these positions; the percentage of entry-level hires that are still with the company after three, five, and ten years; the average starting salaries; medical and additional benefits offered; and contact information for those interested in applying for the job(s) or seeking additional information.

GETTING HIRED

Some organizations recruit on college campuses, and other organizations don't. Some only recruit new hires from select colleges with certain undergraduate majors, while others are looking for people with specific internship or cooperative work experience. Some will only want to interview you over the phone, and others will want to fly you to their headquarters for an entire battery of interviews and may ask you to take a test to boot. This is the admissions process for the organization, and as with colleges and graduate schools, it's different for every place. Compiled using information provided by employees and the organizations themselves, this is where you will learn what you need to know about a company or nonprofit when you're trying to land the job.

MONEY AND PERKS

Let's face it, remuneration is at the top of most every worker's mind, young *and* old. Some jobs offer low salaries, while others offer low salaries with the possibility of making much more in overtime hours. Jobs in finance and a few other industries often offer good salaries and the possibility of large bonuses, but these very same jobs also usually require employees to put in very long hours. Perks are the things that improve the quality of life, or at least make life a little easier, at no cost (or a reduced cost) to the employee. Some jobs offer laundry lists of perks, while other jobs offer none. Some of the most popular perks include 401(k) or similar retirement savings plans, paid time off, and flexible spending accounts (in which you get to use pre-tax dollars to pay for things like transportation and uncovered medical expenses). Additional perks may include gym memberships, tuition reimbursements, and matching donations to charitable causes.

THE ROPES

No matter where you go to work, you will receive training, whether it's an hour or two spent with a human resources representative talking about benefits and company policies or weeks of off-site classes on the different software technologies in which you will have to become an expert. In this section we explain the structure and length of the training you can expect to receive before you actually get to start doing real work.

DAY IN THE LIFE

Once properly trained, employees are expected to work. Here, mostly in their own words, is what first jobbers do all day.

PEERS

What are the people in the position or program like? Are they similar to you in age, gender, or background? Do entry-level workers form close friendships with one another, or are they pretty much on their own because the employees with who they spend most of their time are a little older? Is there a big after-hours social scene, or do people keep to themselves? Does the company do anything, such as sponsor corporate sports teams, to encourage fraternizing? This is where you'll find answers to all these questions.

Moving on

When people have sucked all they can out of a given entry-level position, what do they do next? Do they head to graduate school, get promoted into positions of greater responsibility within the organization, leave for more lucrative or better positions within the same industry, or strike out in completely different lines of work? Many people don't think about what comes after an entry-level job, but they should. This section tries to answer these questions and get you thinking about what your long-term plans might include.

Attrition

We asked employers how many entry-level employees leave their organizations within a year of being hired. In some cases we've provided actual percentages, and in most we've provided an explanation of *why* people depart their jobs so early in their tenure.

Best and Worst

We asked employers to tell us who their best and worst entry-level employees were. Some responded with general descriptions of what makes a good or bad employee, while others gave us specific cases. For the jobs in the "Jobs Without Organizations" chapter, the best and worst employees descriptions were based on our own research and opinions.

Jobs Within Organizations

ABBOTT LABORATORIES
Professional Development Program

THE BIG PICTURE

Global health care company Abbott Laboratories is "devoted to the discovery, development, manufacture, and marketing of pharmaceuticals, nutritionals, and medical products, including devices and diagnostics." Abbott offers a wide assortment of entry-level jobs, including positions in science, information technology, finance/accounting, engineering, and sales and marketing. Many employees enter the company through its rotational Professional Development Program; this allows them to get industry experience in a number of areas before deciding which one best suits their interests and talents.

STATS

LOCATION(S) WHERE ENTRY-LEVEL EMPLOYEES WORK

"Entry-level employees work at Abbott's corporate headquarters in Lake County, Illinois, and at most of Abbott's domestic and international sites."

AVERAGE NUMBER OF APPLICATIONS EACH YEAR

About 125,000 applications are received each year. There is no specific figure available for entry-level positions.

AVERAGE NUMBER HIRED OVER THE LAST TEN YEARS

"More than 5,000 new hires have come on board directly out of college over the last ten years."

ENTRY-LEVEL POSITION(S) AVAILABLE

"They can be grouped into functional areas, including information technology, engineering, finance, science, sales and marketing, and corporate administration (i.e., groups like human resources, public affairs, and purchasing). Specialized opportunities in quality, environmental health, and purchasing also exist."

AVERAGE HOURS WORKED PER WEEK

"Employees work around forty to fifty hours per week."

PERCENTAGE OF ENTRY-LEVEL HIRES STILL WITH THE COMPANY AFTER THREE, FIVE, AND TEN YEARS

90 percent, 85 percent, and 75 percent, respectively. "Abbott has an 84 percent conversion rate for the Professional Development Program, [and] Abbott's voluntary turnover is just 8 percent."

Average Starting Salary

"It is hard to generalize. We have so many hires per year. Abbott is known to have a competitive salary within the top quartile of the industry for base pay and benefits packages. The average base pay for the Professional Development Program is determined by approximating the median in the external market with total cash compensation exceeding this amount when the company performs well."

Benefits Offered

"Every employee starts with three weeks [of] paid vacation, plus medical, dental, disability, pension plan, 401(k), and profit sharing. *Money* magazine rated Abbott number three nationally in their 'Best Benefits' ranking earlier this year [2002]."

Contact Information

Visit the career center at www.abbott.com.

Getting Hired

If you want to apply for a job at Abbott Laboratories, you must do so through their website. "Post your resume [for a] job of interest; recruiters who have open jobs go through our files every day and fill over 90 percent of [available] jobs through Internet postings. This is the main intake point for Abbott." The company also recruits on campus, targeting "top science schools including University of Wisconsin at Madison, Northwestern, University of Illinois at Urbana-Champaign, University of Chicago, and Purdue. [Abbott] also [has] alumni networks working for [them]; for example, the University of Illinois [at Urbana-Champaign] produces forty entry-level hires per year, many of them referred by the 1,100 alumni working at Abbott." One entry-level employee says, "[Interviews are] mostly behavioral-based, and the tone is very relaxed. I was able to ask a lot of questions about the interviewers' career paths and current jobs at Abbott." In all the interview sessions, "Abbott's core competencies (adaptability, initiative, innovation, integrity, and teamwork) were stressed and questions were geared to getting candidates [who] showed aptitude in those areas."

Money and Perks

The Professional Development Programs are rotational, and to be equitable to all participants, all first jobbers start out making the same money as their peers, so "starting salary is not very negotiable." Program participants want you to know, however, that "entry-level salaries are competitive" within the industry and that "Abbott is a meritocracy. High-performing people get ahead quickly here" and earn solid raises in the process. Workers enjoy "a ton of special perks," including "flexible work scheduling, telecommuting, 100 percent tuition reimbursement, a relocation package, a sports and activities program [with] 8,000 employees in leagues and clubs [who] meet outside the workplace, a mentoring program, an employee assistance program, and the Clara Abbott Foundation (scholarship program)."

THE ROPES

The specific training Abbott's entry-level employees receive is relevant to their positions. Recalls one first jobber in information technology, "I started with our Diagnostics division, which has a dedicated training coordinator for each department. Through her, I was able to complete the training requirements (document reviews, computer-based training, and classroom training)." Some workers start with a two-day orientation: "The first day is the regular new employee orientation that all new employees go through, [and] where you learn about benefits, payroll, etc. The second day focuses solely on the program, giving us information on the people involved with the program, expectations, future training, important phone numbers, and websites." After that, "most of the training you receive is hands-on from members of your department—just learning how basic business functions there. Other training consists of soft-skill training through Abbott Training Services." Many new hires are "assigned a mentor, who [they] regularly meet with to discuss Abbott's business model and the general business of business. This is one of the program's biggest strengths and one of the best learning experiences that [they] have had at Abbott."

DAY IN THE LIFE

Newbies at Abbott work in all areas of the company's core business units. A company representative says, "*All* of our new hires jump into meaningful work assignments. Responsibilities are directly related to the success of business. New hires meet periodically with their management team to make sure [they] are properly trained and [are] delivering results. Several areas have structured development programs—rotating assignments that are six to twelve months in duration." Many of our respondents participated in these rotations and all enjoyed the experience. One person writes, "I liked the rotational aspect of [my program]. It's great for college graduates who are not set on what they want their career paths to be because it gives them the opportunity to experience several different options within their field[s] while [still] being a part of the company." Another person adds, "As a member of the Professional Development Program, the job is constantly changing, and we are constantly being challenged and pulled to grow in arenas that make us well-rounded and skilled in several job sets around the company." A third employee adds, "I learned more in each of my six month rotations from my bosses than I could have learned in two years' worth of classes at college."

PEERS

Because Abbott's Professional Development programs are geared toward recent college graduates, there is "a lot of contact with first jobbers at Abbott." One newbie in the finance department writes, "Because of my current assignment, I have three other first jobbers around me who are in their first rotation as well. There are often a lot of invitations to after-hours events, which allow us to socialize and get to know each other better." First jobbers also see each other at "monthly staff meetings, bimonthly luncheons, [and] quarterly social events." Abbott actively encourages employees to participate in intracompany sports and networking groups to build a sense of community throughout the company.

Moving On

Those who leave Abbott are relatively few in number. "Over 80 percent will stay long-term," says one company representative. People who do leave often "go back to school for further education. [They] come to Abbott with expectations of working for a few years, then getting their [graduate or professional] degree. For example, I had two young human resources professionals [who] I mentored and both decided to go to law school. Both are now halfway through law degrees. Both want to return to Abbott. That is desirable turnover that we encourage."

Best and Worst

A company spokesperson describes one of the best first jobbers this way: "He joined the company about twenty-five years ago as an entry-level employee and second-generation Abbott employee. His father worked at Abbott. He performed well and was promoted through many functional roles. Today, he is president of one of Abbott's global divisions. That's not a unique story. Our Professional Development Programs have a great track record for producing corporate officers."

ACCENTURE
Consulting Analyst

THE BIG PICTURE

Consulting analysts are the cavalry of the business world. They save the day by solving problems businesses can't solve on their own. Accenture is well-known for its consulting work in IT services and technology; but with $11.8 billion in annual revenues, there are few areas in the business world where Accenture *isn't* a major player.

STATS

LOCATION(S) WHERE ENTRY-LEVEL EMPLOYEES WORK

Accenture has locations throughout the United States; see http://careers.accenture.com/careers/us for locations.

ENTRY-LEVEL POSITION(S) AVAILABLE

Accenture hires entry-level employees mostly for consulting analyst positions; candidates are chosen according to the company's skill and capability needs, as demanded by individual markets.

AVERAGE HOURS WORKED PER WEEK

Employees generally work over forty hours per week, but this varies based on factors such as level and position.

BENEFITS OFFERED

"Accenture offers total rewards packages that consist of professional growth opportunities, competitive compensation, and a broad and flexible range of benefits that include medical, dental, disability, life insurance, paid holidays, and paid time off. In addition, Accenture provides a range of services to employees that can include financial planning, apartment listings, consumer resources, and many others."

CONTACT INFORMATION

For more details, go to http://campusconnection.accenture.com.

GETTING HIRED

Candidate screening at Accenture is a four-step process. First, the company begins "with a review of resume and qualifications. Selected individuals are then possibly scheduled to begin the interviewing process consisting of three steps. The first round twenty- to thirty-minute interview is a chance for those who wish to work at Accenture to personally present their resume. This initial conversation allows us to get to know each other, understand objectives, and evaluate qualifications. The second round forty-five-minute interview gives the interviewee a chance to share experiences [in] greater detail. This interview will hone in on candidates' educational and personal experiences as they would relate to their potential performance at Accenture. Recruiters may ask for specific examples of situations encountered and how they have been handled. The final step in the process is an office visit. During the office visit, analysts, consultants, and executives further assess qualifications. There will also be presentations to further explain some of the nuts and bolts of working at Accenture." Company officials tell us that "individuals who excel during the interview process are those who are well prepared and demonstrate that they have done research on the company and the position. Many times these candidates have attended an event or talked to company representatives to gain a better understanding of the company and position."

Money and Perks

Accenture offers "competitive compensation;" representatives did not give us more details, but rest assured the pay is pretty good by first job standards. Perks include "many personal and professional development opportunities," a new laptop for business use, personal use of airline miles accrued during business travel, discounts from a variety of vendors, and "a transit transportation program that allows Accenture employees to pay for transportation using pre-tax dollars."

The Ropes

Accenture's orientation program occurs in stages. The first, which lasts several weeks, is called the new employee orientation and the core analyst local course. Once they complete the course, analysts head to core analyst school at the center in St. Charles, Illinois. One analyst describes the experience: "My first few weeks comprised local training with my start group and central training with others from around the world. The local training gave me the opportunity to instantly create a network with my start group and others I met in the office. It also provided an introduction to skills that were very valuable at central training in St. Charles. It was hard work but also fun. The training simulated a real project. It really provided background on what the Accenture culture is like—work hard as a team and play hard as a team." Continuing training is a fact of life for all Accenture employees, regardless of their seniority; "as part of continuous training throughout a career at Accenture, training can be completed either in person or virtually."

Day in the Life

Consulting analysts meet with the businesses they advise, explore the parameters of the problem they are hired to address, and begin solving the problem. One analyst writes, "a typical day at my current project includes meeting with my team leader to ensure all tasks are being addressed, completing those tasks, and raising any issues found along the way. Currently, we are still in the concept phase. The workload will pick up significantly within the next couple of months as we head into the design and implementation phases." The firm adds that "responsibilities can vary across client engagements. On any given day, an analyst may [need to] leverage skills that include building industry skills; developing technology-based solutions; analyzing, designing, and implementing business process improvements; defining user requirements; and specializing in business process design, business validation concepts, testing and quality assurance, system building concepts, programming, and development [skills]." You won't be on your own here, as "many times [older alumni] also make a special effort to ensure that they are progressing. Accenture offers both informal and formal mentoring programs and encourages participation on all levels."

Peers

New consulting analysts at Accenture are "constantly impressed by the people here. Coworkers are intelligent, amiable, helpful, and very committed to the quality of their work. People are always willing to help each other out or answer questions. There is a feeling of camaraderie that always develops when working on a team project, and those friendships extend beyond the workplace." One newbie reports, "The people are fantastically motivated and accept nothing but the highest level of work ethic and achievement. That said, most of the employees are very laid-back and down-to-earth, [which creates] a relaxed but productive work environment." Employees also praise the diversity of their coworkers; one employee reports, "When I attended new analyst training in St. Charles, I was astonished by the diversity of backgrounds, cultures, and nationalities represented by Accenture employees. The company is truly a global one."

Moving on

Consulting analysts make tons of contacts in the business world; thus, it is not surprising that some employees leave the firm to join one of Accenture's clients. Others leave to return to school. Representatives note that "Accenture has a well established alumni program in order to keep in touch with the exciting opportunities that many of our alumni pursue."

Attrition

"Globally, our attrition rate (company wide) is below the industry average."

ACNIELSEN
Market Research Analyst

THE BIG PICTURE

"Researching new, innovative products" is ACNielsen's business; entry-level employees quickly find themselves immersed in the world of product development and marketing. The job, which "combines math, statistics, and analytical thinking," is a great fit both for people "who love puzzles" and for people who love being on the cutting edge.

STATS

LOCATION(S) WHERE ENTRY-LEVEL EMPLOYEES WORK

Westport, CT; Chicago, IL; Covington, KY (Cincinnati metropolitan area); Parsippany, NJ (New York metropolitan area)

AVERAGE NUMBER OF APPLICATIONS EACH YEAR

ACNielsen receives thousands of applications each year.

AVERAGE NUMBER HIRED OVER THE LAST TEN YEARS

"In the last six years we have averaged about twenty to thirty hires per year."

ENTRY-LEVEL POSITION(S) AVAILABLE

"The majority of our entry-level recruiting efforts are focused on the marketing research analyst position. We do, however, fill other entry-level positions that occasionally become available."

AVERAGE HOURS WORKED PER WEEK

Employees work from forty to fifty hours per week.

PERCENTAGE OF ENTRY-LEVEL HIRES STILL WITH THE COMPANY AFTER THREE, FIVE, AND TEN YEARS

"ACNielsen 'BASES' [which is the name of ACNielson's entry-level program] has very little turnover. The vast majority of our college hires stay with the company for years. Specific retention statistics are not available."

AVERAGE STARTING SALARY

"Competitive; salary varies depending upon location."

BENEFITS OFFERED

The company offers "medical and dental insurance, life and disability insurance, vacation and personal days, 401(k), pension plan, tuition reimbursement, flexible spending accounts, and an incentive compensation program."

Visit the careers center at www.bases.com.

GETTING HIRED

ACNielsen recruits on select college campuses; students at campuses that ACNielsen does not visit can apply online for jobs. Company representatives "review your resume and, if [they] feel that your experiences and qualifications may be a good fit [for] the position, [a representative will] contact you to schedule an interview. In addition to multiple interviews, you will also be asked to submit transcripts and a writing sample, as well as complete a one hour analytical skills assessment." One entry-level employee says, "ACNielsen BASES values people who have diverse backgrounds and interests. During my interview process, I was not only asked about my academic and work experience, but also about my extracurricular activities." Another employee reports, "My first interview was with an analyst who had been at the company for [only] one year and had been hired right out of college. This surprised me and at first I thought that the company was not serious about hiring [me] since they sent a fairly new employee to interview me. However, I learned that this is often done and it is representative of BASES culture (young, casual, everyone's ideas and thoughts are respected, etc.). Most of the questions I was asked required me to give a specific event or example from my life (behavioral-based questions). I was later invited to the office for several second round interviews. The second round of interviews included more hypothetical questions specifically related to marketing research and consumer behavior." Company representatives tell us that "interviewers are interested in learning more about the candidate's background and experiences, career interests, analytical skills, communication skills, attention to detail, organizational skills, and work ethic, among other things."

MONEY AND PERKS

"ACNielsen BASES rewards employees based on their contributions and overall performance. All employees receive their first performance appraisal after six months of employment. Annual performance appraisals are accompanied by a salary increase." First jobbers tell us that "the job offer [is] not negotiable in terms of salary, office location, and duties," but that start time is sometimes flexible. First jobbers discuss perks, which include "the laid-back but highly driven atmosphere. Everyone is friendly but takes their work seriously. We deliver a superior product to our clients but enjoy ourselves while we're doing it!" Employees also enjoy "having insider information [about] new product launches. It is a pretty rewarding feeling to have clients look to you for multimillion dollar launch/no launch decisions. It is also gratifying to see a new product on the shelf and know that your insight went into its launch. (Plus, we get a lot of free new products.)"

THE ROPES

Orientation at ACNielsen "is quite quick" and includes some "meet-and-greet" around the office and a day with a human resources representative "learning company policy and filling out paperwork." Training, on the other hand, is extensive and "lasts roughly five weeks. Training sessions have been led by almost everyone in the office, from relatively recent hires to senior-level managers. The first two weeks consist of full day sessions, and the last three weeks consist of half-day training classes. The training sessions comprise presentations, case studies, and various exercises. At that point, we begin working with our managers on small projects, which is a great way to immediately apply the learning from the training. I really enjoyed this training model because it really allowed us to get to know a large number of coworkers very quickly." In addition, "several formal job-specific training courses [are] conducted throughout the first few months of the new hire's employment, [and] other company specific and miscellaneous training opportunities are offered through the year."

DAY IN THE LIFE

ACNielsen market research analysts hit the ground jogging and soon after hit full stride. One analyst says, "When I was first hired, my responsibilities mainly entailed data gathering and summarizing. However, as soon as training was over, I was given more extensive responsibilities. While my manager reviewed all of my work (from reports to emails), it was [ultimately] my work that was being sent to our clients. This was a great feeling: to have an entry-level job that really allowed you to think for yourself and contribute to the success of the company." Another analyst agrees and adds, "The responsibility curve at BASES is incredibly steep. I was put on my own project right away, which entails analyzing in-market and consumer data, checking marketing plan inputs, entering data into a complex model, drafting emails to clients, and writing toplines and lengthy (100-page) reports and presentations." First jobbers appreciate that "there is no typical day." One first jobber reports, "I am always working on something new. I am typically on one to four projects at a time. There is no set schedule to follow. I have a lot of independence as to how I spend my time."

PEERS

"I feel like there is a definite 'BASES personality," writes one market research analyst. "Nearly everyone I have met here is young, intelligent, and fun. No one tries to get ahead by stepping on other people's toes. Even though everyone is obviously trying to get ahead, no one is willing to do so at the expense of others. There is a definite team feeling at BASES." Another analyst adds, "I am constantly interacting with peers at the office. BASES encourages employees to bounce ideas off of one another. I would say I interact with my peers half (or more) of the hours I am at work." The camaraderie continues even after the computers are shut down for the day: "Socializing outside of the company with coworkers is big," explains one entry-level employee. "There is an organized off-site happy hour at least once a week and frequent weekend parties. There are also several company sports teams."

MOVING ON

Most new hires come to ACNielsen expecting to stay for the long haul, and few are disappointed. Most first jobbers like the work and stick around as long as opportunities for growth and advancement exist. "The majority [of people who leave the firm after a few years do so to] return to school and obtain a master's degree. Others leave the company to start a family or pursue outside interests."

ATTRITION

Dropouts from ACNielsen's entry-level job program are rare. Some who do leave "have voiced concerns about lack of managerial training—that people are promoted to management levels but not properly taught how to manage their direct reports. This leads to frustration among the newer hires." Others "complain about the workload or high expectations [from their managers]. However, the people with these types of criticisms are far less common than people who hold a positive view of their job here at ACNielsen BASES."

ÁEGIS ASSISTED LIVING
Various Positions

THE BIG PICTURE

Named America's third-fastest growing private company by *Inc.* magazine in 2003, Áegis Assisted Living is a business that should be creating many new jobs for years to come; it hopes to expand the number of communities it oversees by 50 percent between 2003 and 2004. If you're interested in working for Áegis, that's especially good news, since employee satisfaction levels there translate into a turnover rate that's among the lowest in the assisted living industry.

STATS

LOCATION(S) WHERE ENTRY-LEVEL EMPLOYEES WORK

Corporate headquarters is located in Redmond, WA; regional offices are located throughout Washington, Nevada, and California.

CONTACT INFORMATION

Visit the website at www.Áegisal.com/Positions.html.

GETTING HIRED

Áegis advertises job openings on its website and on www.monster.com. Most applicants undergo multiple interviews before the company decides whether to hire them. Explains one support staffer, "The office manager, director of recruiting and retention, chief marketing officer, and the accounting manager all interviewed me. My interview process began with a call from the office manager. She asked me a few basic questions over the phone and then invited me to a group interview. The group interview consisted of approximately sixteen candidates and was conducted by the office manager, the director of recruiting and retention, and the chief marketing officer. My third interview was conducted by the office manager, director of recruiting and retention, and the accounting manager. This was a panel interview. My fourth interview was one-on-one with the president of Áegis." While not *everyone* we spoke with interviewed with the president, all our correspondents were vetted by many layers of company hierarchs prior to receiving a job offer.

MONEY AND PERKS

Most entry-level job offers at Áegis aren't negotiable, employees tell us, although some found the company flexible on the start date. Our correspondents speak highly of Áegis' Enhanced Benefit

Program; they also tell us that "the company offers a lot of soft benefits such as luncheons, group activities, etc." Those who work at corporate headquarters feel that hometown Redmond is a major plus.

THE ROPES

Orientation at Áegis, one worker reports, "begins on your first day of work. I met with everybody in the office separately and sat with them for a little while to learn about their role in the company. This gave me a better feeling for the culture of Áegis and also the business itself. My orientation lasted for the first few days on the job." After that, "you sit down and dive right in." Most employees receive some specialized training early on to teach them how to deal with Áegis' clients; writes a chef, "I was new to Alzheimer's/dementia care and to Áegis itself, but the company took the time to train me on the aspects of care and the company so I felt comfortable and informed of what to expect. I also received training in CPR and first aid."

DAY IN THE LIFE

Áegis hires first jobbers in almost all areas, from client care (activities director, care manager, concierge, cook, wellness nurse) to behind-the-scenes business management (bookkeeping, marketing, office staff). As such, there is no typical day, although most would agree that "as the company is growing, so is the challenge of keeping up with it." Nearly all the employees we spoke with feel they have ample contact with higher-ups in the company. Writes one typical employee, "I have plenty of access to upper management. I feel as though I can approach any of them if I need some information. We have an all-staff meeting once a month, which allows everybody to find out what is going on in the other departments."

PEERS

There is "a fairly high degree of camaraderie" among coworkers at Áegis; few of the people we spoke with distinguished between their relationships with fellow first jobbers and the workforce at large. Everyone agrees, "the camaraderie is very strong, and it doesn't matter how long someone has been with the company. It feels [as if] we've all been here forever. It's a very family-oriented atmosphere." Most employees enjoy getting together after-hours; says one, "Everybody is outgoing. I have met a couple of coworkers outside [of] the office for social occasions."

MOVING ON

Áegis has a very low employee turnover rate, a testament to the satisfaction level of its employees. Writes one exuberant Áegis booster, "I don't hear anything but praise about the company. It's a really great place to be. It's challenging, busy, friendly, caring, funny, and sometimes [it is] better to be at work than at home!"

AMERICAN BIOPHYSICS CORPORATION
Various Positions

THE BIG PICTURE

If you hate mosquitoes—and besides frogs and bats, who doesn't?—and love the idea of a growing business, American Biophysics may be the right place for you. The producer of the Mosquito Magnet, a machine capable of capturing up to 1,500 of the pesky biters in one night, was the number one growth company on the 2003 *Inc. 500* list. This company plans to continue growing, but don't expect it to strike out in wild new directions. According to its website, American Biophysics is "single-mindedly focused and dedicated to the business of biting insect control."

STATS

LOCATION(S) WHERE ENTRY-LEVEL EMPLOYEES WORK

North Kingstown, RI (corporate headquarters)

AVERAGE NUMBER HIRED OVER THE LAST TEN YEARS

There are 108 employees, twenty-five of which are entry-level employees. Based on company strategy, the company predicts a 30 percent increase in the amount of new hires.

ENTRY-LEVEL POSITION(S) AVAILABLE

There are anywhere from fifteen to twenty entry-level positions available.

AVERAGE HOURS WORKED PER WEEK

Depending on the position, employees work over forty hours per week.

PERCENTAGE OF ENTRY-LEVEL HIRES STILL WITH THE COMPANY AFTER THREE, FIVE, AND TEN YEARS

After two years, 90 percent of all entry-level hires remain with the company; after three years, 80 percent of all entry-level hires remain.

AVERAGE STARTING SALARY

The average starting salary ranges from $25,000 to $30,000.

BENEFITS OFFERED

The company offers Blue Cross/Blue Shield (20 percent employee contribution) and Delta Dental (20 percent employee contribution). Additional benefits include a 401(k) and 529 college savings plan.

CONTACT INFORMATION

Rebecca Green

Human Resources Manager

140 Frenchtown Road

North Kingstown, RI 02852

401-884-3500 ext. 139

401-884-6688 (fax)

GETTING HIRED

The company is "in the beginning stages of developing roles for entry-level candidates who have the drive to learn, accept challenges, and are looking for future growth in their careers." American Biophysics representatives tell us that many things may change quickly. For now, they seek candidates who are "adaptable to ever-changing environments, have an entrepreneurial spirit, are willing to make decisions, have a drive to succeed, and have excellent communication skills." Currently the company does not advertise job openings on its website (www.mosquitomagnet.com), but it does recruit at area campuses. One of the company's recruiters says, "Applicants who stand out are [candidates] who have researched the company already, who seem confident and natural, [who don't give] canned answers to questions, and who have insightful, creative answers to our questions. We ask them how they handle pressure, ask them to describe a high stress situation they feel they handled well, and why, and then describe one they feel they didn't handle as well and what they would have done differently and what they learned. We also talk to them a lot to see how well they listen, which is very [crucial]." One successful hire says, "The interview process was very casual. Both people who interviewed me explained the history and the goals of the company. The human resources manager called me a few weeks later and told me I had the job."

MONEY AND PERKS

Because the company is quickly growing, new opportunities become regularly available for current employees. The company bases pay increases on "annual increases and changing roles." The benefits package is "evolving," and the company is working to expand and add extras as it grows more profitable. According to some employees, the greatest perk is the excitement of working at a fast-growing company; it's "the best company in the world at what we do, and we're sitting on the verge of helping to create something truly groundbreaking," gushes one new entry-level hire.

THE ROPES

As with most everything else at American Biophysics, orientation and training is a work in progress. According to company representatives, "We have some established training for our specialized products that involve hands-on experiences with our product. Training in regard to specific jobs is still being developed." Most of the employees we spoke with tell us that at first they "did not receive much training at all." One person says, "I was definitely thrown into the mix and left on my own to find my niche. How I dealt with that is what enabled me to advance in the company." Others add that they "receive constant training on company policies, procedures, and products, but none specifically on the job functions" and that, because the company is so small, "all employees have some knowledge of all operations."

DAY IN THE LIFE

American Biophysics is still in the process of defining the jobs its new hires will fill. If the company continues to grow at its current rate, the experiences of new hires will be much like those already working at the company. A current employee explains, "My responsibilities varied from day to day. The company was moving so fast with so few employees that everyone had to pitch in." Because American Biophysics workers usually have several coals in the fire at any given time, "there is always a level of multitasking that needs to occur so you can get each of your projects completed on time and [within] budget." One of the great things about working at such a small company, entry-level employees agree, is the relatively easy access they have to everyone from the shipping room to the board room. One worker reports, "There is no isolation at American Biophysics. All departments have close contact. The high-level executives know everyone's first name. They regularly interact with all employees on both a business and personal level."

PEERS

There's "a mix of young and old workers" at American Biophysics, which "helps maintain a balance of youth and experience" and maintains a level of comfort in an otherwise hectic work environment. "We're all good friends, even when things get intense in the office," writes one employee. "Everyone respects each other even when there's a conflict. At the end of the day all issues are forgotten." Workers "spend a lot of time together inside and outside of work. We all go out a few times a month after work."

MOVING ON

American Biophysics was founded in 1991, but its business has only moved into high gear since it introduced its first mosquito trap in 1998. As such, it doesn't have much of a history of employees who "move on," and few people could offer any insights into where departed employees have gone. In fact, the vibe we get from them is that most people are happy to work here and bullish about their prospects of advancement within the company. Their few complaints concern poor communication. One first jobber says, "When a company is growing as fast as we are, some things slip through the cracks without all the appropriate people knowing about them. When the customer knows and you don't, it can be embarrassing. That's the main issue that comes up."

ABC NEWS
Desk Assistant

The Big Picture

To get to the top of any skyscraper, you have to enter through the ground floor. In network news, the job of desk assistant is the ground floor; it's where everyone who wants a career in broadcast journalism begins. It's a low paying, extremely demanding, and sometimes tedious job, but if your dream is to make it in the news biz, well, this is the way to go. The good news is that if you impress your bosses, you will be eventually promoted to a better position.

Stats

Location(s) Where Entry-level Employees Work

Los Angeles, CA; New York, NY (most of the jobs are available in New York City); Washington, DC

Average Number of Applications Each Year

ABC News receives from 700 to 1,000 applications per year.

Average Number Hired over the Last Ten Years

ABC News has hired 150 to 200 people per year over the last ten years.

Entry-level Position(s) Available

Entry-level hires work as desk assistants.

Average Hours Worked Per Week

Employees work from fifty to sixty hours per week.

Percentage of Entry-level Hires Still with Company after Three, Five, and Ten Years

50 percent, 40 percent, and 30 percent, respectively.

Average Starting Salary

Entry-level hires earn $26,000 base pay, plus overtime.

Benefits Offered

The company provides medical, dental, life, and disability insurance.

Contact Information

Nissa W. Booker

ABC News Recruitment Coordinator

47 West 66th Street, 6th Floor

New York, NY 10023

GETTING HIRED

The job of desk assistant is among the most competitive low paying positions to obtain, so finding some way to distinguish yourself from the pack is crucial. One desk assistant writes, "Once I knew that I wanted to pursue a network job, getting one was quite the challenge. Every desk assistant has become one through a different channel and brings with them different experiences. I believe what got me an interview was that I had a good producer resume tape that showed I had a decent amount of experience writing and editing. Plus, my resume demonstrated my other journalism experiences through internships, summer jobs, etc. I do believe, however, that you must bring something different to the position other than journalism skills. I was a Spanish and journalism double major and had completed a semester abroad. I think traveling and knowing another language helped me in that I could bring a wide variety of knowledge and passion for another subject other than broadcast to ABC." A passion for the news is also crucial, of course. ABC is on constant lookout for good candidates, "even when there are no positions available." Network representatives tell us that "resumes are screened and interviews are conducted on a regular basis. If certain qualifications are met after an initial review of the resume, the candidate is invited to set up an exploratory interview. Resumes of interest are kept on file for one year. Resumes from the strongest candidates are flagged and reviewed again when a position becomes available. A hire is then made from that select group." ABC also holds "several job fairs" that "specific[ally] focus on minority recruitment."

MONEY AND PERKS

Desk assistants earn a pretty poor salary, especially considering the big-city location of the jobs. The best desk assistants, however, can earn much more (yet, still at a poor hourly rate), since they "make [a great deal] of their money in overtime earnings, which are largely dependant upon how good they are at the job. The best desk assistants are asked to work more and therefore make more money." Regardless of the pay, all desk assistants are happy to have the job, since "in journalism the supply is much greater than the demand. [They] take what [they] can get and work [their] ass[es] off." The biggest perk, according to one desk assistant, "is that every day you are witness to and involved in the incredible process of making the news. It is very gratifying to know that you contributed in some way to a product that millions of people see. This is only amplified when major news breaks. I was a desk assistant during Election 2000, and even though the work wasn't that challenging, I had a front row seat to how this historic event was reported to the public. You are also exposed to a talented array of news professionals and news stars. Simply observing them is an education."

THE ROPES

At ABC, orientation is a quick review of "benefits, company policies, company history, etc. It lasts only a few hours with a human resources representative." After that, work begins; you train as you work. Explains one desk assistant, "I was trained by my peers on the job. Outside of the heavy packet of information we were expected to study, there was no formal training process." ABC News representatives explain why: "There is no way to prepare an individual for the chaos of covering a breaking news story, so we immediately throw them into an environment [that] helps them to build a level of confidence that will carry them through the chaos. A typical day can range from reading several papers and developing story ideas to being sent to the World Trade Center to cover the towers collapsing."

Day in the Life

Desk assistants' duties depend on their assignments. "If they are assigned to a show like *World News Now* or *World News Tonight,* they are responsible for supporting the show so that it runs smoothly. This means organizing scripts, routing calls appropriately, and collecting editorial information. If a desk assistant works on the assignment desk, the responsibilities include helping to coordinate news coverage, obtaining and retaining very specific editorial information about several important stories, and knowing how stories are staffed." Writes one assignment desk assistant, "I had to learn where everyone was at all times and had to be up to speed on all news, especially breaking news, and who from our team was covering what stories. I worked with an assignment editor. Some nights it was so busy I couldn't get up to go to the bathroom. The phone would be ringing off the hook, and you just have to manage. The night of the blackout [in New York] was crazy but incredibly fun 'cuz I love this stuff!" All of the desk assistants we spoke with agreed that they needed to take on jobs beyond their own to get ahead; explains one assistant, "I took a lot of initiative, and I pitched story ideas that aired, and I got to go on shoots (this is rare). You need to be aggressive or else you could get stuck. Most importantly people have to like you and have confidence in you. Network! If you don't network, you won't move. Talk to anyone who will talk to you, [and] make sure you have mentors."

Peers

Desk assistants get to see a lot of each other at work. "We do not hang out that much after work, since we're here on average sixty hours a week together." One desk assistant writes that because they spend so much time together, "there is a lot of camaraderie among the desk assistants. During the day, we'll discuss the various ABC shows as well as what's happening in our personal lives. I also think we offer a support network for one another since we all have our days of struggling as desk assistants and the stress of worrying about moving up the ABC ladder." Desk assistants like each other, in part, because they are so alike. One desk assistant interviewed notes that "ABC News—maybe news in general—attracts smart, interesting people with drive and talent. It generally takes a certain type of personality to withstand the pressurized environment, so while people have diverse interests, they generally share a sense of adventure, humor, and curiosity. The desk assistants I worked with all went to good schools and were your typical overachievers."

Moving On

According to company representatives, "The majority of the people who leave the desk assistant position are promoted to the next level job at ABC News. Some people who leave the company leave to go back to school or for other jobs in the industry." You should be aware that promotions don't always happen quickly. In fact, "promotions among desk assistants typically occur at a glacial pace. There is not a lot of movement among production staff; they don't leave, and they aren't promoted regularly, so people can be desk assistants for some time, maybe a year to two years. The unhappy people were those who had a sense of hopelessness that they would never move on to have greater responsibilities and do more interesting work."

Attrition

"Less than 5 percent" of desk assistants quit within a year of taking the job; "everyone stays at least a year with the hope that they will be promoted to the next level job." Employees who leave, as well as many who stay, "complain about working too many hours and not really doing tasks that represent their true capabilities." Ultimately, though, "people know being a desk assistant in New York is a golden opportunity [that] can lead to so much."

Best and Worst

Pick your favorite as your own personal "best-ever" desk assistant from ABC's news staff; one first jobber explains, "Everyone has been a desk assistant at one point. All executive producers and vice presidents of news are former desk assistants."

AMERICORPS
Various Positions

THE BIG PICTURE

Say AmeriCorps representatives: "This year [AmeriCorps will] engage 75,000 people in service to their communities and country. Every AmeriCorps member gains the personal satisfaction of making a difference by helping others. You can teach or mentor youth, build affordable housing, teach computer skills, clean parks and streams, run after-school programs, and help communities respond to disasters. You can also put your college skills to work strengthening the capacity of charitable organizations by recruiting volunteers, expanding programs, providing training and technical assistance, and updating technology, thereby helping grantees to become more self-sustaining."

STATS

LOCATION(S) WHERE ENTRY-LEVEL EMPLOYEES WORK

All fifty states, Washington DC, Puerto Rico, and other U.S. territories

AVERAGE NUMBER OF APPLICATIONS EACH YEAR

People apply directly to the nonprofit organizations where AmeriCorps members serve, and there isn't a centralized database of all applications; therefore, the number is unknown.

AVERAGE NUMBER HIRED OVER THE LAST TEN YEARS

AmeriCorps currently hires 50,000 people a year (2004 will support a record 75,000 members).

AVERAGE HOURS WORKED PER WEEK

Full-time members work forty hours per week. A full-time member works 1,700 hours over ten to twelve months. Some part-time members work 900 hours over ten to twelve years.

PERCENTAGE OF ENTRY-LEVEL HIRES STILL WITH THE COMPANY AFTER THREE, FIVE, AND TEN YEARS

"AmeriCorps members typically serve for a year. Some of them, however, continue for another year or accept positions as employees with the nonprofit organizations where they've served."

AVERAGE STARTING SALARY

Members receive "a living allowance of about $10,000 a year, plus a $4,725 education award that can be used to pay back student loans or put toward future tuition. Each member receives the [education] award after completing a year of service."

BENEFITS OFFERED

Health care coverage is included in the living allowance. Additional benefits include forbearance on interest for student loans during the term of service.

CONTACT INFORMATION

To learn more or apply online, visit www.americorps.org or call 800-942-2677 or 800-833-3722.

GETTING HIRED

There is no surefire route to getting an AmeriCorps position, since "the hiring criteria are determined by the nonprofit organizations [that] select AmeriCorps members. The only general criteria is that you must be at least seventeen years old and a United States citizen, national, or legal permanent resident alien of the United States. For some programs, such as the AmeriCorps National Civilian Community Corps (AmeriCorps NCCC), members must be between eighteen and twenty-four years old, but for most [programs] there are no upper age limits." Openings available through AmeriCorps are listed on the website. Successful applicants recommend that interested candidates post their resumes online. Writes one applicant, "I posted [my] resume and cover letter on the AmeriCorps Web page. This was the better way to go since there was a much quicker response time than sending any application via mail."

MONEY AND PERKS

AmeriCorps representatives describe the living allowance that makes up its pay as "modest," so you know you won't be getting rich from this job. You will gain valuable experience, however, and you may also be eligible for other helpful perks such as student loan deferments, a grant toward paying off student loans (paid at the end of your term of service), health insurance, child care assistance, and money to relocate. For most, though, the greatest perk is the experience itself. As one AmeriCorps veteran tells us: "I really met some great people. I am still in contact with fellow members six years after we served together. I have gained valuable skills that transfer into everyday life and my current positions. Finally, I have gained confidence in my abilities and myself."

THE ROPES

As with the hiring process, orientation for AmeriCorps jobs varies depending on the organization with which members are placed. A two-term AmeriCorps veteran reports, "Orientation was an intensive experience for the two AmeriCorps programs I participated in. The concept was to challenge the corps to learn about diversity, conflict, and other challenges they would be facing in the coming year. For one of my assignments, we actually went on a three day retreat as part of the orientation process—which allowed for quick and deep bonding to occur." For many organizations, corps members receive training through various federal, state, and local agencies; the training sessions can focus on everything from intensely practical skills (i.e., how to fight a fire or how to build a house) to maddeningly bureaucratic chores (i.e., how to complete government forms).

DAY IN THE LIFE

Because AmeriCorps workers undertake so many different projects for so many different organizations, there is no typical day. According to organization representatives, "Some typical assignments for AmeriCorps members are running after-school programs, tutoring, developing and maintaining nature trails, addressing issues of homelessness, and responding to natural disasters." The work can certainly be gratifying, as the experiences of one graduate who worked at a domestic violence center illustrate: "I was responsible for answering the crisis hotline. I went to court with victims who needed help in obtaining restraining orders against their abusive partners. I did shelter intakes and talked with people who needed someone to talk to. I provided information and support to victims and survivors of domestic violence. I also did outreach events in the community to help spread awareness of the issues. Over time, I was given more and more things to do. I came up with projects that I wanted to do. I was able to really branch out and find my own niche. The experience I received was invaluable and has helped me in every position I have had since."

PEERS

Peer relationships at AmeriCorps also depend on the assignments members have. One member says, "We are spread out around the state, so there is no peer network." Conversely, an alum of AmeriCorps NCCC reports, "The corps bond was very tight. I was a team leader, and this group was also very close-knit. This was my social circle, since I had moved to a new city to participate in the programs. To this day, I still maintain contact with many people with whom I served. Despite the fact that we are spread out all over the country, we commit to getting together at least once a year for a reunion." Another first jobber sums up the situation this way: "[During] the months you spend on projects, you are limited to interaction with your team, or if you are working at a site with other people, then [you interact with] coworkers. Some projects are team-based and during other [projects], you work individually. Most after-work hours are spent privately or with your team if you chose to fraternize."

MOVING ON

AmeriCorps is a one-year program, and most people leave after their term is finished. Quite a few people, however, sign up for a second and third tour of duty. An organization representative says, "One of the benefits of AmeriCorps is that it provides members with the opportunity to explore different career paths. Many members discover a love and talent for the service they have provided as members, including teaching and nonprofit management."

ATTRITION

About one in five people who start an AmeriCorps assignment don't make it through the year of service. Some members find themselves working on projects they deem trivial; other members find they can't handle the demanding work and/or the low pay.

AP

Various Positions

THE BIG PICTURE

The Associated Press (AP) is the framework that holds the world news industry together; the organization maintains 242 bureaus around the globe, providing copy, photographs, graphics, audio, and video to over 1,700 newspapers and 5,000 television and radio outlets. If you want your stories to be seen, there's no better place to work: AP news services reach a billion people every day.

STATS

LOCATION(S) WHERE ENTRY-LEVEL EMPLOYEES WORK

"Generally speaking, every major city has a bureau. We hire at all locations, if there are appropriate openings."

AVERAGE NUMBER OF APPLICATIONS EACH YEAR

The AP receives "hundreds" of applications per year.

AVERAGE NUMBER HIRED OVER THE LAST TEN YEARS

The number of people who the AP hires "depends on turnover and various economic forces."

ENTRY-LEVEL POSITION(S) AVAILABLE

Entry-level employees work as editorial assistants, temporary news people, and interns.

AVERAGE HOURS WORKED PER WEEK

Entry-level emplyees work full-time hours.

AVERAGE STARTING SALARY

"[Starting salaries] depend on location. Salaries are covered by a collective bargaining agreement."

BENEFITS OFFERED

The AP offers "health, dental, mental health/substance abuse, [and] life insurance."

CONTACT INFORMATION

Email the AP at apjobs@ap.org.

GETTING HIRED

The AP makes its hiring decisions locally; "The bureau managers generally review the applications," organization representatives tell us, and the three qualities they look for are "experience, experience, experience." The AP visits "a number of colleges, especially those with strong journalism/communications departments." The most important part of the application process, first jobbers tell us, is the AP test. One new hire explains that "among other things, it has exercises in spelling, grammar, AP style, and current events. There are hypothetical situations posed that require you to write a news story based on tidbits of information provided. The AP also expects its news staff to write for broadcast media, so there are exercises related to that as well." Passing "puts your name in the AP system as someone who [is] interested in working for the AP and has passed their test. After that, it's a matter of a position opening up. If they call you up for an interview, it's already a done deal; they've already formed an evaluation of you because they've seen your test." Many employees begin with temporary assignments; people who make a good impression have the inside track when a permanent position becomes available.

MONEY AND PERKS

Salary at the AP is entirely determined by its union contract. Available jobs usually require first jobbers to work in specific locations on specific shifts; only in rare cases are start time or location negotiable. First jobbers point out that "AP does, however, have posts in every state and most countries, so sometimes people will take the test in one bureau, then wait for a position to open up somewhere else." Young employees love "being exposed to breaking news over the world on the wire (it's an extremely exhilarating feeling)" and "the feeling of learning nonstop." One person says, "You have to [have] a very humble attitude. Sometimes a topic will be thrown [at] you that you know nothing about." Employees also say, "It's neat to see your copy in newspapers around the state and sometimes around the country, even if it isn't credited."

THE ROPES

Each local AP bureau runs slightly different. At some bureaus, first jobbers are thrown into the job with little preparation or training; others receive an orientation and training that lasts several weeks. A first jobber at one end of the spectrum tells us, "I was sent out on a story on the very first day. I didn't even know how to use their internal computer system. You learn as you go. They're so short staffed; when they need you, they need you." At the other end was the writer whose orientation "involved a couple of weeks of work on each part of the job—writing and reporting, dictating stories from the scene, writing broadcast copy, and working a supervisory shift that requires heavy editing." A former first jobber states, "Training [at most bureaus] is in the form of shadowing more experienced staff. For instance, I worked several broadcast shifts with the broadcast editor before I was left to man that desk on my own."

DAY IN THE LIFE

Working at the AP means you'll always be in the middle of the action. Explains one first jobber, "One of my first jobs was driving to the scene of an explosion in downtown St. Cloud, Minnesota. I collected information from people at the scene, law enforcement officials, and rescue workers, and then phoned in a story to the day supervisor. I also gathered information from energy companies about gas leaks. I phoned in a story to the broadcast desk, then updated both the newspaper and broadcast stories throughout the day." The sheer volume of work required is often overwhelming; many of the writers tell us they are expected to "write two or three stories on happenings of the day. There is also the expectation that you will write more extensive weekend stories a couple of times a month." Promotions usually mean more responsibility, higher-profile stories, the responsibility of coming up with original stories (rather than simply covering stories assigned by an editor), and more work. It's a news junkie's paradise.

PEERS

AP peer networks vary from bureau to bureau. In the larger bureaus "there is ample camaraderie." "I often socialize with my colleagues," explains one first jobber in just such a bureau, adding "I constantly interact with my peers at work, and I probably spend two or three nights out with at least one other AP person." At some bureaus, social life is limited by the demands of work; "There isn't much on the social plane here, since we're all at work twenty-four hours, and if you're not on, someone else usually is," writes one newbie. At smaller bureaus, there may not be any other young hires; "There weren't any other entry-level people when I started," reports one staffer.

MOVING ON

AP first jobbers are generally future lifers in the news industry. People who leave get jobs with newspapers or in broadcast news; however, many people stay with the organization and work their way up the ranks.

ATTRITION

Most AP writers know what they're getting into, so the attrition rate is low. The "pressure from editors," the "heavy workload," and the "tedium of some routine jobs, such as editing" are things that might drive others to leave this organization; but AP employees generally take these issues in stride and accept them as the cost of working for a world-class news outlet.

BANK ONE
Development Programs and other Entry-level Programs

THE BIG PICTURE

Bank One spans much of the financial universe, and it provides not only traditional savings and checking services, but also credit cards, insurance, financial planning, mutual funds, and annuities. The bank offers a variety of programs designed to integrate recent college graduates into each of its divisions.

STATS

LOCATION(S) WHERE ENTRY-LEVEL EMPLOYEES WORK

Various cities in Arizona, Colorado, Delaware, Illinois, Indiana, Kentucky, Louisiana, Michigan, Ohio, Oklahoma, and Texas.

ENTRY-LEVEL POSITION(S) AVAILABLE

There are numerous entry-level positions available, including Bank One Scholar Program: Card Services' Business Associate Program and First Leader Program; Capital Markets Analyst Program; Finance, Accounting, and Audit Development Program; Chicago Sales Management Development Program; National Retail Management Development Program; Relationship Banker Development Program; National Enterprise Operations Management Development Program; and the Technology Development Program. Other opportunities may exist at any given time.

AVERAGE HOURS WORKED PER WEEK

Hours vary per the position.

AVERAGE STARTING SALARY

Salaries vary by position; they range from $25,000 to $50,000 for people with bachelor's degrees and from $51,000 to $85,000 for people with master's degrees, depending on the program.

BENEFITS OFFERED

Bank One and its employees share the cost of medical and dental insurance, 401(k) plans, training and education benefits, and adoption assistance. Bank One pays the full cost of disability, business travel accident insurance, and a wellness program. It also pays the full cost of life insurance and pension accounts. It provides sick leave, vacation time, holidays, and service awards.

Visit Bank One at www.bankone.com/careernav.

GETTING HIRED

Bank One "actively recruits on campus at many schools in the midwest and south (a copy of our recruiting schedule can be found on our website)" and also accepts online applications. An entry-level employee in the National Enterprise Operations Management Development Program describes the process: "I got the interview after turning in one of my standard resumes. I believe that my past work experience and GPA are what got me the interview. I was interviewed first by a Bank One finance manager on campus. After passing that first round, I was invited to the operations center for a tour and two more interviews, one with an operations manager and the other with a senior vice president and division manager. All of the interviews used a standard Bank One format consisting of behavioral questions like, 'Describe a time when . . .'" Interviews for full-time jobs "typically occur in the fall of each year; internship interviews are conducted in the spring. Offers are typically extended in November and December for full-time positions and in March and April for internships."

MONEY AND PERKS

Entry-level salaries vary at Bank One by program: "Each program determines if and how bonuses will be distributed as well as how salaries will increase. Some individuals receive increases once they graduate from their specific programs; others receive merit increases at their annual performance reviews." Starting salaries are rarely negotiable, although they can be for candidates with well-developed skills (i.e., in technology areas). Respondents to our survey praise the long-term financial benefits of working for Bank One: "There are great 401(k) and pension plans. Also, we get fees waived or better rates on other financial products." One entry-level employee adds that "the best fringe benefit[s] for the short-term [are] the discounts. Bank One is partnered with several companies, from restaurants and cell phone companies to clothing stores and gyms." Other fringe benefits include "exposure to senior management of the company (their guidance was invaluable and very motivating)" and "four weeks' vacation!"

THE ROPES

Everyone in Bank One's development programs starts off with "a weeklong orientation, which includes an in-depth overview of Bank One as well as exposure to the heads of our lines of business. Each line of business continues from there with some form of orientation [and] training for their new hires during the individual's first 120 days of employment." One undergraduate hire reports, "The orientation process was the very best part of the program. They bring you in first to the corporate orientation, where you have an overview of the company and meet people from all different departments. The second day was the in-store orientation, where we were introduced to the program manager and were given our training schedules for the next 120 days. It made me feel very secure and eased my nerves about coming into a bank, knowing basically nothing about banking!" Training continues throughout the development programs, often including substantial amounts of classroom learning.

DAY IN THE LIFE

A typical day depends on the program in which the entry-level employee participates. Bank One scholars work six-month rotations in various positions by day, then attend an MBA program in the evening. Card Services Business Associates is a "fast-track management program" that places trainees in one of the bank's many credit card related areas. Capital markets analysts rotate through positions in the bank's Capital Markets departments, supplementing their training with formal classroom instruction. Development programs also entail rotations that expose participants to all the different specializations within their selected area. A participant in the Technology Development Program describes his work experience this way: "My job has been to take graphs of metrics [that] are reported manually each week and help automate them and make them viewable in a Web environment. In order to accomplish this task, I have spent a large [amount of] time learning the Java language and other technologies [that] I do not have much experience with. A typical day consists of learning new technologies, applying them to my metrics reporting projects, and a daily meeting with the team on the project to go over our progress."

PEERS

"There is a huge camaraderie within the members of our program," writes one program member. "I think the main reason is because for all of us, this is our first real introduction to the corporate world, so we have lots we would like to discuss, but more as friends than as coworkers." Adds another, "We spent a lot of time together in Chicago [during training], and that was a real bonding experience for all of us. A few times, we have gotten together after work, and most days I eat lunch with at least one or two people from the program."

MOVING ON

Most entry-level employees remain with Bank One. "I plan to stay for as long as I can continue to grow and feel satisfied with my job," is how one person puts it. Typically, they advance through the ranks of the area for which they received training. "I left after graduating from the six-month program when I was placed in a supervisory position," writes one such entry-level hire. Others move elsewhere within the bank; "I have moved through the program to [become] an assistant manager, a branch manager, and now I'm moving to a different program—the In-Lines—as a branch manager," explains one employee.

ATTRITION

According to Bank One representatives, fewer than 5 percent of first jobbers leave within twelve months. "Given that the majority of the new hires are recent college graduates with limited work experience, those that choose to leave the bank do so to pursue career opportunities outside of banking," write company representatives. First jobbers add that some people leave because they "feel they were placed in a department that didn't utilize their skills, [feel] undervalued, or [feel] there was poor communication about [things] happening within the program"

BEST AND WORST

Bank One representatives tell us that "individuals who are successful at Bank One tend to possess our core values [and] competencies: a customer focus; interpersonal effectiveness and teamwork; a drive for quality and results; ethics, integrity, and character; and courage."

BOEING

Various Positions

THE BIG PICTURE

Boeing, maker of commercial airplanes, military aircraft, satellites, spacecraft, and missiles, is the United States' largest exporter; it conducts a pretty tidy business within the nation's borders as well. There are a myriad of opportunities to work on groundbreaking projects and advance through the ranks for a go-getter with a flair for aeronautics or the aeronautic business. And they can be had in many far-flung locations, as the company has operations in seventy countries and twenty-eight states.

STATS

LOCATION(S) WHERE ENTRY-LEVEL EMPLOYEES WORK

"Most all company locations have opportunities for entry-level work. Boeing operates in more than seventy countries and thirty-eight states within the United States, with major operations in the Puget Sound area of Washington state; Southern California; Wichita, Kansas; and St. Louis, Missouri."

AVERAGE NUMBER OF APPLICATIONS EACH YEAR

Boeing receives "thousands" of applications every year.

AVERAGE NUMBER HIRED OVER THE LAST TEN YEARS

Boeing has over 150,000 employees total. There are no figures for the number of new hires per year.

ENTRY-LEVEL POSITION(S) AVAILABLE

Entry-level hires work in engineering, information technology (IT), and business.

AVERAGE HOURS WORKED PER WEEK

"Forty hours is the typical workweek for Boeing employees, with part-time work options also available. Boeing also offers virtual work options, allowing employees to telecommute from their homes or use 'hoteling' or transit work spaces at company work sites."

AVERAGE STARTING SALARY

Engineering salaries start at $50,000, IT salaries start at $46,000, and business salaries start at $41,000.

BENEFITS OFFERED

"Boeing offers a competitive program of health and welfare plans to help take care of employees and their families. Employees in most locations can choose from among several types of medical plans. Prescription drugs, vision, dental, mental health, and substance abuse also are covered. For more information, please visit www.boeing.com/employment/benefits/index.html." Additionally, "Boeing offers competitive total compensation. Employees represented by labor unions negotiate their pay and benefits—including incentives—through collective bargaining. Nonunion employees enjoy salary reviews, retirement and 401(k) plans, stock options, profit sharing, vacation time and holidays off, [and] other financial/recognition programs."

CONTACT INFORMATION

Visit us at www.boeing.com and www.boeing.com/employment/flash.html.

GETTING HIRED

Although Boeing "does target schools and maintains an on-campus visit schedule based on curriculum and locations of schools," the company values all schools. "By having an online application process, every student is able to apply for open positions." The company seeks new hires who demonstrate the ability to work with a team, "integrity, technical proficiency, and the ability to communicate effectively." The hiring process can drag on from start to finish. Writes one electrical engineer, "A few weeks after submitting my application, Boeing gave me a phone interview. The interview was behavior-based ('Tell me about a time when . . .'). I'm sure that my having had a couple of these already, and having brainstormed and practiced answering some of those questions helped. Shortly after that, I was invited to an interview/recruiting event in St. Louis for three days (Thursday evening through Sunday morning, right before Thanksgiving). There, they presented information about Boeing, put us through a group discussion/business case-style interview, did another round of behavior-based interviews (this time with two interviewers), and provided [us with] some time for relaxing and socializing. They also asked us what our interests were—what type of job we wanted. The atmosphere was upbeat, mostly structured, and relaxed. On Saturday, after all the interviews were finished, they locked themselves in a room and matched up all the job openings and candidates (some people getting none, [and] others getting one or more), and slipped letters or offers under each student's door during the night while we slept (or waited up). The next morning, they had optional feedback sessions. There, we were allowed to ask how we did, why we did or didn't get a specific offer, etc., based on the information that had been collected in our file. I found this really helpful."

MONEY AND PERKS

The negotiability of Boeing positions varies widely from function to function; obviously, the more specialized your skills, the better your negotiating chances. Most first jobbers find that "location, activity, and salary are specified [in] the offer." One first jobber explains, "In my case, the first two [offers] were specific and seemed nonnegotiable. I did ask to negotiate the salary. They listened to my arguments, but didn't change it." A new hire in one of Boeing's rotational training programs reports that "the program is flexible in terms of the job you're hired into. You get to choose [what] department you start in and have a large degree of discretion in where you go over the two-year rotational period (mandatory rotations occur every four months)." Newbies love Boeing's flex-time arrangement, which "with proper approval (that is usually given), allows you to take a whole Friday off, and make up the hours during the rest of the two-week pay period. Or, you can work an extra hour one day and leave an hour early the next." They also appreciate "the Learning Together Program, known as one of the most generous corporate tuition reimbursement programs. It offers 100 percent paid tuition at accredited schools."

THE ROPES

Boeing offers "a standard half-day schedule for orientation used by all company locations" that is "designed to congratulate and celebrate with the employee on the success of their newly obtained position at Boeing. In addition, it is an opportunity for Boeing to impart some very important values, responsibilities, and standards of conduct." In addition, "certain regions (such as Long Beach or St. Louis) may add an afternoon session that is specific to their own region." Participants in the rotational training program have a longer formal orientation; writes a person in the Business Career Foundation Program, "We had a week-long orientation seminar that gave us an overview of the company and of the positions we would be rotating through." Other new hires complete the four-hour orientation, then jump right into their new jobs. Subsequent training is a mix of "on-the-job training as well as formal training," including some online instruction. How much of each an employee gets depends on his or her job. The more technical the position, the more likely it is to require specialized training classes.

DAY IN THE LIFE

Entry-level employees work in just about every department in every location where Boeing does business; as company representatives explain, "The responsibilities for newly hired employees vary; there is not one standard set of responsibilities." Much of the work at Boeing is project-oriented, so new hires often jump in *in media res;* writes one engineer, "When I was first hired, there was a project that most of my coworkers were working hard to finish up. So, at first, I spent a lot of time doing the online training and learning the computer tools from coworkers. My first assignment was to draw up the wiring to install a new device, following the example of one that had already been done. Most of that time was spent using a 2-D drawing package on the computer, as well as using other tools to look up information I needed (guided, again, by my coworkers)." Mentoring plays a large part in the life of a new Boeing employee, as does "a program that is a network for new college hires. It allows college hires to network with others that are in the same circumstance." Those new hires participating in a rotational program tell us that "the benefit of a rotational program is that each position only lasts for four months, which gives you a chance to figure out where you fit."

PEERS

Because Boeing is such a big company, there are plenty of first jobbers. The company is even large enough to hire a number of students from the same school; writes one Texas A&M graduate, "Contact and camaraderie among the new hires from the same school [are] extremely good. There is a big after-hours social scene organized by different people from Texas A&M." Regardless of your alma mater, though, "there is definitely contact and camaraderie with other young workers. Not all of them are first jobbers but several are still around [the same] age." Everyone we spoke with agrees that they "have a great group of supportive, intelligent, and driven peers. Friends are easy to make here."

MOVING ON

Most first jobbers stay in Boeing; reports one, "I've been told it's relatively easy to move around in the company." People who do leave, according to company representatives, go to work for "competitors in the aerospace industry and/or companies requiring technical professionals such as Lockheed, Raytheon, Northrop Grumman, BAE Systems, Honeywell, Microsoft, Rockwell, Sandia National Labs, Los Alamos National Labs, and Ball Aerospace."

ATTRITION

Boeing representatives report that some employees who leave the company do so because "the work was not what they expected." Concurs one electrical engineer, "One or two of my peers have commented that this job doesn't seem to use our training." Company representatives also tell us that "money, level, and promotion ability" sometimes compel first jobbers to seek work elsewhere; agrees one of our correspondents, "Some who left were not too happy with the new hires coming in due to salary discrepancies."

BOOZ ALLEN HAMILTON
Junior-level Consultants and Researchers

THE BIG PICTURE

Booz Allen Hamilton is a very big and very well-known "strategy and technology consulting firm" that offers aspiring consultants opportunities in numerous cutting-edge fields. One entry-level employee explains the appeal of this demanding, but rewarding, program: "[The company has] a very good reputation in the government business sector."

STATS

LOCATION(S) WHERE ENTRY-LEVEL EMPLOYEES WORK

"With more than 14,000 employees serving clients on six continents we are truly a global organization. The majority of our undergraduate new hires join the firm in our Washington, DC, metro area corporate headquarters in McLean, Virginia (also known as our McLean Campus). We also have undergraduate opportunities in our Atlanta, San Diego, Colorado Springs, and Omaha offices."

AVERAGE NUMBER OF APPLICATIONS EACH YEAR

For the undergraduate program, "we receive between 8,000 and 10,000 [applications] each year."

AVERAGE NUMBER HIRED OVER THE LAST TEN YEARS

The company has hired an average of 150 undergraduates each year for the last ten years.

ENTRY-LEVEL POSITION(S) AVAILABLE

"We offer two entry-level positions: junior-level consultants and researchers with concentrations in functional areas such as IT, systems, business, economics, public policy, and engineering within our national security, civil, and defense business segments."

AVERAGE HOURS WORKED PER WEEK

Employees work between forty-five and fifty hours per week. The firm "is committed to helping our staff keep their lives in balance. Our team members enjoy flexible schedules."

PERCENTAGE OF ENTRY-LEVEL HIRES STILL WITH THE COMPANY AFTER THREE, FIVE, AND TEN YEARS:

After three years, 72 percent of all entry-level employees remain with the company, and after five years, 70 percent of all entry-level employees remain with the company.

AVERAGE STARTING SALARY

"We offer very competitive starting salaries ranging from $35,000 to $60,000, depending upon specific job function and skills."

Benefits Offered

"We offer generous medical and dental benefits from top providers with plans that fit individuals." Furthermore, the company offers profit sharing and 401(k) plans, income protection, reimbursement accounts, tuition assistance ($5,000 per year per employee), an award-winning training program (that offers technical and business strategy certification courses), work/life programs, family centers, family-friendly policies, and a generous paid leave policy.

Contact Information

Interested students should visit www.boozallen.com. Access "Careers," then "College Opportunities" to create your profile and submit your resume.

Getting Hired

Booz Allen Hamilton does much of its undergraduate recruiting at select college campuses. You can also submit applications online, so you don't need to attend one of the company's "core schools" to land an interview. First interviews are held on campus, with subsequent interviews conducted at a Booz Allen office. Interviews typically consist of "behavioral questions; some examples are, 'Tell me about a time when you had a deadline for an assignment, you had many other things that interfered with meeting that deadline, and how you handled it?' Another question is 'Tell me about a time when you had to work in a team and rely on other people to deliver a final project and how you handled conflict within the group.'"

An entry-level hire describes the entire experience: "I submitted my standard resume and was interviewed by a recruiter and a senior consultant. They were both very friendly and fairly laid-back. I was asked to come back for a second interview at their McLean, Virginia, headquarters. I went to a nice dinner with about thirty other candidates, stayed in a hotel overnight, and then went through a pretty tiring day of interviewing. They set us up to interview with teams they thought we would be compatible with based on our resumes and previous interviews, and they also had a mini career fair with the other teams if we wanted an interview with them. I received my offer a couple of months later."

Money and Perks

Undergraduate hires disagree as to whether their starting salaries were negotiable. One "negotiated a higher salary and signing bonus," while others say that "there was no negotiation." All agree that location "and assignments were not negotiable," but that new hires are "able to move onto different tasks that better suit [their] interests" once they've been with Booz Allen for a while. By all accounts, the best perk is flex time: "We can work from home or work more on one day to make up the hours from another day," explains one consultant. The firm also offers "tuition assistance, an award-winning training program, employee discounts and special buying services, mentoring, benefits for domestic partners, tax-deferred reimbursement accounts for medical and dependant care, family centers, paid parental leave for new parents (mothers *and* fathers), and a plethora of [minority and interest] groups and forums."

THE ROPES

Orientation is relatively brief at Booz Allen. Firm representatives tell us that initial training consists of "a half-day training class that helps staff become familiar with the culture and what to expect in the beginning of their career at Booz Allen. Within the first thirty days, new hires attend a two-day training class. Within the next few months, employees attend another two-day training class focused on consulting skills." Here's how one beginning consultant describes the process: "The orientation included filling out benefits paperwork and learning more about Booz Allen and getting our badge printed. We had a four-hour orientation and my peer team member came to meet me at noon and we had lunch and she got me situated at my desk. I met my boss after lunch to find out what specific project I was going to be working on."

DAY IN THE LIFE

Booz Allen Hamilton representatives tell us that "Most new hires will work within a team environment, have frequent interaction with clients, and be challenged to make change happen. Functionally, they are often assigned roles requiring keen data gathering and analysis skills." Because the firm consults for such a wide range of businesses and government offices, there is "a vast variety of opportunities for new hires with different functional skills, [and] each role requires different responsibilities." Here's how one entry-level employee describes her integration into the firm: "I supported a couple different projects here and there for my first couple weeks until I was tasked on a project full-time. My typical day on my first project was meeting with military subject matter experts to gather requirements for an integrated HR system for the Department of Defense." Another entry-level employee's says, "[My first task] was to debug this application that we are investing in as a new service offering. I would come in and do Google searches, ask other team members for their expertise, and keep trying new solutions to debug the entire application that was created by another company. Now I am solely developing Web portals by myself, I lead the code review team, and I am the team's graphic designer." The longer you're at the company, the greater your responsibilities. All the consultants we spoke with praise the mentoring skills of their supervisors and approve of their frequent contact with upper-level management.

PEERS

Consulting is all about teamwork, so it should come as no surprise that "[Booz Allen Hamilton] managers encourage us to go out after-hours." One newbie reports, "We go to happy hours on Thursdays, and on Fridays or Saturdays we go out to clubs. Sometimes we [take] weekend trips like white-water rafting or barbeques at coworkers' houses." Another young consultant adds, "We are a very close group of friends and colleagues."

MOVING ON

The entry-level employees we interviewed have little intention of leaving Booz Allen Hamilton; they all hope to remain with the company as long as possible. Firm representatives explain one possible reason: "Our people don't have to leave the firm to try something new. Booz Allen offers an internal transfer process through our Career Mobility Program. Staff can transfer between teams to pursue new opportunities and learn new skills." When entry-level staff members do move on, they usually do so to return to school or to "pursue a technical concentration versus consulting."

ATTRITION

Firm representatives say, "Naturally, people pursue new passions and new opportunities—and we encourage our staff to explore the world around them. Booz Allen has an active 'Come Back Kids' program that works with people who want to come back to the firm, and some might even say that many of our best clients were once Booz Allen employees who have taken the expertise they gained serving many clients to one institution."

BOSTON BEER COMPANY
Account Manager

THE BIG PICTURE

Remember when you stopped dreaming of being a fireman or an astronaut and instead started dreaming of a life surrounded by beer? Dream no more, stalwart brew-phile! Boston Beer Company offers you the chance to promote, sell, and, yes, drink beer, *and get paid for it*. Homer Simpson, eat your heart out!

STATS

LOCATION(S) WHERE ENTRY-LEVEL EMPLOYEES WORK

Boston Beer has locations in major metropolitan areas throughout the United States.

AVERAGE NUMBER OF APPLICATIONS EACH YEAR

The company receives 1,000 applications each year.

AVERAGE NUMBER HIRED OVER THE LAST TEN YEARS

The company has hired approximately forty entry-level employees per year for the last ten years.

ENTRY-LEVEL POSITION(S) AVAILABLE

There is an entry-level account manager (outside sales) position available at the company.

AVERAGE HOURS WORKED PER WEEK

Employees work over forty hours per week.

PERCENTAGE OF ENTRY-LEVEL HIRES STILL WITH THE COMPANY AFTER THREE, FIVE, AND TEN YEARS

After three years, about 70 percent of all entry-level employees are still with the company.

AVERAGE STARTING SALARY

The base salary is in the $30,000 range, with a 10 percent bonus potential.

BENEFITS OFFERED

The company offers medical and dental insurance, long- and short–term disability, life insurance, and a flexible spending account. Furthermore, the company offers a 401(k) plan (the company matches), gym membership discounts, paid vacation, discounted movie tickets, tuition reimbursement, and a car allowance (for sales personnel only).

CONTACT INFORMATION

Visit the website at www.samadams.com/company.

GETTING HIRED

Boston Beer Company recruits on campuses and through its website, which offers valuable information to potential candidates. One current employee writes, "I thought it was important to find out what skills [the company] was looking for in a college recruit candidate and then pull out and magnify those skills on my resume. For example, I knew they were looking for someone with high levels of customer service, especially in the restaurant/bar area. Obviously, I focused on my bartending experience both on my resume and in interviews." The interview process itself can be extensive. One entry-level employee reports, "I interviewed with four different employees, and each one of them asked numerous questions about my college career and work history. Questions like: 'Provide me with a time when you had to manage your time between work and school in order to more efficiently and effectively accomplish both? What questions do you have about the company?' The interviews were all about one hour long. The entire process took about three months, from the career fair to the actual start date." Part of the interview process includes spending a day in the field with an account manager. One employee writes, "The great thing about [the company] is that a step in the interview process is actually riding with an experienced sales rep, so you know exactly what the job is like."

MONEY AND PERKS

Account managers say, "The area where we [were first assigned] and what we actually did were pretty much nonnegotiable. You knew the requirements for both these things throughout the interview process." Starting salary is negotiable, but only within relatively narrow parameters. Everyone agrees that the best fringe benefit of all is the product itself, and their access to it. "If anybody tells you it's not the free beer, they're lying!" agrees another respondent. "The great relationships you build with accounts" is also cited as a big plus.

THE ROPES

Aspiring account managers agree that "the training program at Boston Beer Company is awesome!" Here's how one new hire describes the process: "Our orientation class was held in Boston at the main office. It lasted an entire week, with five days of extensive information about brewing, beer, brief sales training, and how it all works together." One entry-level employee notes, "I was definitely on information overload." The highlight of orientation, according to one new hire, is "getting to sit down one evening with Jim Koch [the founder of Boston Beer] and having him sample and taste-profile the products with us." After the weeklong orientation, trainees return home and "receive three full months of training from [their] managers. We began reviewing information from orientation and then gradually worked our way into accounts, watching our managers deliver sales presentations, doing it all together, and from then on presenting on our own."

DAY IN THE LIFE

Account managers are responsible for managing and developing business within a specified region. Here's how one person describes his job: "I was in charge of developing business in seventy core accounts, most of which already carried our product. Half of the accounts were grocery or liquor stores, and the other half were bars and restaurants. My job was to drive availability and visibility by gaining new or additional distribution and selling the customer on how displays, extra visibility, product position, and features could help their business. A typical day for me would start in a grocery store at 8:00 AM. I would try to get into five stores to sell displays and get better visibility. My afternoon might be spent in the bars trying to get accounts that [carry] our beer in the bottle to put it on draft or [to bring] in some additional Samuel Adams products. I would set up staff beer educations, features, and promotions. Three evenings a week I would have a promotion set up to help support an account that had brought in a new product of mine."

PEERS

Account managers work in the field, so they don't have much daily personal contact with their peers as employees in many of the other jobs featured in this book. Even so, "the camaraderie was there throughout training, and five of the six college recruits I trained with became close and have remained in contact over the phone and/or email." One employee adds, "Most of my contact with my fellow trainees has been via cell phone; phone conversations asking advice or sharing ideas were the norm for me. The camaraderie was still there despite the distance. I still keep in close contact with my original college recruit class." One entry-level employee writes, "To this day, the other college recruits that I started with are some of my best friends. They are all going to be at my wedding, and one is actually in my wedding party."

MOVING ON

Boston Beer doesn't track where employees who leave its account manager program end up, and all the account managers we spoke with hope to remain in the company. This is not a two-and-out program; most who take the job do so with hopes of building a career and apparently many do. An employee who's been with the company for several years writes, "My job has changed several times in four years, as I have been promoted three times and relocated four times in four years (from Colorado to Chicago, to Indiana, to Chicago, and back [to] Colorado again). With each new position, I was challenged with another area, gaining new responsibilities, including managing point of sales materials, distributors and their inventories, and now managing people (three account managers)."

ATTRITION

"Some employees resent having to relocate as part of the job, even though the company makes this aspect of the work clear from the beginning. One current employee writes, "It made a couple of the college recruits a little apprehensive to have to move to another market, but that is the main requirement of the program: You *had* to be willing to take a promotion and relocate to another market where we needed reps. Other than that, everyone loved everything else about the program: the company, the peers we worked with, our bosses, the level of training we were receiving, [and] how fun the industry is."

BEST AND WORST

One of the company's best recruits rose through the ranks, beginning as a sales manager and then becoming an account manager, then a senior account manager in New York City, and finally ascending to the position of district manager in Boston ("one of our most visible and high-impact markets."). The worst first jobber never really got started; "he decided that he did not want to relocate and resigned in the midst of moving."

BP

Various Positions

THE BIG PICTURE

"BP is a new company formed by the union of British Petroleum, Amoco, ARCO, Castrol, and Vastar." It hires many entry-level workers every year; its blue-chip entry-level opportunities are in the early development programs found in every segment of the company. BP's Exploration and Production segment, for example, offers a three-year rotational program called Challenge. According to people in the company, "all university hires are immersed in a formal development program that includes extensive training opportunities, a variety of work experiences, and an induction event with university hires from all over the globe."

STATS

LOCATION(S) WHERE ENTRY-LEVEL EMPLOYEES WORK

"BP has offices or operations in all 50 states. States with the largest number of employees are Alaska, California, Illinois, and Texas."

AVERAGE NUMBER OF APPLICATIONS EACH YEAR

BP receives 4,000 applications every year.

ENTRY-LEVEL POSITION(S) AVAILABLE

There are 125 to 150 multiple hires per entry-level position at BP.

AVERAGE HOURS WORKED PER WEEK

New hires work forty hours per week.

BENEFITS OFFERED

BP offers "several medical plan options, depending on job and location." Additional benefits *may* include a "dental plan, vision plan, basic [and] supplemental life insurance, short- and long-term disability plans, 401(k), [and] retirement accumulation plan."

CONTACT INFORMATION

Visit the website at www.bpfutures.com/us.

Getting Hired

BP representatives report, "There are a number of ways for students to apply for entry-level jobs. Each discipline decides [what] schools its teams will visit, but since we can't send teams to every school, we have an online process that is available to all students. Our recruiters are also active with the student chapters of numerous professional organizations and associations." An engineer who ultimately landed his dream job in Alaska describes the vetting process this way: "I don't recall much about the interview other than that it went well and seemed more like a conversation than a grilling. The interviewer invited me to dinner with the rest of the BP folks and interview candidates that evening. I went (knowing full well that it was an additional step of evaluation) and was invited shortly thereafter to come to Anchorage on a site visit with other candidates from around the country. During the visit, BP put us up in great hotels—really wined and dined us. They showed us around town and nearby areas, and introduced us to lots of staff, from the newest hires to powerful managers. Interactions were mostly social and informal. There were a few actual interview sessions during the site visit. Some of the questions were clearly designed to catch you a little bit off guard—but nothing truly underhanded. The interviews were predominantly conversational in nature, each conversation focusing specifically on some portion of my preparation for the job." A number of employees we spoke with had previously interned or worked co-op jobs with BP while they were in college.

Money and Perks

Entry-level workers at BP tell us that their job offers were "somewhat negotiable." Explains one, "Essentially, I gave them my preferences on where and what and communicated my priorities. BP then took those priorities and preferences and placed me in the organization. In my case, my top priority was honored." Adds another, "Starting salary was excellent, so I didn't bother to negotiate." Most people agree that the best fringe benefit is the "Flex Fridays" work schedule. Here's how it works: "We work nine hour days instead of eight, and then we get to take every other Friday off. Two three-day weekends a month goes a long way toward home/work life balance."

The Ropes

Orientation and training at BP is a combination of formal courses, on-the-job training, and mentoring. For one employee, "On day one I had a number of briefings starting with job location safety, team/business orientation, benefits, and meeting my team. By six months, I had a mentor, a junior staff 'buddy,' and had attended an induction event at another BP location. All together, I received about one month's worth of training in my first year, away from the office, at courses. The courses were either recommended for my job function by my manager or were health/safety/environment related. After my first several years, I ventured out into other courses that were outside of my core job function or behavioral/leadership related." There's a lot of information for newbies to process; as one explains, "The nature of the petroleum industry is that college is where you learn the very basic material, and then your work life builds on the fundamental understanding that you have. I didn't come in on day one and understand everything. It probably took me six months to feel like I had a good idea [of] what I was doing—looking back, I understand that I still had a lot more to learn (and probably still do). [I have] no regrets about what I did or didn't know."

DAY IN THE LIFE

BP hires entry-level workers in many different areas for many different jobs; all require newcomers to be prepared to learn a lot quickly. Explains one, "My responsibility was to look after about fifty oil wells, the same as other more experienced engineers. I did my job by asking a lot of questions and getting a lot of help. I was learning to use new software packages, find information on the company networks, analyze available data, and use the analysis to move toward a solution (a solution is usually a project of some type to improve production)." Some newcomers to BP spend their first three years in the Challenge Program, a rotational program that places them in three different assignments; one participant we spoke with spent a year as a reservoir engineer, later moved into a position as a production engineer, then finally worked as a petroleum engineer and production coordinator. Most people tell us that they rarely interact with upper-level people in the company, but none saw this as a major issue; as one puts it, "I don't need face time with bigwigs right now. I need to be technically proficient, and if I want to progress, it will be my skills in concert with my networking that will get me there. Networking is very important in BP, but skills are more important. An emphasis is placed on contact with folks from other teams and departments. We do a lot together."

PEERS

"The social scene is pretty good" for BP newcomers, although the particulars vary depending on one's placement as well as "your status: single/married, kids or not, where you live relative to work, and interests." Reports one typical newbie, "The majority of my friends now are from the company, and I interact more with my peers outside of work than I do at work. At work, the focus is with my team (though we will meet up for lunch a time or two each week). Outside of work, something is going on virtually every weekend, and occasionally on weeknights." Our correspondent in Alaska tells us that "I'm on two hockey teams made up solely of young BP folks, and there [are] always parties, hikes, runs, climbing, and all sorts of activities going on. Most of my friends in Alaska also work at BP, so I spend the majority of my time outside of work with them."

Moving On

BP did not provide us with data on former entry-level employees, and those we spoke with have no plans to leave the company.

Attrition

"The frequency of downsizing exercises," as one employee puts it, is a major reason some newcomers don't stick with BP. Some people leave because they find their jobs too demanding, while other people leave because they feel that opportunities for advancement and interesting assignments are too difficult to come by.

CATERPILLAR
Various Positions

THE BIG PICTURE

Come work for the company that makes the big machines. You'll join one of America's most successful industrial companies and enjoy a salary employees call "competitive" and a benefits package they rate "top notch."

STATS

LOCATION(S) WHERE ENTRY-LEVEL EMPLOYEES WORK

"Caterpillar [Inc.] is a global company, with nearly 250 company facilities worldwide. While many of the entry-level new hires would begin their career at the company's Peoria, Illinois, headquarters, Caterpillar has independent dealers and customers on every continent."

AVERAGE NUMBER OF APPLICATIONS EACH YEAR

"Caterpillar receives about 50,000 applications each year for all positions across the company. About one-third of those applications would be from recent college graduates."

AVERAGE NUMBER HIRED OVER THE LAST TEN YEARS

"Over the last ten years, Caterpillar has hired about 1,000 people per year on the management payroll, which is where the majority of entry-level hiring takes place."

ENTRY-LEVEL POSITION(S) AVAILABLE

"Caterpillar hires entry-level employees in a variety of disciplines. The primary areas would include engineering, information technology, manufacturing, marketing and communications, business, accounting, and finance."

AVERAGE HOURS WORKED PER WEEK

"The majority of positions within Caterpillar are full-time, forty hours per week minimum. Many jobs offer varying degrees of travel as a part of the position responsibility. Management employees are expected to manage their time and workload appropriately, often requiring time at work beyond the forty-hour minimum."

PERCENTAGE OF ENTRY-LEVEL HIRES STILL WITH THE COMPANY AFTER THREE, FIVE, AND TEN YEARS

"Among employee management, which is where the majority of entry-level position hiring takes place, 92 percent of new hires are still with the company after three years. After five years, 79 percent of new hires are still with the company. After ten years, 73 percent of new hires are still with the company."

Average Starting Salary

"At Caterpillar, you'll earn what you're worth—we're firm believers in higher rewards for higher performers. In addition, our more-than-competitive salary package includes a base salary along with incentive compensation."

Benefits Offered

"Caterpillar offers one of the most generous benefits packages in the corporate world, including: 100 percent matching on 401(k) contributions; portable pension equity plan; paid vacation and personal time; tuition reimbursement; comprehensive medical, dental, and vision coverage; a preventative care program; and life and disability insurance."

Contact Information

For more information about opportunities and how to apply, visit www.catcareers.com. General company information is available on www.cat.com.

Getting Hired

Caterpillar recruits on campuses and also accepts applications through its website. Company representatives tell us that "the development of a diverse, global workforce within an environment that encourages innovation and rewards individual and team performance is critical to its future success. Caterpillar values diversity, not only in the race or gender of employees, but also in background, skills, and experience." First jobbers from Caterpillar's more than twenty different business units describe the hiring process similarly. Here's how one newbie in human resources recalls it: "The director of compensation and benefits, the director of succession management, the corporate [human relations] manager, and the director of human relations interviewed me. Each interview was one hour in length and was a structured behavior-based interview. The questions revolved around how I have responded in the past to given situations (i.e., 'Tell me about a time you had to convince a boss or coworker of your idea'). During my interview, the program coordinator gave me an overview of the program. She also took me to lunch. At the end of the day I was given a drug test. The program coordinator contacted me approximately a week later with a job offer."

Money and Perks

"Salary increases are based on business conditions and strongly tied to job performance" at Caterpillar. "The highest performers are rewarded with the highest salary increases," company representatives report. First jobbers rave about the benefits package; one new hire tells us that "the entire package is excellent. If I were forced to pick one as the best, I would say the 401(k) plan. Caterpillar matches employee contributions to the 401(k) plan dollar-for-dollar up to the first 6 percent of gross salary. These contributions are immediately vested." Other new hires say the best perk is "working in a team environment. This allowed [us] to meet a large group of [our] people in a short time. Also, there were after-work sporting and social events that allowed everyone to get acquainted with each other outside of the work environment."

THE ROPES

Orientation and training regimens at Caterpillar "vary by business unit or functional area." Many of the employees we spoke with describe a one-week orientation period; however, some (such as those in marketing) recount orientation periods that lasted over three months, and others describe being briefly introduced to their bosses before getting to work. For most positions, orientation and training are both thorough and rigorous, designed to ensure that new hires are familiar with both Caterpillar's corporate culture and the tasks for which they were hired; these processes typically involve classes and seminars, team-building exercises, plant tours, and equipment-specific training. New hires in manufacturing participate in a special three-year rotational development program, as do some beginners in human resources.

DAY IN THE LIFE

Caterpillar is a huge company that hires entry-level employees for numerous jobs in most of its divisions. There is no typical day for all of these employees; they do, however, participate in a common corporate culture. Part of that culture involves close contact with upper management. As one new hire tells us, "One of the best things about this program is the amount of exposure you get to leadership. I've met with several vice presidents and upper-level managers." Agrees another, "It is sometimes scary the extent to which I have interacted with high-level employees within the company. So far in my career, I have interacted with [many] vice presidents, a group president, and have given presentations to division managers. When averaged on a weekly basis, the time would be very minimal (not even an hour), but the time spent is very valuable." Another aspect is the emphasis on taking initiative. Supervisors, one entry-level worker reports, "are not afraid to let me take on as many challenges or responsibilities as I want (as long as I demonstrate that I'm capable of handling them). They do a great job of providing coaching and support as I take on tougher, more demanding responsibilities."

PEERS

Caterpillar's emphasis on teamwork helps build strong relationships, both among entry-level workers and between entry-level workers and their bosses. Reports one employee, "There is definitely camaraderie with our new hires. Part of my responsibility in my current position is to organize events for our new hires. These events have ranged from facility tours to bowling outings." After-hours socializing varies from division to division and from city to city. A manufacturing trainee says, "There is a large after-hours social scene at Caterpillar. I usually interact with my peers about ten to twenty hours a week at work, and after work I usually spend about eight hours a week interacting [with them]". A new hire in accounting tells a different story and says, "I do not live in the same city as most of my peers, so my social interaction with them outside of work is limited, but it [does exist]."

MOVING ON

Caterpillar doesn't lose many employees; over 90 percent of new hires remain with the company for at least three years. Company representatives brag that "the average length of service for full-time Caterpillar employees in Illinois is 18.7 years—nearly *four times* the manufacturing industry average of just five years. Since 1972, more than 17,000 current and retired employees have reached their thirty-year service anniversary." The few people who fly the coop usually do so "for personal reasons because they determine that the job isn't a good fit for them or because they identify another opportunity that they feel better meets their goals."

BEST AND WORST

"Four of the five group presidents started with Caterpillar soon after college. Their first jobs were in accounting, engineering, finance, and marketing. Today, their years of service with Caterpillar range from twenty-nine to thirty-six years, and each of these senior executives has administrative responsibilities for a group of business units."

CENTRA
Various Positions

The Big Picture

Centra provides software and support for real-time business-to-business collaboration via the Internet and corporate networks. The company conducts everything from one-on-one virtual classroom sessions to meetings of over 500 executives from across the globe. Only eight years old, Centra could develop into a major growth company. If it does, today's first jobbers could be tomorrow's fat cats, since—as they say on Wall Street—a rising tide lifts all boats.

Stats

Location(s) Where Entry-level Employees Work

Mostly in Lexington, MA; some positions available in other locations

Entry-level Position(s) Available

Various entry-level positions are available.

Benefits Offered

Centra offers its employees medical and dental insurance. Additional benefits include life and disability insurance, flexible spending accounts, a 401(k) plan, stock options, an employee stock purchase plan, a tuition reimbursement program, paid time off, holidays, vacation days, and sick days.

Contact Information

Visit the website at www.centra.com/corporate/jobs.

Getting Hired

Centra posts available positions on its website. One employee we spoke with found his job online; several others say they found their jobs through placement agencies. Some people were attracted by "the company, the people, and opportunities available at a small, fast-growing company." The hiring process is fairly standard; explains one employee, "I interviewed in two rounds; the first interview was with the hiring manager and human resources. The second interview was with the chief financial officer, to whom the department I would be working for reported. I was then called to confirm references and then called [with the] verbal offer by the hiring manager, which I accepted." Interviewers "ask very basic questions about computer skills. The interviews were very friendly. I think the interviewers were just trying to get a read on my long-term interests, my working style, and my work experience." Successful hires suggest you "express a willingness to learn and an interest in the industry."

MONEY AND PERKS

Centra first jobbers tell us that their "start date was somewhat negotiable" but that "salary, what [we] did, and where [we] did it were not." Employees appreciate the company's extensive benefits package. They also praise the "informal work environment" with "lots of young people, which makes it easy to make friends." One newbie especially likes how he "was able to interact with all of the different departments and talk with people in various positions to determine areas of interest for [himself]. This was invaluable to [him]."

THE ROPES

Most of the employees we spoke with started at jobs that didn't require much training. Since those we spoke with moved on to better positions relatively quickly, they didn't really mind. Writes one, "I think the receptionist position [I held] was a perfect entry-level job. I learned a lot from this position, interacted with everyone in the company, and learned how the company worked." Agrees another, who also began at a reception desk, "I viewed the position as a means to get to other positions in the company. My duties were very much day-to-day administration and not too difficult to learn or perform." Another new hire adds, "[That orientation and training is generally informal] because it's a young, small company. On my first day, I walked around and met everyone. By my second day, I was contacting customers and prospects." She also tells us that she had "no formal training, but [she] learned a lot from [her] coworkers."

DAY IN THE LIFE

The core of Centra's business is facilitating e-Learning (college courses, training sessions, etc., conducted via the Internet) and virtual business meetings. Many first jobbers play a crucial role in these Web events as event managers; they "host" the event by coordinating logistics, training clients to use Centra software, and serving as moderators. Other new hires provide the type of support found in all businesses: clerical, human resources, sales, [and] customer service. While some consider this "mostly grunt work, it *is* important. Every company needs someone to manage those day-to-day tasks. Centra is very busy since it is growing. There are many interviews taking place and new hires coming on board, lots of equipment that has to be ordered on a daily basis, and many other tasks to complete."

PEERS

As do many young companies, Centra has a large population of fresh-faced go-getters, many of them first jobbers, among its employees. These workers enjoy "a lot of contact with other first jobbers at the company. There's a big after-hours social scene." One new hire says, "I guess I interact with peers at work maybe five hours per week, but probably ten or more outside of work." Others tell us about "weekly after-work parties, going out on weekends, and partying at each others' apartments."

MOVING ON

Centra does a good job of promoting from within, and many first jobbers find themselves quickly moving on to better jobs in the company. Two of our correspondents began as receptionists; today, one works in human resources, and the other became a marketing specialist.

CITIZEN SCHOOLS
Teaching Associates and Teaching Fellows

THE BIG PICTURE

Citizen Schools offers after school programs that "deliver a creative and effective learning model that addresses community needs while building student skills through hands-on experiential learning activities" primarily in poor, urban settings. It's the kind of company that advertises its employment opportunities on websites like Idealist.org. In short, this is a job you get if you seek much more than financial fulfillment.

STATS

LOCATION(S) WHERE ENTRY-LEVEL EMPLOYEES WORK

Tucson, AZ; San Jose, CA; Boston, MA; Lowell, MA; Malden, MA; Worcester, MA; New Brunswick, NJ; Houston, TX

AVERAGE NUMBER OF APPLICATIONS EACH YEAR

The company receives from 200 to 300 applications per year.

AVERAGE NUMBER HIRED OVER THE LAST TEN YEARS

"We have only been in existence for eight-and-a-half years and have increased our staff from five full-time employees to approximately ninety full-time equivalent employees and from forty to fifty part-time employees. This past year, we hired nineteen new Teaching Fellows (TF) and thirty new Teaching Associates (TA) to complement returning TF and TA staff."

ENTRY-LEVEL POSITION(S) AVAILABLE

"We hire approximately thirty to forty new Teaching Associates in the fall and an additional ten to twenty in the spring. Every summer we hire twenty new AmeriCorps-funded Teaching Fellows. The Teaching Fellows position is a two-year position."

AVERAGE HOURS WORKED PER WEEK

Hours vary according to the position. Teaching Associates work from twenty to thirty hours per week, program staff (including Teaching Fellows) work from forty to fifty hours per week, and headquarters staff work from twenty-four to fifty hours per week.

PERCENTAGE OF ENTRY-LEVEL HIRES STILL WITH THE COMPANY AFTER THREE, FIVE, AND TEN YEARS

After three years, about 80 percent of all entry-level hires remain with Citizen Schools.

AVERAGE STARTING SALARY

"Compensation varies by position and is commensurate with experience. AmeriCorps Teaching Fellows earn a salary of $19,200 per year."

BENEFITS OFFERED

"All full-time employees have the opportunity to enroll in [a] health care plan (currently HMO Blue, a provider of Blue Cross/Blue Shield). Citizen Schools pays 80 percent of the monthly premium, and the employee pays 20 percent. This amount is deducted from his or her paycheck on a pre-tax basis. Health insurance, like all benefits, is pro-rated for part-time FTE staff. Part-time Teaching Associates are eligible to enroll in health insurance upon entering their fifth semester with Citizen Schools. Citizen Schools offers both individual and family plans, which includes health insurance benefits for domestic partners." Furthermore, while working with Citizen Schools, "staff can concurrently receive a master's in education with a specialization in out-of-school time from Lesley University (assistance provided by Citizen Schools)." They have the "opportunity to enroll in a 403(b) retirement plan (currently with TIAA-CREF). Citizen Schools matches up to $500 annually after one full year of employment." Time off includes "fifteen vacation days, nine sick days, three personal days, and eleven paid holidays per year. After four years of continuous employment, employees are eligible for a twenty day vacation splash." There is also an "opportunity to enroll in Section 125 flexible spending account (for non-reimbursed medical expenses) and dependent care account program. Long-term disability insurance [comes] at no cost to the employee." When junior comes along, staff members are eligible for "six weeks paid parental leave for primary caregivers [and] two weeks paid parental leave for secondary caregivers."

CONTACT INFORMATION

Joanna Varholak

Recruiting Specialist

Museum Wharf

308 Congress Street

Boston, MA 02210

Tel. 617-695-2300 ext. 144

Fax 617-695-2367

joannavarholak@citizenschools.org

www.citizenschools.org

Emily McCann

CFO

Museum Wharf

308 Congress Street

Boston, MA 02210

Tel. 617-695-2300 ext. 120

Fax 617-695-2367

emilymccann@citizenschools.org

GETTING HIRED

Citizen Schools scours its applicant pool for candidates who demonstrate "experience in education/working with kids; commitment to nonprofit/social service work in urban communities; flexibility and patience; excellent communication skills (written and verbal); enthusiasm; and entrepreneurial spirit. Bilingualism/multilingualism is a plus." All applicants fill out the online application available on the organization's website, and submit a cover letter and resume with the application. One successful candidate writes, "I emailed my cover letter and resume and followed [up] with a call to the human resources specialist. The director of development called me back to arrange an interview. I then met with her, along with the manager of individual giving. The interview was casual and they inquired about my goals, interests, and intent for the position. They stressed the importance of enthusiasm, flexibility, and dedication. The energy around the office was high, and I was impressed by the fact that employees seemed to be enjoying their jobs." Sample interview questions include: "What about Citizen Schools most excites you? After reading and filling out the job application, what is your understanding of the impact we are trying to achieve? Tell me about your past work experience and how it relates to this position? What are your three greatest strengths and weaknesses for this job?"

MONEY AND PERKS

Teaching Associates earn $10.75 per hour during their first semester of work; the starting salary for Teaching Fellows was slightly under $20,000 for the 2003–2004 school year. According to organization representatives, "salary reviews occur on an annual basis. Annual increases typically are in the 2 to 5 percent range." The best perk, employees tell us, is "working with kids!" The organization also touts its "$2,000 housing adjustment benefit [for AmeriCorps Teaching Fellows]."

THE ROPES

"When an employee arrives on his or her first day, he or she already has a voicemail account, an email account, a network log in, and a mailbox. All new employees meet with the human resources manager for an in-depth review of benefits and policies (typically one hour). New employees also receive technology training on computer systems, email, voicemail, etc. New employees are also given an office tour by the office manager. This orientation usually takes about half a day." One new hire adds, "I got a thorough overview of the job and what my responsibilities were [before I started work], so I felt like I knew what I was getting into. Everyone was very accommodating to me [considering] the fact that I was both new to the organization and new to the workforce. I learned by asking questions, watching others, and using my best judgment. All of these things have helped me do my job well and improve many projects and processes with my own ideas."

DAY IN THE LIFE

"There is no real typical day at the job" at Citizen Schools. As organization representatives explain, "Citizen Schools turns children into community heroes: children apprentice with lawyers, Web designers, [and] architects and culminate their learning apprenticeships by arguing trials before federal judges, designing websites for their school, organizing public events, publishing newspapers, and much more." Citizen Schools' Teaching Fellows "work primarily as front-line educators and community builders, leading hands-on activities for small and large groups children; designing and teaching curriculum; leading peers in planning and implementation of educational activities; recruiting students and volunteers; communicating with and engaging parents; and fostering partnerships with school faculty and community organizations." They also recruit volunteer Citizen Teachers from the local community. Teaching Associates also handle a wide range of duties, including leading curriculum, designing and leading learning games, organizing sports activities, and directing hands-on learning experiences. They also confer with students' parents to keep them apprised of their progress.

PEERS

"Citizen Schools attracts a wide variety of people. Most are very intelligent, friendly, and come with a unique array of past experiences," offers one employee with the organization. They're the type of folks who believe "that all communities are blessed with thousands of born teachers (old and young, professional and laborer, athlete and artist); [these are] people who would like to enrich their own lives and contribute to their community by sharing their skills with children." Many are young; one employee writes, "There is large camaraderie largely due to the young age of the Teaching Fellows. My peers are the coolest cats in town."

MOVING ON

Among those employees who use Citizen Schools as a springboard to land another job, "approximately 70 percent are involved in community-based education initiatives as program directors and teachers. Some are involved in graduate studies. Several graduates have become campus directors or start-up captains at our affiliate sites. Because of their excellent teaching, leading and community organizing skills, and Citizen Schools' strong reputation, Teaching Fellows are highly sought-after employees."

ATTRITION

Current employees warn that teaching for Citizen Schools is hard work. "I wish I had known about the amount of hours that would be needed after work," one employee tells us. The organization adds that "Teaching Associates often leave to find more full-time employment or because of scheduling conflicts. Other staff may leave due to new opportunities and/or better salary."

BEST AND WORST

According to organization representatives, the best new hire ever "began with Citizen Schools as a Teaching Associate, became a Teaching Fellow, and is currently a successful campus director." The worst new hire was "a recent college graduate who moved to Boston to become a Teaching Fellow and was overwhelmed by living in such a big city and not prepared to work with children nine to fourteen years old. She resigned after only six weeks. This shaped how we recruited for Teaching Fellows. All potential candidates now spend a day at a Citizen Schools campus as part of their interview process."

CITY YEAR
Corps Member

THE BIG PICTURE

City Year is one of the bigger volunteer programs falling under the AmeriCorps umbrella. Through a year of community service, leadership development, and civic engagement, participants mentor and educate children in public schools; they also lead community service projects. Budget problems from AmeriCorps stymied some City Year operations in 2003 and 2004, but the federal government has increased funding for AmeriCorps in the coming year, indicating a bright future for City Year for 2004 and 2005 (and beyond).

STATS

LOCATION(S) WHERE ENTRY-LEVEL EMPLOYEES WORK

"In the 2004–2005 corps year, City Year will have service opportunities at fifteen sites: Boston, MA; Chicago, IL; Cleveland, OH; Columbia, SC; Columbus, OH; Detroit, MI; Little Rock, AR; New Hampshire; New York, NY; Philadelphia, PA; Rhode Island; San Antonio, TX; San Jose/Silicon Valley, CA; Seattle/King County, WA; and Washington, DC."

AVERAGE NUMBER OF APPLICATIONS EACH YEAR

"City Year receives 17,000 inquiries and about 3,000 completed applications for 750 to 1,000 corps member positions."

AVERAGE NUMBER HIRED OVER THE LAST TEN YEARS

"Corps member enrollment in the 2003–2004 corps year is 750. This reduction, from 1,000 corps members in 2002–2003, was due to federal funding cuts to AmeriCorps, which have been reversed for the 2004–2005 corps year; City Year now expects to enroll more than 1,000 members in the coming year."

ENTRY-LEVEL POSITION(S) AVAILABLE

"Corps members work full-time in service to community and country as tutors and mentors to children in the classroom and after-school programs and as leaders of physical service projects (such as painting schools, planting community gardens, building play spaces, [and] revitalizing urban spaces.)"

AVERAGE HOURS WORKED PER WEEK

"Corps members serve full-time every week for ten months to complete at least 1,700 hours of service."

PERCENTAGE OF ENTRY-LEVEL HIRES STILL WITH THE COMPANY AFTER THREE, FIVE, AND TEN YEARS

"The City Year model is a one-year term of service, with approximately one-third of City Year corps members returning to serve a second year in a leadership capacity."

AVERAGE STARTING SALARY

"Corps members receive a very modest living stipend, based on the region's cost-of-living and other factors."

BENEFITS OFFERED

"City Year provides corps members with standard health care benefits." Additional benefits include "a $4,725 education award that can be applied toward existing student loans or future higher education tuition. Meeting the 1,700-hour service requirement secures this full education award."

CONTACT INFORMATION

For general information visit www.cityyear.org.

For application information visit www.cityyear.org/joinus/joincorps.cfm.

GETTING HIRED

City Year scans each application for evidence of "the four C's: character, cooperation, commitment, and competence." Volunteers must be between the ages of seventeen and twenty-four; according to the organization, such people are "young enough to want to change the world—[and] old enough to do it." A complete application includes personal information, two letters of reference, and three personal essays. A screening interview follows, with most applicants receiving a second, in-depth interview later in the process. One successful applicant tells us that the process "was a real mix between an application for school and an application for a job. There was a standard form with questions and essays. I also had to send in letters of recommendation. [Subsequently] I got a letter from City Year offering me an interview, and I set one up while I was home for winter break. I interviewed with the recruitment director. She provided me with a lot of information about the job that I couldn't get from the website. She told me about the particular challenges that the type of work presented and asked how I would deal with them. The process was formal but not intimidating."

MONEY AND PERKS

No sane person would take a position with City Year for the money. You may be able to negotiate the location in which you work, but all other aspects of the job offer are "a take it or leave it proposition." Several of the volunteers we spoke with said that City Year offers "great networking opportunities. With all of the community service we do and with all the service partners that we work with and attract to the organization, [we] get to make a lot of connections, if [we] put [ourselves] out there." Others feel that the best perk was "being able to put your idealism to work." Organization representatives note that "alumni have a well-earned reputation as hard-working, dedicated, and idealistic leaders who bring passion, competence, and a can-do attitude to subsequent endeavors," so City Year service should be a help on future job applications.

THE ROPES

City Year orientation, one newbie tells us, "lasts for five weeks and is provided by a host of people. Some training is given by local City Year staff, but at least half is not. We have members of the community and representatives from numerous agencies come in and speak to us. We also go out to several places for workshops and lectures. Each team also has its own particular training with the community service organization it works with on a regular basis. For example, the Case Foundation Young Heroes Team (my team) had several training sessions with an organization [called] For Love of Children (FLOC)." Ongoing training continues throughout a volunteer's ten-month tenure; explains one first jobber, "We receive all kinds of training from all kinds of people, and it goes on throughout the year. Every other Friday all the teams are together for training in self-defense, different social issues, the government process, health, and wellness. We [corps members] could suggest themes for any of these days as well."

DAY IN THE LIFE

Notes one corps member, "There really is no such thing as a typical day, or even a typical week, which is one of the great things about the job." While some volunteers spend the bulk of their time teaching in the classroom or producing educational dramas for school children, many others shift from role to role, serving whatever project the local City Year office has undertaken that day, week, or month. Those projects could include anything from delivering meals to shut-ins to serving as course guides on a homeless walk to providing day care to organizing press conferences and other media events. As one volunteer puts it, "The job changes every day, and the teams achieve more and more independence throughout the year both for individual service and initiatives (our service projects) and within our schools. The work itself doesn't really change but the level of independence and individual initiative does increase throughout the year."

PEERS

Most City Year volunteers enjoy a strong peer network. Offers one, "The camaraderie is excellent—[there is] a ton of outside-of-work social gathering, hanging out, etc. Some of my best friends are corps members I serve with." Of course, the amount of peer interaction varies according to the individuals involved and the locations; in some areas, "because teams have different focuses, there are times when we can go without seeing a team for a week or more. Regardless, there is some camaraderie across teams since we spend so much time in training together." Many people tell us that corps members "have such different backgrounds," which they see as a major plus. As one member puts it, "One of the cool things about working with so many different people is that there is always somebody to go to with a unique perspective on things or with information that you don't have. My peers, for the most part, are nothing like me, and it is really the first time that I have been in a situation like that."

Moving On

City Year is a ten-month program, and many members move on after one term of service, "having earned their education award." Some use their education awards to "bear the costs of higher education, making college and graduate school the top destination after City Year." One volunteer says, "Some people do come back for a second year, and that's something I'm seriously considering." Returnees constitute about one-third of the volunteer force; those who return usually find themselves "in a leadership capacity."

Attrition

Members who leave early generally complain about "the staff and the hours of the work. Those people looked at the experience more as a conventional job than as a learning experience that would lead to other things." Some people leave when they discover they cannot survive on the living stipend.

Best and Worst

According to organization representatives, "some of City Year's most successful corps members now advocate for social justice, lead foundations, work in schools, and create new opportunities for service. Other very successful corps members are those who incorporate an ethic of service and commitment to community in their work as doctors, lawyers, and businesspeople. City Year alumni are also in government and on City Year staff."

DELOITTE
Various Positions

THE BIG PICTURE

Enter the expanding universe of professional services and advice at Deloitte, a firm that serves more than half the world's largest companies. Deloitte's services include everything from assurance to enterprise risk services to management solutions to tax services. Does this sound intriguing? Then maybe you're perfect for one of the nearly 2,000 entry-level jobs that open at Deloitte each year.

STATS

LOCATION(S) WHERE ENTRY-LEVEL EMPLOYEES WORK

"Deloitte hires entry-level candidates in nearly all of our eighty U.S. offices."

AVERAGE NUMBER OF APPLICATIONS EACH YEAR

"We review more than 10,000 resumes [and] applications each year."

AVERAGE NUMBER HIRED OVER THE LAST TEN YEARS

Deloitte hires 1,900 people per year.

ENTRY-LEVEL POSITION(S) AVAILABLE

"We hire a range of entry-level candidates [who have majored in] accounting, finance, information systems, computer science, business, marketing, economics, and others."

AVERAGE STARTING SALARY

Employees earn from $45,000 to $50,000, depending on the market.

BENEFITS OFFERED

Deloitte offers a comprehensive medical benefits plan for employees, their families, and domestic partners, and includes a prescription drug plan, dental plan, and discount vision care. Additional benefits include a 401(k) plan, flexible spending plan, pre-tax transportation program, various forms of flexible work arrangements, parental leave, adoption assistance, adoption reimbursement, child care resource and referral program, elder care consultation and referral service, mortgage assistance program, and paid time off programs.

CONTACT INFORMATION

"Students can either visit us on the Web (www.deloitte.com) and apply online or apply through their campus career center."

GETTING HIRED

Deloitte seeks candidates "who can provide evidence of excellent client-service skills; marketing, sales, and communication skills; management effectiveness (time management, project management, people management); and leadership skills (team playing, driving results)." If that describes you, apply through your campus career center or online. "All resumes and applications are reviewed and selected for interview," firm representatives tell us. They use "a structured, behaviorally-based interview to hear real experiences that provide evidence of the skills/attributes that we're interviewing for." One successful hire in tax services describes the application process this way: "On my resume, I focused on experiences and knowledge that were specifically related to the job I was applying for. I was very truthful and genuine in my cover letter. I had a total of five interviews, and they were with partners and senior managers during first and second rounds. The tone of the interview depended on who I was interviewing with. They were all very friendly and asked questions to get to know who I was and why I wanted to be at the firm."

MONEY AND PERKS

Newcomers to Deloitte tell us that "the start date is definitely negotiable and the office where you work is also, to some extent, but that typically requires another interview in that office." As for salary, everyone we spoke with agrees with the first jobber who states, "I do not think that if I asked for more, I would have gotten it." Company representatives note that "salary increases are based on performance, business growth, and marketplace." Full-time workers "generally start in August, September, and January." Most of our respondents say the best perks are "the great people who you work with" and "being able to work [with] so many clients from so many different industries."

THE ROPES

A first jobber in tax services tells us that orientation at Deloitte "lasts, on the whole, about two weeks. We had one-day new-hire orientation that covered benefits, general overview of the firm, different support functions, etc. Then we went to a national training for four days. Although it was technically training, the new hires and I were all so new it was like an orientation into the firm as well as tax training. When we got back into the office, we had a week-long new-hire training that focused on more technical tax training as well as software training." Once orientation and initial training is done, newbies "are assigned 'buddies,' 'counselors,' and 'mentors.' These individuals are generally selected and developed for their roles—often based on their team-working skills and their involvement in recruiting generally. We consider the involvement of our client-service professionals as personal and professional development."

DAY IN THE LIFE

After orientation and initial training, "New hires commence working on teams dealing directly with clients" at Deloitte, and "they fulfill these responsibilities through a fairly structured team-support approach." Explains one entry-level worker, "A typical day involves coming in and checking our emails, then we start on our work. Sometimes we work on more than one project, so we have to balance our workload. The day involves our preparing the work papers and then getting them reviewed by our seniors. During this whole process there is also a lot of communication between the staff and the senior staff." Adds another, "My responsibilities [from day one] were to have a good attitude, learn from every engagement I was assigned to, and ask questions. A lot of this job is on-site, learn-as-you-go training." There's rarely down time; one newbie tells us, "I am almost never bored. When I am at work, I am always thinking and keeping myself busy and the time flies by. Sometimes the amount of work can be a little overwhelming but that makes the time go by faster."

PEERS

There are many first jobbers; therefore, new hires describe an atmosphere that is "like a college class. We have a great camaraderie. We usually go out together for a while at least every Friday, and more often than not we get together for something on the weekends." One worker says, "[Other new hires are] smart, nice, and hardworking. We also share a lot of similarities because I feel that every company has its own culture of people, and all of us were hired by Deloitte." Those in accounting tell us that they enjoy their peers' support and help in preparing for the CPA exam.

MOVING ON

Many entry-level employees come to Deloitte in the hopes of building a career. Those who use it as a way station often go on to business school, capitalizing on their experiences to build a more compelling business school application. Others "wind up working with clients they met through their work engagements; so in a sense, they continue to work with Deloitte."

ATTRITION

According to Deloitte representatives, "there's no over-arching reason that stands out" for why some entry-level hires don't stick around long, "but generally when a person leaves that early in the process, it's because of a disparity between the job responsibilities and the person's goals or expectations." Some new hires, we're told, simply can't take the long hours required of them. "It isn't for everyone," concedes one audit associate.

DEMOCRATIC NATIONAL COMMITTEE
Various Positions

THE BIG PICTURE

The Democratic National Committee (DNC) coordinates the political party's presidential nominating convention; supports Democratic candidates for public office at the national, state, and local levels; and publicizes and promotes the positions of the Democratic party as a whole. Working here is a great way to break into politics and an equally great excuse to move to Washington, DC, a fun town and a good place to start a career.

STATS

LOCATION(S) WHERE ENTRY-LEVEL EMPLOYEES WORK

First jobbers work in Washington, DC.

AVERAGE NUMBER OF APPLICATIONS EACH YEAR

The DNC receives 100 applications per year.

ENTRY-LEVEL POSITION(S) AVAILABLE

Entry-level hires work as administrative assistants to directors and offer administrative support.

AVERAGE HOURS WORKED PER WEEK

New hires work fifty hours per week.

PERCENTAGE OF ENTRY-LEVEL HIRES STILL WITH THE COMPANY AFTER THREE, FIVE, AND TEN YEARS

After three years, 5 percent of new hires remain with the DNC.

AVERAGE STARTING SALARY

New hires earn $30,000 per year.

BENEFITS OFFERED

The DNC offers its employees major medical, dental, and vision insurance. Additional benefits include life insurance, short-term disability, and supplemental medical insurance; a 401(k) plan; and flexible spending accounts.

CONTACT INFORMATION

Jewelle Hazel

Director of Human Resources

hazelj@dnc.org

GETTING HIRED

The DNC lists job openings on its website; internships, first jobbers tell us, are an excellent gateway to subsequent employment (according to DNC representatives, "Most of our entry-level hiring is done by word-of-mouth. We also hire prior DNC interns and people who have prior campaign experience."). Because interns are already known by human resources and other staffers, they usually avoid a prolonged vetting process (including resumes, letters of recommendation, etc.). All other applicants, however, must take the conventional route. Here's how one applicant describes it: "I sent my resume via email, actually for another position at the DNC. However, my resume was noted and sent to the director of the Women's Vote Center, where I was eventually hired. When I heard that my resume was drawn from a pool of other resumes, it appeared that the DNC internally communicated; this impressed me. Since I was in Texas at the time, I interviewed via teleconference with the director. The questions were both vague and specific, ranging from, 'Why do you want to work with the DNC Women's Vote Center?' to specific questions about my previous work experience." At DNC "individuals who are [good at multitasking] and who are quick and creative thinkers are DNC material."

MONEY AND PERKS

The primary goals of most first jobbers is to accumulate experience and gain a foothold in democratic politics; accordingly, few people worry much about their starting salaries. "I didn't try to negotiate. I was perfectly happy with the start date and salary," writes one first jobber in the research department. One employee says, "The health benefits [we] receive [are] unbelievable. I am covered so completely that I have nothing to worry about." Other excellent perks include "working at the pulse of the DNC, so you get to interact with the entire staff. It's also a great way to make connections."

THE ROPES

When candidates accept an offer, "a human resources package is mailed to them at least one week before the start date. This package includes their confirmation letter, benefits, and personnel information. On the first day a welcome package is awaiting the new employee, which includes information technology information, basic DNC information and policies, information on public transportation, and places to eat. Department directors conduct specific department orientation on the first day. Each department's orientation is different, based on how the department works. A human resources orientation is scheduled for several days after." While most DNC employees receive some formal training during their tenure, it is primarily "a learn-as-you go process. As I was working and questions arose, I asked them and had them answered by my colleagues."

Day in the Life

The first jobbers we spoke with at the DNC work on a wide range of assignments; for example, some assist senior strategists and organizers, others supervise and coordinate events for interns, and others perform basic clerical and administrative tasks. What they all share in common is that they're very busy; explains one, "There is always something to do in our office. I always have a lot of work and long- term projects. While anyone can get bored during office work, I know that I have things I can be doing. If I find myself either overwhelmed or bored, a quick Internet read, such as a newspaper or clips, can help with that. It's about pacing your day and allowing yourself to merge into the day and your work." They all also get to mix and mingle with party bigwigs. As one newbie tells us, "Even as an intern I was given the opportunity by my boss and other high-level people to sit in on meetings. I have the opportunity to work directly with them on a regular basis, depending on what we are working on and what kind of meeting is being held."

Peers

DNC staffers tell us that their peers "are extremely friendly. We often hang out at happy hours and events, and we have other outside contact. Sometimes it is just our department, and other times it's the entire staff." Notes one first jobber, "One thing unites all of us, even if our personalities differ: All of us [are] determined to win back the White House in 2004. From there, great, and even unexpected, relationships can form." The ubiquity of "mostly young, diverse individuals" on the staff means first jobbers have "people with whom one can talk with if [they feel] overwhelmed."

Moving On

"Since we are a campaign headquarters and a fundraising operation, employment with the DNC is very cyclical," officials tell us. "Most people move on after a particular campaign cycle to either work for candidates who have won a particular campaign or to work for other democratic organizations or nonprofit organizations to expand their campaign portfolio." Some leave to go back to school. The average tenure of a DNC first jobber is two years.

Attrition

Turnover rates are high at the DNC, where approximately 50 percent of employees leave within a year of starting. Most people find work with an elected official or another political organization.

EDWARD JONES
Various Positions

THE BIG PICTURE

Named in *Fortune* magazine's "100 Best Companies to Work For" six years running, Edward Jones is one of those rare companies that continued to grow rapidly throughout the recession. It isn't just the growth-related job security that employees love, though; the *Fortune* ranking reflects worker satisfaction on a whole range of quality-of-life issues, including benefits, workplace culture, and advancement opportunities. Many new hires start in a rotational program—ideal for those who know they want a career in the world of finance but aren't sure what area best suits them.

STATS

LOCATION(S) WHERE ENTRY-LEVEL EMPLOYEES WORK

Edward Jones has offices in St. Louis, Missouri; home offices in Tempe, Arizona; and many other locations for branch-office work.

ENTRY-LEVEL POSITION(S) AVAILABLE

New hires work as investment representatives and hold positions in accounting, compliance and licensing, human resources, information systems, marketing, operations, products and sales, research, and training.

AVERAGE HOURS WORKED PER WEEK

Employees work forty or more hours per week.

BENEFITS OFFERED

Benefits vary according to the position.

CONTACT INFORMATION

Visit the website at www.edwardjonesopportunity.com/usa_home.html.

GETTING HIRED

Many first jobbers get their start at Edward Jones through the rotational development program, "a year-long rotational program through four different product and marketing areas of the firm. During the course of the year, [employees] were also required to become Series 7 licensed [Series 7 is an exam that qualifies an idividual to trade in corporate securities]. The program has recently changed to include areas beyond product and marketing." Many new hires find their way into the rotational program through internships they held while they were still in college; "The internships helped me get the initial interview," explains one trainee. The interview process, a first jobber reports, "is pretty unique. They have a three-interview minimum. The first one is just a sit-down, face-to-face interview; nothing complex. Then they do a phone interview/personality profile. What I liked about that was they knew what they were looking for, and I was able to answer the questions the way I felt. They were asking about my childhood, how I looked at things, that sort of thing. After that, if they think you're a good match, they extend an offer for a final interview. Then you sit down with an investment representative."

MONEY AND PERKS

As far as working in the company's rotational program goes, one new hire says, "The salary is pretty much set. They were willing to negotiate the start date; they were really willing to work with me on that. [Rotations] were set when I got hired. However, I was told by my department leaders I would do better somewhere else and was able to move. A lot of people don't end up where they originally thought they would. The program is flexible in that way." According to company representatives, hard-working, first-year investment representatives "can net an average income of $55,000." Since that takes long hours and above average work, "the firm has developed a unique 'first year' compensation package: regular paychecks during training, salary support during the first twelve selling months, and bonuses." First jobbers love "the fact that there's a lot of flexibility. If you need to go to an appointment, you just tell your leader. If [you] need to get something done, it's not like they're going to make you take away from vacation time or sick days." They also "like that it's a very big local company. Somewhere down the line, if [you] want to expand [your] horizons, [the company has] campuses in St. Louis, Tempe, Toronto, and London."

THE ROPES

"Edward Jones does a terrific job with orientation," writes one first jobber, and adds: "We had a week-long orientation in which they told us about the culture of the firm. We learned about the history of the firm, where they come from, what they do. Orientation sucks at most places, but everybody in the room was like 'This is great. There's a great corporate culture here.'" Following orientation, "You go to the main campus where you start your job. You're told ahead of time who and where, so you know where to go. I sat down with my department leader and she told me what was in store for me. Being part of the rotational program, I was encouraged to visit other departments." Ongoing training is a major component of the rotational program. Another first jobber explains, "I still get training to this day, long after I started. During each of the three-month rotations, my first year I worked very closely with one or two associates in the department I was in and was trained by them. I also attended training sessions both internally and externally, ranging from diversity training to Web-content workshops. There are also a plethora of learning courses to sign up for on the learning site of our Intranet. They offer both independent study and class courses on the applications and software, presentation skills, leadership courses, etc."

DAY IN THE LIFE

According to one trainee, most first jobbers' daily tasks "really depend on the department. You come in at the assigned time, maybe seven or eight. If I had a meeting, I'd go to that. If not, I'd work on old projects, try to get information on upcoming projects, and have meetings with other associates in the department to get ideas [from] them." Agrees another trainee, "My responsibilities changed, of course, with each rotation. Although, looking back on it, I had some pretty important responsibilities for an entry-level training position. My responsibilities included working on ideas for a redesign of the public website entry page, designing fliers and posters, creating Web pages, designing and implementing contests for the branches, setting up a Trade Show Booth program for our branches, designing the trade show booths, and many more projects. I don't really have an example of a typical day because each and every day is different." One new hire warns that "when you start a new rotation, it sometimes takes awhile to get going and you can get a little bored, but from then on, you stay busy. I always have something exciting going on. I have felt overwhelmed a few times, but everything always works out great in the end."

PEERS

First jobbers at Edward Jones "see each other a lot, especially with rotational associates, which is the number-one entry-level position." The company provides plenty of opportunities to socialize; explains one associate, "What's good about being a big company is they have tickets to every sporting event, every concert, any outing you want. We do an annual Founders' Day; we have baseball and softball tournaments. Our division took us to the Cardinals game. It's definitely a fun atmosphere." Another associate adds, "During our rotations, we had to all work in groups on a competitive-strategies project together and present it to management. That was work, but a good experience to work with others." Associates usually remain close with their work group for the first year: "After a year, you're placed in your own department, and you've moved on to your other 'real' job, and you're kind of wanting to work as hard as you can to be beneficial to your department."

MOVING ON

Edward Jones is a great place to start a career, but it's not for everyone. Writes one trainee, "It's just not a good fit for some. Maybe the rotations aren't what they thought they'd be. Maybe they thought they'd be earning more than they get here." People we spoke with agree that "there are more positives than negatives" but also explain that "sometimes people just don't like their actual job duties. It may not be what they really wanted to do or may not be related to what they studied in school, but it's the job they were offered." Some are turned off by the fact that "it's very challenging. If you're a slacker, it's not going to work for you. Also, it's a very conservative atmosphere. [People] wear suits every day. It's very structured." Some people who leave return to school for an MBA; others seek opportunities elsewhere in the world of banking and finance.

ELECTRONIC ARTS (EA)
Various Positions

THE BIG PICTURE

For many, it's a dream come true: a job that pays you to develop and test games for PCs, PlayStation, Xbox, and Nintendo. Electronic Arts (EA) is a major producer of sports games, role-playing games, war games, driving and flight simulators, and all other manner of blissful diversions. It's kind of like the way you spent your free time in college except that EA pays you for it.

STATS

LOCATION(S) WHERE ENTRY-LEVEL EMPLOYEES WORK

Los Angeles, CA; Redwood Shores, CA; Walnut Creek, CA; Maitland, FL; Austin, TX; Montreal, Canada; Vancouver, Canada; Chertsey, United Kingdom

AVERAGE NUMBER OF APPLICATIONS EACH YEAR

Approximately 82,000 applications are submitted to EA every year.

AVERAGE NUMBER HIRED OVER THE LAST TEN YEARS

EA hires approximately 2,100 people over the last ten years.

ENTRY-LEVEL POSITION(S) AVAILABLE

New hires work as software engineers, computer graphic artists, financial analysts, marketing assistants, public relations assistants, and production assistants.

BENEFITS OFFERED

Comprehensive medical benefits are available. Additional benefits include a 401(k) plan with matching program, employee stock purchase plan, $100 toward a game console, and ten "EA points" per year for use toward games.

CONTACT INFORMATION

"Please visit our website at www.jobs.ea.com to register on our EA Recruiter system."

GETTING HIRED

EA posts available positions on their website, "where an applicant can complete a profile and electronically attach a resume. The EA Recruiter system will automatically notify each applicant of an opening that matches his or her skill sets and interests via email." The company visits "several campuses during the fall and spring seasons;" find out which ones on www.eaacademy.ea.com. Many first jobbers we spoke with begin their tenure with the company as interns; internship opportunities are also posted on www.jobs.ea.com. Reports one former intern, "I was not interviewed for my full-time position, but when applying, I attached screenshots of my personal projects, and I believe this helped set me apart from the rest of the applicants."

Money and Perks

Entry-level workers at EA warn that little is negotiable in the job offer: "The position is quite popular given the number of gamers out there, so [the company] can be picky," explains one first jobber. Most newbies tell us that the "start date was flexible and accommodative," but other aspects of the job were not. Key perks include "working in a field that is very much 'now' and the center of attention in many homes and media. This kind of experience right out of school seemed almost impossible." Employees also enjoy "game rooms on-site to play the latest games, $100 toward the purchase of a gaming console, world-class facilities (state-of-the-art gym, cafeteria, indoor basketball court, sand volleyball courts, etc.), and free games!"

The Ropes

Orientation at EA takes a half day and includes "completing the required paperwork, information on benefits, corporate culture, ergonomic equipment available, and travel and events." Subsequent training depends on the position. Newbies inform us that "Electronic Arts offers a variety of courses in all areas of game production. These are open to all employees." A designer we spoke with, for example, explains that he had "attended a couple of seminars/conferences. They were all related to design. One was a seminar on interface and another was on Flash." A 3-D production artist reports, "I'd learned 3-D fundamentals from school, but most of what I do at work I learned during my Electronic Arts internship. Training was a steep and hectic process, but I'm really glad I came through."

Day in the Life

There's much more to creating and selling games than you might imagine, and there are a myriad of tasks for first jobbers to perform at EA. One software engineer tells us her typical day consists of "working with the game designers to figure out how they want the enemies to act, then working out how to implement that, and finally working with the artists to get any new animations that this behavior may require." An artist on the production team often spends the day "modeling props and environments for the game. I receive my task(s) in the morning, complete the task(s) by the afternoon, and receive critiques from [an] art director, then refine the model based on the feedback. Sometimes certain tasks may take up to three to four days." Other positions at EA might require an employee to "resolve player disputes, take report information about hacked accounts, report bugs, fix bugs that affect the general player base that are easily resolvable, action customers that use harassing language, fix doors; if they did not have us, the game world would be anarchy." No matter what the task, new hires are "expected to strive for the goals that their supervisor has set for them and learn as much about the project and skill sets needed for the task they are working on."

PEERS

"Most people here are really smart and cool," say EA entry-level employees. "We also play a lot of video games!" According to one worker, "[They are otherwise] a diverse group of people from all around the world, so I've gotten to work with people from all ages, walks of life, and several different cultures." EA "provides many opportunities for social and personal interaction. This is not only for first jobbers, but anyone in the company and on your team. You can become great friends with producers and executives; no one is out of reach professionally or personally."

MOVING ON

Because "EA is very successful and constantly growing in every way," few first jobbers are anxious to move on. They like the security EA provides, as well as the excellent on-the-job training they receive. People who leave most often move on to other gaming companies or return to school for an advanced degree.

ENTERPRISE RENT-A-CAR
Management Trainee Program

The Big Picture

Entry-level employees in Enterprise's Management Trainee Program love the "company's extremely performance-based philosophy for business" under which "everyone at the company starts [at] the same place and succeeds through [his or her] own work and determination." The chance for advancement and a solid, well-nurtured sense of community combine to make Enterprise a great place to begin your working life and perhaps even build a career.

Stats

Location(s) Where Entry-level Employees Work

"Enterprise Rent-A-Car hires entry-level employees company wide in five countries."

Average Number of Applications Each Year

The company receives 200,000 applications per year.

Average Number Hired over the Last Ten Years

Enterprise hires from 5,000 to 6,000 people per year.

Entry-level Position(s) Available

Entry-level hires work as management trainees.

Average Hours Worked Per Week

New hires work from forty-five to fifty hours per week.

Average Starting Salary

"Though starting salaries vary by location, all are highly competitive and range from the high $20,000s to high $30,000s."

Benefits Offered

"Enterprise offers a complete benefits package. Employees have a choice of medical benefits through either an EPO or a PPO. Full-time employees can also participate in a health care reimbursement [or flexible spending] account, which sets aside up to $3,000 in pre-tax dollars to pay for noncovered medical expenses such as deductibles and co-payments. Additional medical benefits include a dental, prescription drug, and vision savings plan." Additional benefits include "A pre-tax [flexible spending] account for dependent care in which employees can set aside up to $5,000 pre-tax to pay for child care; 401(k); profit sharing; ChoiceTime (paid time off for illness or personal use); discounts on renting, purchasing, or leasing a car; monetary rewards for new employee referrals (up to $2,500); education assistance; adoption assistance; clothing allowance; LifeMatters Resource program (a professional service that assists employees in finding resources for any number of needs—from serious matters such as child care or parental care to other issues like finding a realtor, pet care, and a health club).

CONTACT INFORMATION

Go to www.enterprise.com/careers.

GETTING HIRED

Enterprise tells us that "we hire management trainees that have already been out in the workforce; our company [also] regularly visits campuses across the nation looking for management trainee candidates. If an applicant proactively decides to apply for a position, an application is available online at www.enterprise.com/careers. The company welcomes candidates from all backgrounds, schools, and experiences." It seeks candidates who display "a strong work ethic, team player mentality, self-motivation, leadership potential, confidence, a customer service–centered attitude, flexibility, persistence, and social deftness." One trainee explains, "I posted my resume [at my school's career website], then logged onto the Enterprise website. I had to take a test online, and then I waited for a phone call. I had three interviews. The tone was professional. I felt very comfortable, and they asked many questions about my ambitions." Agrees another, "The tone of the first interview was serious, yet laid back. The interviewer was very nice and personable; he encouraged me to relax and talk to him as if I [were] an old friend. He asked me situational questions as well as questions about my experience in sales. I then spoke with a regional recruiter; I asked her for more specifics about the position. She was very excited and energetic and passed that along to me. I then interviewed at the branch where I'd be working. That interview was very short; I was offered the job the next day."

MONEY AND PERKS

All management trainees at Enterprise are "initially taught how to manage an Enterprise location. Normally, employees who successfully complete this training program can expect to become assistant managers after one year. Their next step is to become a branch manager. They typically attain that level two to two-and-a-half years after joining Enterprise." Trainee salaries vary slightly depending on location (i.e., trainees earn more in expensive locations such as San Francisco than in areas where the cost of living is lower) and whether they have completed internships at Enterprise. Subsequent pay raises occur "as employees become management assistants, assistant managers, or branch managers; their management compensation is determined by the success of the business. Managers receive a base salary plus a percentage of profits from their operation, and they have the potential to earn a lot more by driving the growth and increasing the profitability of their operation." Employees agree that "the best perk is the opportunity to be promoted based on performance;" they also appreciate how "Enterprise does a great job of taking care of people through office outings, a summer party, and a Christmas party. In addition, the 401(k) plan, profit sharing, and generous vacation times are also nice fringe benefits."

THE ROPES

Orientation at Enterprise is a one-week program. Explains one entry-level employee, "The experience was extremely positive and informative. There were nine other management trainees and the overall feeling from all of us was that orientation introduced us to the start of our careers." Enterprise officials tell us that "because of the decentralized nature of the company, orientation programs vary by region of the country. While the orientation is designed by and catered to specific regions, each program teaches the basics of the business and introduces employees to the philosophy of the company." Following orientation, trainees are sent to a branch location, where they "develop skills in sales, marketing, customer service, accounting, and finance. Managers meet with trainees weekly to go over their progress and any questions they may have. Throughout the seven to twelve month training program, the trainee will receive opportunities for increased responsibility, bonuses, and pay increases." Notes one first jobber, "Enterprise understands the importance of continuous employee development. Every employee undergoes some type of formal training at least once a month. These training sessions are designed to inform the employees of other departments of the company and how they relate to the functions of the rental branch."

DAY IN THE LIFE

The management trainee program at Enterprise is designed to teach trainees every aspect of running a business. This means that trainees must master a wide range of duties. Here's how one trainee describes a typical day: "In the morning before opening, we have to make sure all the cars for the day's reservations are ready. After opening, it's a balancing act of helping customers who come in, picking up customers who need rides, marketing, cleaning cars as they're returned, and making sure the cars get their regular maintenance. I spend just as much time on the road as I do in the branch—this helps break up my day so I am not burned out. Every day the same concepts of business are applied, but to different situations. The ability to multitask is essential to this job." Because of its unique business model, "Employees at Enterprise have an opportunity to essentially run their own business; in essence, to have a franchise without paying a fee. To prepare employees for that opportunity, we offer an extensive training program, which many employees make reference to as the 'virtual MBA.' Every employee serving customers at the front counter is quietly learning the ins and outs of the business world, including profit-and-loss statements, controlling expenses, and implementing a comprehensive business plan."

PEERS

One new employee says, "There is no separation among 'first jobbers' and other employees at the company. Each branch becomes a team that depends on each member. The company provides chances for employees to interact outside of work, which takes the pressures off of the daytime grind by providing a more social atmosphere. I spend a good amount of my free time with those I work with, whether it be just hanging out or participating in an organized flag football team." Adds another new employee, "Besides knowing the people who work at branches near yours, the training sessions are one way to network and get to know other management trainees. There is a big 'after-hours' social scene. Many managers will reward performance by offering a happy hour after work. It is very easy to make friends mainly because the majority of employees here are very outgoing."

MOVING ON

Company officials report, "Realizing the potential for growth that exists within the company many first jobbers stay on to become the company's leaders. Regardless of background, employees at Enterprise progress purely on their own merit." The employees we spoke with confirmed the company's assertions; all of them told us they plan to stay here, work hard, and rise through the ranks.

BEST AND WORST

"Pam Nicholson began her career at Enterprise Rent-A-Car in 1981 as a management trainee. Fresh out of college with a bachelor of arts degree, she started in St. Louis behind the rental counter learning the importance of customer service, an Enterprise trademark. Within nine months, Pam was promoted to assistant branch manager, and within a year, accepted a position in the company's fast-growing Southern California group. Over the next twelve years, she was promoted through the ranks to one of the top operating positions in Southern California: regional vice president. While there, she assisted in growing the region's fleet from 1,000 to more than 27,000 vehicles. Her efforts were rewarded with a position back in her hometown of St. Louis as a corporate vice president at Enterprise's world headquarters. Proving that professional growth with Enterprise is constant, Pam was soon promoted to general manager of the New York Group, a top job in that region. Overseeing rental car, fleet services, and car sales operations for the company's second largest operating group, Pam led the group to double its profitability. In acknowledging her top performance in New York and throughout her career, Pam was promoted back to St. Louis as senior vice president, North American Operations, and soon after to executive vice president, North American Operations. Today she oversees the activities of 50,000 employees; 500,000 rental cars; 100,000 fleet services vehicles; and 5,000 branch offices in the United States and Canada. She is a corporate officer and one of the company's top operating employees."

GE

Corporate Leadership Development Programs

THE BIG PICTURE

General Electric (GE) offers Corporate Leadership Development programs in many divisions. All of them are "two-year rotational training programs [that] consist of formal classroom, digital, and on-the-job training" and prepare participants to continue their careers at GE when they end.

STATS

LOCATION(S) WHERE ENTRY-LEVEL EMPLOYEES WORK

There locations in over 100 countries.

AVERAGE NUMBER OF APPLICATIONS EACH YEAR

The company receives about 50,000 applications per year in the United States alone.

AVERAGE NUMBER HIRED OVER THE LAST TEN YEARS

About 1,000 people are hired in the United States per year.

ENTRY-LEVEL POSITION(S) AVAILABLE

Entry-level positions are available in communications, engineering, finance, information management, and operations.

AVERAGE HOURS WORKED PER WEEK

The amount of hours vary by position.

PERCENTAGE OF ENTRY-LEVEL HIRES STILL WITH THE COMPANY AFTER THREE, FIVE, AND TEN YEARS

After three years, about 80 percent of all entry-level employees remain with the company; after five years, 60 percent of all entry-level employees remain with the company; and after ten years, 50 percent of all entry-level employees remain with the company.

AVERAGE STARTING SALARY

The average starting salary ranges from $35,000 to $65,000 per year.

BENEFITS OFFERED

The company offers competitive, full medical coverage and a generous tuition reimbursement program.

CONTACT INFORMATION

Submit resumes online at www.gecareers.com.

GETTING HIRED

Applying for one of GE's corporate leadership development programs requires two interviews. The first, conducted on campus or over the telephone, is with a human resources representative and involves "many questions about working in teams, situations in which failure occurred, and how it was dealt with." Next, "candidates selected for on-site (second) interviews will be interviewing for a position with a specific GE business. Students are given the opportunity to choose up to three GE businesses they are interested in joining. We try our best to align student geographic and business preferences with internal business hiring needs; however, there is no guarantee that you will be offered a position at your preferred location." A former program participant who now organizes recruiting says, "I'd encourage candidates to be energetic and engaging. Ask a lot of questions! The goal of the process is to determine whether there is a fit between the candidate and the organization. Sometimes it is clear that a candidate has the technical and nontechnical skills to exceed, but [it is] unclear whether the candidate is engaged with the environment and really wants the job. Asking questions about the work, organization, and program is the best way for both parties to accurately predict whether there is a fit." Another entry-level employee adds, "Entry-level positions at GE usually require work that isn't a direct outflow of previous work, so specific technical skills are less important than a strong and consistent demonstration of capability to learn, adapt, and excel."

MONEY AND PERKS

Participants in all GE development programs tell us that "the job offer is negotiable in terms of when you start, but nonnegotiable in terms of salary and placement." Many hasten to add that "the offer [GE makes] is highly competitive, so there's no need to negotiate the compensation." Pay increases come semiannually and are based on performance. One entry-level employee says, "Those raises are based [on] your on-the-job evaluations and your class grades, and they add up quickly during the two-year program." Perks include "discounts on products, ranging from GE appliances to gym memberships to Dell computers to automobiles." Program participants also love the educational package; as one student explains, "GE paid for my master's degree, [gave me] two full-time quarters off work with full salary, and paid for [all my books]. It was a great opportunity; I got a masters degree at a top twenty-five engineering graduate school in about two-and-a-half years."

THE ROPES

General Electric's Corporate Leadership Development programs start with a brief orientation, usually half a day or one day long. Writes one entry-level hire, "My orientation process was a three-hour long seminar-style event that entailed a presentation about the big picture of GE and how the research center [where I was assigned] serves the business, overviews of how programs are funded, how the time accounting should be performed, procedures related to security and safety, and other rather unexciting, but necessary, topics." Orientation is only the beginning of a long and thorough training process, however. In fact, since first jobbers rotate through jobs throughout the two-year program, the training period never really ends. Offers one engineer, "I received so much training it's hard to recall it all, so I'll give the highlights: two trips to [a] GE corporate training facility at Crotonville [in Ossining, New York] for business leadership courses and jet engine teardown training [where] we disassembled and re-assembled aircraft engines. In addition, Six Sigma green belt classes and training also were provided." Six Sigma is the management philosophy that all GE employees are supposed to subscribe to, in which the goal of constantly improving operational efficiency is held sacrosanct. Many employees also pursue master's degrees while working for GE; the company offers substantial support in this area [see Money and Perks].

DAY IN THE LIFE

GE is number five on the *Fortune 500* list, which means that it is very big and generates a great deal of revenue. Accordingly, the variety of tasks performed by entry-level employees is incredibly broad. According to company officials, "The average program member works about fifty hours per week. Additional time commitments may be required depending on job assignments. Course work, on average, will add another five to eight hours to your week." Writes one program participant, "Responsibilities vary depending on the area of the first job assignment, but typically program members are directed [or] given work by a manager and given a mentor or engineer in the area who provides help [and] advice. As a program member progresses onto different assignments and gains more on-the-job engineering competency, the program member is typically given the same amount of work and responsibility as any other engineer in the area of work." Everyone in the program rotates positions within their business every six months; company officials tell us that "rotations outside your function or your GE business do exist, but [they] are an exception, rather than a rule, for all program participants. Assignments of these types are dependent upon the GE business need and participant preferences and are also often based on merit."

PEERS

"One attractive thing about a big program like this is that there is a continual stream of young, bright, and motivated folks coming in," notes one first jobber. The scope of the after-hours scene varies widely by division and location, program participants tell us, but all agree that there's "a tremendous amount of camaraderie" among people starting out at GE. Explains one, "You're in classes with twenty to thirty people [who are] your age every week, so it's kind of like being in college again. All of us made friends pretty quickly, went out after work [or] on weekends; and still, now, three years later [we] are still going out to happy hours and dinners together. We've all been to each other's weddings and have established a very close group of friends through this program."

MOVING ON

GE regards its Corporate Leadership Development programs as stepping stones to careers with the conglomerate. Its website states, "GE's Leadership Programs prepare graduates for positions with a significant level of responsibility and challenging off-program assignments. Some graduates join the GE audit staff. Others enter positions in one of the GE businesses. Cross-functional assignments are also a possibility. If someone successfully completes one of our leadership programs, other advanced educational degrees or certifications are not required to succeed at GE. Training and experiences gained while on program may accelerate an individual's career growth in much the same way an advanced degree might at another corporation. Inevitably, some program graduates feel the need to seek further education. In these instances, GE's support, whether it is in the form of tuition reimbursement, leave of absence, executive MBA, etc., is considered on a case by case basis and differs according to the GE business."

ATTRITION

People who leave GE site the lack of "work/life balance" as their reason, "which is something that GE as a whole struggles with. Most jobs require pretty long hours, especially during programs where you have to work until late at night on homework every week. There's not much time for friends or spouses outside of work." Also, "the traveling aspect of the program turns a lot of people off, even after they take the job knowing they might move every six months. Above all else, [employees] say the lack of [geographic] stability is the number one criticism."

GOLDMAN SACHS
Various Positions

THE BIG PICTURE

Goldman Sachs is "a leading global investment banking, securities, and investment management firm." It hires entry-level employees in all of its divisions, although the majority wind up in the firm's Analyst Program. The hours are long and the work is demanding, but those with "the right stuff" will find plenty of opportunities for advancement and remuneration.

STATS

LOCATION(S) WHERE ENTRY-LEVEL EMPLOYEES WORK

"We hire a vast majority of first-year analysts into our New York and London offices. While analysts could be placed in any of our offices throughout the United States, Europe, and Asia, other top hiring cities are Paris, Frankfurt, Chicago, Hong Kong, and Tokyo. For more information on our offices, please visit www.gs.com/careers/about_goldman_sachs."

AVERAGE NUMBER OF APPLICATIONS EACH YEAR

Approximately 42,000 applications are submitted to the company every year.

AVERAGE NUMBER HIRED OVER THE LAST TEN YEARS

Anywhere from 600 to 1,000 people are hired per year.

ENTRY-LEVEL POSITION(S) AVAILABLE

Available entry-level positions vary by year.

AVERAGE HOURS WORKED PER WEEK

The hours vary widely, depending on the position. Generally, a Goldman Sachs employee can expect substantial workdays, with the rewards commensurate to the commitment.

PERCENTAGE OF ENTRY-LEVEL HIRES STILL WITH THE COMPANY AFTER THREE, FIVE, AND TEN YEARS:

"Most of our new hires begin in our Analyst Program. We regard the Analyst Program as a two- to three-year experience. After completing the Analyst Program, analysts pursue various exciting opportunities." Some stay, while many return to business or law school or move on to other career opportunities, as an analyst position at Goldman Sachs opens doors in the financial services community.

AVERAGE STARTING SALARY

New hires earn from $45,000 to $60,000 per year.

Benefits Offered

"We offer a competitive benefits package. We also offer [an] on-site fitness center or subsidized memberships at local clubs; on-site health units for physician-ordered testing, vision testing, prescription services, facilities for nursing mothers, and Lamaze classes for expectant parents; on-site physician services; wellness/health fairs and seminars; free on-site screenings such as flu vaccinations, cholesterol, skin cancer, [and] prostate cancer [tests] and mammograph[ies]." In addition, "a partial list of the services we provide for employee convenience, professional development, and charitable efforts [includes] online employee discounts to stores such as Barnes & Noble and Sharper Image; complimentary admission to many New York museums and discounts at gift shops; no-fee ATM machines on site; discount banking and mortgage programs at Chase, Citibank, and other participating institutions; and Series 7 and Series 63 prep classes (with manager approval) provided on-site or off, for those who need certification. [Furthermore,] second and third year analysts have access to a How to Apply to Business School seminar and on-site receptions with admissions officers from top business schools; GMAT Princeton Review classes; numerous classes available on various topics (with manager approval); and one paid day off a year to volunteer in the community."

Contact Information

Visit www.gs.com/careers, or visit your campus' career services office.

Getting Hired

Goldman Sachs "actively markets and has a physical presence on campus at a select number of universities across the United States, Europe, and Asia but hire from a greater number of universities. Students from all colleges and universities are encouraged to apply." The firm reviews all applications, which can be submitted online (see "Contact Information" above), then invites the most likely candidates to interview. The first-round interview "consists of a Goldman Sachs 'firm wide' interview, rather than a divisional one. The interview focuses primarily on past candidate experiences and accomplishments and is designed to help [the firm] get to know the candidate, and for the candidate to ask questions." The second-round interview "focuses on candidate suitability for a particular division and may be more technical in nature" than the first. Writes one entry-level employee of the experience: "The interviews were, in general, challenging but fair. I did not receive any trick questions, but the nature of the questions did force me to be thoughtful and think on my feet. Overall, it was an extremely positive experience." Notes another, "Prior to the interview, I scoured the GS website for information on what the interviewers might ask of me as well as tips for a successful interview. I found the website to be extremely helpful in my preparation."

Money and Perks

Salaries, according to Goldman Sachs officials, "generally move according to 'class.' Typical packages consist of a base salary, discretionary bonus, private health care, pension, and other benefits." The employees we interviewed say the firm's initial offers were not negotiable but also note that "the pay-scale and other employment terms were competitive with the other industry players." Perks include the extensive benefits package outlined above, as well as extensive travel ("which means that I can reconnect with friends in different cities") and "the extremely high quality of coworkers, both in terms of intellect and motivation/dedication."

The Ropes

Orientation programs at Goldman Sachs "vary by division" and "are designed to provide the skills, background, and tools candidates need to do their job within their chosen division, business unit, or product group." They can last "anywhere from two to twelve weeks." An investment banking analyst reports that her program "was taught by both university-level professors as well as internal presenters and revolved around long days of economics, financial math, and business products and services, as well as soft skills training. There were also a number of social and networking events." Training is also facilitated by "formal mentoring programs that are administered by human resources professionals working within our divisions" and a "big buddy program" in which newbies have contact with "an experienced associate who answers questions, helps [them] figure out how to complete [their] work, shows them where to find the information they need, and, more generally, looks out for their well-being."

Day in the Life

Although their duties differ depending on the division in which they work, all starting analysts "learn a great deal about [Goldman Sachs'] businesses, develop important relationships, and build the skills necessary to carry them through to the next level of their careers." Starting jobs are designed to "help analysts learn critical business skills while gaining fundamental skills in their respective divisions." Here's how one employee describes his experience: "Upon first joining the group, my responsibilities were typical of those of an entry-level analyst, and included general administrative tasks such as setting up calls and preparing notes/slides for meetings, coordinating meetings, spreading numbers and running models for various counterparties or banking clients, and making sure that I was being diligent and retaining the significant volume of information that was being presented to me." Another employee writes, "As a first year, I was assigned to three industry teams (Financial Institutions/Hedge Funds/ Private Wealth Management) and one product team (Bank Loans). On any given day, I could have been working on projects on any or all of the four teams. This aspect of the work kept things interesting, fast paced, and challenging, and really made working a pleasure. Over time, I have taken on more responsibility; people expect more of me in terms of value-added opinions and critical analysis, and people seek me out as a source of information. My work has gotten more challenging, and I have been able to begin weaning [myself] off the administrative tasks I was performing as a first year."

PEERS

Friendships among newbies are forged during Goldman Sachs' intensive training programs, according to the analysts we surveyed. Writes one, "Just like at the start of college, the groups getting together after work and on weekends tend to be very large at the beginning and for the most part eventually dwindle down to your closest friends." Because "everything is done collaboratively here," close working relationships are key. Fortunately, "coworkers are definitely friends, and there is a young, fun atmosphere at work. Not a single hour goes by without interaction with my peers."

MOVING ON

Goldman Sachs officials say, "Some of our departing analysts are often accepted into top graduate business and law schools, or receive offers from private equity shops, hedge funds, or other outstanding companies throughout the world. Our program has an excellent reputation among academic and business leaders worldwide." Many employees who complete the analyst program stay on; officials note that "the analyst program is also an integral component of our associate recruiting strategy. After completing the analyst program, some top performing analysts are promoted to the associate level. We also keep in touch with our departing analysts, and frequently rehire them back to Goldman Sachs at a later time in their careers." As one analyst tells us, "At this point, and given my extremely positive experience thus far, I cannot imagine why I would really ever want to leave Goldman Sachs for good. I *would* eventually like to go back to business school. However, following that, I would ideally like to return to Goldman Sachs."

ATTRITION

"On most nights, I don't get out of work until at least midnight," warns one analyst, who has stuck with the firm despite the demanding work schedule. People who quit usually cite the unusually long hours and the "seemingly endless workflow" at Goldman Sachs; as one analyst told us, "Even the jobs with 'good' hours are still much more intensive than your standard forty-hour workweek. This is a firm where people work hard, play hard, and then go back and work harder."

BEST AND WORST

Successful employees at Goldman Sachs "create and sustain positive working relationships with others," "show initiative," "earn and deserve increased responsibility," and "maintain high ethical standards." Failures are those who just can't cut it in Goldman Sachs' high-pressure, high stakes atmosphere.

GREEN CORPS
Field Organizer

THE BIG PICTURE

"Hey, you titmice, let's have a little more chirping, okay? Frogs, don't all bunch up in one spot—spread out! And who in blue blazes cut the grass so short?" No, that's *not* what Green Corps field organizers do, but wouldn't it be cool if it was? But, what they do is just about as cool: They coordinate with local activists to affect Green environmental goals. Working with this organization is a great introduction to the world of ecoactivism.

STATS

LOCATION(S) WHERE ENTRY-LEVEL EMPLOYEES WORK

"Nationwide—placements are temporary (usually two to three months), and entry-level employees move to a couple of locations throughout the year."

AVERAGE NUMBER OF APPLICATIONS EACH YEAR

Green Corps receives 800 applications each year.

AVERAGE NUMBER HIRED OVER THE LAST TEN YEARS

The organization hires twenty-four people per year.

ENTRY-LEVEL POSITION(S) AVAILABLE

New hires work as field organizers.

AVERAGE HOURS WORKED PER WEEK

Hours are "highly variable based on campaign schedule[s]." When big events approach, field organizers work "approximately sixty to seventy hours [but] less during other times."

PERCENTAGE OF ENTRY-LEVEL HIRES STILL WITH THE COMPANY AFTER THREE, FIVE, AND TEN YEARS

"The program is a year-long training program, so all employees leave for other organizations after one year."

AVERAGE STARTING SALARY

New hires earn $19,500 during their year-long program.

BENEFITS OFFERED

Field organizers get health insurance. Additional benefits include a loan repayment program, paid vacation, holidays, sick days, and job placement assistance.

Jenna Perry

Assistant Recruitment Director

jobs@greencorps.org

617-426-8506

GETTING HIRED

Green Corps interviews "on as many college campuses as possible and conducts first-round phone interviews for all other qualified applicants." A successful applicant describes the process this way: "Green Corps has a three step application/interview process. First, there's a short, written application, at which point you provide your resume. It was helpful that my resume showed that I had been active on campus. Second, I interviewed on campus with the assistant director of the program. What made my first interview work was that I made a personal connection with the person interviewing me. I told stories that got her attention, made her laugh, and showed her that I was smart and motivated. On that basis I was invited to the interview weekend. Third, Green Corps takes the best candidates from the round of first interviews and invites them to group interview weekends. There are about five around the country during the hiring season, and they have about forty to fifty candidates per weekend. Over the two days, Green Corps runs you through a couple of skills sessions and another individual interview and evaluates overall chemistry and social skills. Even those who don't get hired generally agree that it's inspiring to meet so many smart, committed people like them."

MONEY AND PERKS

For Green Corps field organizers, "the salary and length of employment are fixed. Because Green Corps is a fellowship program, it runs thirteen months, and all of the thirty or so fellows [who] are hired each year work from the beginning of August until the end of the following August, when Green Corps staff helps them find more permanent positions in the environmental or social-change fields." The best perks include "a loan repayment program (for student loans), full staff subsidized vacation in Aspen, Colorado, in December, spending time organizing in communities around the country, and a great outplacement service. Because Green Corps has such a great reputation in the environmental field, other organizations end up competing with each other for the chance to hire Green Corps organizers."

THE ROPES

All field organizers start at the beginning of August with a four-week orientation in Boston. The training is run "by Green Corps staff, alumni, and veteran leaders from across the environmental field. That's where you learn how to write a press release, run a meeting, recruit and develop volunteers, organize an event, build a coalition, etc." Adds one corps member, "Green Corps is very much based around building a team among the organizers and on learning by doing, so we jumped right into classroom training the day after we arrived. There were different social events every night where all of the fellows could hang out—the people in each Green Corps class remain close friends, and a lot of times people become close friends with other Green Corps alumni who weren't in their class." Organizers then set off on two-month campaigns in the field, after which they "meet for a week to debrief the previous campaign, get some additional training, and prepare for the next project."

DAY IN THE LIFE

Perhaps the most appealing—and intimidating—aspect of Green Corps' program is the amount of responsibility first jobbers take on. Explains one, "Basically Green Corps organizers are the directors of their campaigns in the cities where they work—so they don't have a boss overseeing them on the site, and they recruit and train everyone they work with. On my first campaign, I was responsible for signing on dozens of organizations to a coalition letter, holding media events, meeting with reporters, and recruiting and training citizen volunteers. On a typical day, I'd come into the office at 8:30 AM or 9:00 AM and make a detailed plan for my day. I'd spend the next two hours calling potential coalition groups and talking to them about the campaign. At noon, I'd take a break for lunch and meet with one of my student interns about her plan for the week and what she was going to accomplish for the campaign. In the afternoon, I would nail down logistics of a press conference in the coming week, including the site and permit, and prepping the speakers for the event. I would talk to existing coalition partners about turning out members to the press event. In the evening, I would spend a couple of hours phone banking volunteers to [get them to] turn out for the press event."

PEERS

Because "most Green Corps organizers are in their campaign cities without any other Green Corps organizers there," the organization lacks the regular after-hours social scene present at many entry-level jobs. Even so, the peer network is a potent one. One organizer explains: "One of the biggest perks about the job is that you are in a class with an incredible group of Green Corps organizers. You bond with them during the classroom training in Boston. Then you keep in touch via phone and email during the campaigns. When you get back together between each campaign for the follow-up trainings, it's like a mini-reunion. And then after the year is over, these people become your friends and colleagues and support system. It's incredible to have such a tight network of such talented, motivated, creative people who are out there making a difference day in and day out."

MOVING ON

According to Green Corps, about 85 percent of its program graduates continue in "the social change and environmental field." Others travel, study abroad, or head to graduate school. Some of the graduates we spoke with now work for the Sierra Club, the Campaign to Ban Landmines, and Physicians for Human Rights.

ATTRITION

Green Corps isn't for everyone. Those who don't make it through the program usually cite "being overwhelmed, having too much responsibility, [and] working hard when their friends [who] care less about their jobs leave at five" and get paid much more. As one Corps graduate puts it, "The same things that are great about the job also make it tough."

BEST AND WORST

"Anna Wagner, now an organizing director with Green Corps, helped stop the privatization of the New Orleans water supply during her first job out of college. Anna's first campaign with Green Corps partnered her and four other Green Corps organizers with ACORN and Public Citizen on a campaign to stop the bids of three large corporations attempting to privatize the city's water. The environmental track records of all three companies did not bode well for the future of New Orleans' water quality; moreover, privatization introduces risks to the average citizen who is trying to find clean and affordable water."

HP

Various Positions

THE BIG PICTURE

Hewlett-Packard Company (HP) is a manufacturer of computers and provides much more, like "technology solutions for consumers, businesses, and institutions across the globe; IT infrastructure; global services; and imaging and printing for consumers, enterprises, and small and medium businesses." The company stresses a comfortable, positive work environment in its literature.

STATS

LOCATION(S) WHERE ENTRY-LEVEL EMPLOYEES WORK

Cupertino, CA; Palo Alto, CA; Roseville, CA; San Diego, CA; Sunnyvale, CA; Colorado Springs, CO; Fort Collins, CO; Atlanta, GA; Boise, ID; Marlborough, MA; Corvallis, OR; Austin, TX; Houston, TX; Vancouver, WA

AVERAGE NUMBER OF APPLICATIONS EACH YEAR

Approximately 22,000 applications are submitted every year.

AVERAGE NUMBER HIRED OVER THE LAST TEN YEARS

Hewlett-Packard hires approximately 700 people per year.

ENTRY-LEVEL POSITION(S) AVAILABLE

Entry-level hires work as chemical engineers, software design engineers, mechanical product engineers, hardware/firmware design engineers, research and development engineers, IT analysts, financial analysts, product marketing analysts, and sales representatives.

AVERAGE HOURS WORKED PER WEEK

New hires work forty hours per week.

AVERAGE STARTING SALARY

"HP researches the market each year and adjusts its college compensation guidelines accordingly. Our research shows that we offer competitive salaries appropriate for entry-level college hires. The details of this information are confidential."

BENEFITS OFFERED

The company offers medical, dental, and vision coverage. Additional benefits include flexible spending accounts, 401(k) and retirement medical savings account, share ownership plan, vacation and paid holidays, and an employee purchase program.

Apply online at www.jobs.hp.com, or contact your university's career services office to see if Hewlett-Packard recruits there.

GETTING HIRED

HP "focuses its proactive campus recruiting efforts and long-term relationships on forty-seven HP partner schools;" students at other schools can apply via the company website. Company officials tell us that it most highly values a prospective employee's ability to work in a team, to take initiative when required, and to write and communicate effectively. Many jobs require technical expertise: "They asked a lot of C++ questions, so if someone didn't nail those I suppose they probably wouldn't get the job," writes one successful hire. The interview process proceeds in several stages; recalls one employee, "Originally I did a phone interview with the recruiter, then a phone interview with the hiring manager. I was then flown in for a round of interviews with several people currently working in the group. The phone interviews were about gauging interest and job/education background. The on-site interviews [focused on] job and education experience, along with [my] technical abilities." Many newbies told us that working as interns during college is a great way to get your foot in the door.

MONEY AND PERKS

According to the company, salary "changes are based on employee performance and business conditions, and vary each year." New hires tell us that their starting date can be "totally flexible" and that there's occasionally some leeway in their choice of location; the company representatives report that "there is a lot of flexibility offered to employees [regarding] work/life options, arranged between manager and employee." Favorite perks include "discounts associated with a large company and local discounts (percent off, reduced price tickets, etc.), free books and tons of online technical material, [and] the work/life balance: Your personal life is valued very, very highly here."

THE ROPES

New HP hires begin their tenures with the Succeeding at HP program, in which they "learn about the company mission, vision, goals, and values. They are also given individual [orientation] by their manager and mentor (if assigned) to help learn about working at HP and to have someone to go to for questions." The amount and kind of training workers receive varies from department to department. A software/firmware developer tells us that he "spent a month working with the group that tests the firmware that [his] group develops" before doing any work on his own; a marketing manager received "no training—we must get the info from the portal. It took me a long time to figure things out." Mentor relationships are not uncommon and often serve as a new hire's informal training; writes one first jobber, "I learned about some of the software processes by reading documentation or books. The majority of what I learned was guided by a team leader that was designated as my mentor."

Day in the Life

As already mentioned, HP offers a wide range of positions to first jobbers. They're responsible for designing and developing software, hardware, computer systems, and components; coordinating manufacturing and product development processes; managing the supply chain; and conducting research and development in chemistry, physics, and material sciences. For many employees, a typical day consists of "research, attending meetings, talking with partners, and thinking (on [their] own)." One developer says, "Some days I work alone; others I work with other people from my group." Over time, workers "get more and more freedom in making decisions." An atmosphere of positive reinforcement encourages workers to take initiative. "Every so often I fall on my face and make a mistake, but if I get up and recover quickly I am congratulated, not scolded," explains one newbie.

Peers

Most first jobbers wind up in offices with much more experienced employees. "There are no other first jobbers in the department," writes a typical survey respondent; adds another, "This is one of the biggest weaknesses of working at Hewlett-Packard. I don't know any other first jobbers at this time. I hang out with guys on the team sometimes, but a lot of them are married, so they don't want to do the same things I do." Even so, newbies describe their coworkers as "very smart, hardworking, and willing to teach."

Moving On

HP reports a "low attrition rate of 2 percent in 2003;" people who leave head to various technology companies, with others heading back to school (an increasingly popular option during the down period the job market has experienced in recent years). Other people have left due to issues in the computer industry; workers have growing concerns that outsourcing and sluggish computer sales may ultimately erase jobs at HP. The company is confident, though: "HP is a global company," says an HP representative, "[and] at the end of the 2003 fiscal year, all [HP's] businesses posted strong revenue and record unit shipments, and all [the] businesses were profitable."

HOME DEPOT
Business Leadership Program

THE BIG PICTURE

Home Depot's Business Leadership Program (BLP) is a two-year rotational training program into which only an elite few are accepted each year. The four six-month cross-functional rotations the program encompasses are designed to "develop [program participants] into the next generation of business leaders. BLP gives top management candidates the chance to reach higher levels of achievement by joining the most outstanding talent in business today." The program, which began in 1998, has graduated four classes; today, some of these graduate members hold prominent positions throughout the Home Depot organization.

STATS

LOCATION(S) WHERE ENTRY-LEVEL EMPLOYEES WORK

Atlanta, GA

AVERAGE NUMBER OF APPLICATIONS EACH YEAR

Approximately 4,500 applications are submitted to BLP every year.

AVERAGE NUMBER HIRED OVER THE LAST TEN YEARS

Home depot hires about fifteen people per year for BLP.

ENTRY-LEVEL POSITION(S) AVAILABLE

"We have multiple entry points for entry-level hires, with BLP being just one. We also direct hire associates into functional roles (i.e., finance, marketing). Those needs are determined annually by business need."

AVERAGE HOURS WORKED PER WEEK

New hires work from forty to about fifty-five (or more) hours per week (varies by project assignment).

AVERAGE STARTING SALARY

"Starting salaries for BLP [hires] are competitive with the market and vary with the experience and [educational background] of [the] candidate[s]."

BENEFITS OFFERED

The company offers comprehensive medical, dental, vision, etc. Additional benefits include stock options, 401(k), employee stock purchase plan, and paid vacation.

Apply on-line at http://careers.homedepot.com/ur/.

GETTING HIRED

With only fifteen candidates chosen from over 4,000 applicants, Home Depot's BLP program makes Cal Tech look like a community college, at least in terms of selectivity. What magic key opens this door? According to one employee who has breeched the wall, "the company is committed to attracting not only high potential people, but also those who will be a culture fit. Applicants interview first on campus with current and past members of the program. If the candidate is asked to the second round, they are invited to an all-day session at the Atlanta Store Support Center (i.e., our global headquarters). That round [is] very extensive—[applicants] interview with BLP associates, [human resources] professionals, and associates from across the enterprise. Home Depot puts its BLP candidates through an extensive screening process." Notes one BLP participant, "The interview process was intense. They required an on-campus interview followed by an hour-long exam that tested my comprehensive, logic, and basic behavioral tendencies." This job requires excellent people skills: "It's not just about the 4.0 GPA. We like solid grades but truly look for leaders, especially those who can motivate others and work well on teams. [We] would much rather see a 3.5/4.0 GPA with strong leadership experience than a 4.0 with little community involvement."

MONEY AND PERKS

Participants in the BLP program "start in mid-August. You rotate four times and your interests as well as BLP Logistics Committee input drive where you are placed for each assignment. Business need and professional development are the key determinants with respect to BLP rotation placement." One participant tells us that "there can be some salary variance among BLP participants. The overall package the candidate presents helps to determine this range (i.e., advanced degrees, professional experience, etc.)." The best perk is the employee stock purchase program; adds one wry BLP participant, "The stock options would be the best fringe benefit . . . if they were worth anything."

THE ROPES

The BLP program commences with "three weeks of orientation, which begin on the first day of employment. These sessions include introductions to company history, values, priorities, and benefits, as well as presentations from leaders across all functional areas (i.e., finance, merchandise, human resources, IT, operations, etc.) External faculty facilitates classes on corporate strategy, operational excellence, and corporate finance." During this orientation period, "You meet leading executives and even spend time working in a store to develop perspective" and "learn the business from the retail floor." Sums up one first jobber, "The three-week orientation covered a little of everything. We sat in seminars with a finance professor from Emory who taught us everything from market fundamentals to engaging us in a business simulation. [We spent one week] in the stores. That's right, the stores; you can't understand Home Depot until you serve on the front lines. So there I was mixing paint six days into working at the company. I was struck by how wonderful the associates are in the stores—caring, patient, and mentoring. It was a terrific way to begin the experience. The last week we focused on project management and other skills necessary to be successful at Home Depot."

DAY IN THE LIFE

"Each BLP associate's responsibilities vary by functional group and project assignment," Home Depot representatives report. "No two rotations are alike." Assignments often carry a great deal of responsibility; writes one BLP participant, "My first job at Home Depot was managing the national rollout of a merchandising fixture to 1,500 stores. I was the single point of contact at Home Depot for vendor partners, contractors, and fixture manufacturers. A typical day would be managing all the parties involved and managing the process, which varied depending on the point in the rollout that we were in." Reports another participant, "My first project was to optimize the way our stores handle inventory management. It was a company wide project with a scale in the hundreds of millions of dollars. Pretty cool for being in my early twenties!" Your assignment and your role within your assigned area can change quickly, so "you must be flexible. This program will stretch you to work on projects in disciplines where you have no previous experience. These experiences often teach you the most." As one program graduate summarizes, "You are limited only by your own potential at Home Depot, not years of experience."

PEERS

The BLP program creates an instant support network for participants, especially since "the majority of participants in the program have relocated to Atlanta and are in a similar, new environment." While "most BLP participants do not typically work directly with one another," they "have an internal network, which is a great asset. There's a great collaborative feel. Everyone wants to help each other, and the manager of BLP makes it clear that it is the expectation that you succeed as an individual and as a team." Strong friendships are forged through BLP, many here tell us. Writes one participant, "They are an amazing group of people, and I can't imagine making the transition from school to work without them. All of us hang out as much as possible. Some weeks are hard to get everyone together, but so far we haven't gone two weeks without setting up a dinner or gathering after work. Our group loves to celebrate birthdays. When we do get together it is for at least three or four hours." Another participant offers an even more telling fact: "Three of eight groomsman in my wedding were BLP participants. I have made lifelong friends."

Moving on

Home Depot has graduated four groups of BLP participants, and "most of those associates are still with the company." Alumni currently serve as finance managers, human resources directors, store managers, auditors, strategic business development analysts, safety managers, supply chain managers, and in numerous other positions within the company. Some of the first jobbers we spoke with say they hope to remain with Home Depot for a while, then return to business school to earn a master's degree.

Attrition

Home Depot tells us that "associates do not typically leave while still in the program. In the few rare cases, associates have left to pursue nonretail or corporate careers, (i.e., nonprofit and sales [commissioned]). People who leave [Home Depot] after graduating the program typically leave to pursue a graduate degree." Notes one BLP participant, "There will always be some bit of dissatisfaction in any program; the majority of the complaints are usually related to poorly managed expectations. Anyone who approaches this program with open eyes would realize that it is a great opportunity to get your foot in the door at a Fortune 500 company. We have the ability to work hard, get recognized, and climb quickly."

IRC
Various Positions

THE BIG PICTURE

"Refugee relief, respect, renewal" is the slogan of the International Rescue Committee (IRC), an international organization that provides housing, food, water, medical assistance, and other essentials to people uprooted by war, violence, disease, or natural disasters. The organization also offers long-term relief in the form of education programs, job training, and employment services.

STATS

LOCATION(S) WHERE ENTRY-LEVEL EMPLOYEES WORK

"[There is] potential for entry-level positions in any IRC office—domestic (including headquarters in New York or any regional resettlement office) or international."

AVERAGE NUMBER OF APPLICATIONS EACH YEAR

The IRC receives "roughly 2,600 applications per year (domestic and international) for entry-level positions."

AVERAGE NUMBER HIRED OVER THE LAST TEN YEARS

The IRC fills "roughly 100 (domestic and international) entry-level positions per year."

ENTRY-LEVEL POSITION(S) AVAILABLE

Domestic new hires work as "volunteers, administrators, and specialists." International new hires work as "volunteers, interns, and officers."

AVERAGE HOURS WORKED PER WEEK

New hires work a little over thirty-seven hours per week.

PERCENTAGE OF ENTRY-LEVEL HIRES STILL WITH COMPANY AFTER THREE, FIVE, AND TEN YEARS

"After three years: domestic, 28 percent; international, 5 percent (these are, by nature, short-term positions)."

AVERAGE STARTING SALARY

"International volunteers/interns, [earn an] average $500 [per] month. International officers [earn from] $20,000 to $24,000 per year. Domestic [officers earn from] $27,000 to $30,000 per year."

BENEFITS OFFERED

"International [hires receive] major medical, life insurance, emergency evacuation, travel insurance, and workers' compensation. Domestic [hires receive] major medical, dental, life insurance, emergency evacuation, travel insurance, workers' compensation." Additional benefits for "international employees including volunteers and interns [are] round-trip transportation, housing, travel within country, coverage of visa expenses, immunizations, medical exams, 403(b), and pension plan. [Additional benefits for] domestic employees [include] options for a 403(b) plan, transit saver program, and cafeteria plan."

CONTACT INFORMATION

Visit the website at www.ircjobs.org.

GETTING HIRED

"Volunteering is a great way to start with IRC—both in the United States and overseas," employees tell us. Writes one, "[Volunteer work] gave me the opportunity to show my interest in the organization and my commitment to working with refugees. When a position opened, I already knew a lot about the organization and the programs in Atlanta, and had already demonstrated some of my strengths." Internships are also an excellent gateway to full-time work. Outsiders (i.e., those without volunteer or internship experiences) may attempt to penetrate the citadel by applying through the organization's website. The organization seeks in its prospective hires "international experience, strong writing skills, excellent interpersonal and communication skills, [an] ability to work productively in a team environment and independently, flexibility, and a sense of humor." So how do you wow IRC's recruiters? "I definitely think that my enthusiasm for the work, matched by my studies at college and extracurricular activities, as well as the fact that I had found IRC on my own demonstrated to the recruiter that I was very serious about working for this organization, and that it fit into my long-term career plans," reports one successful hire.

MONEY AND PERKS

Your IRC salary is "not really negotiable," but "at the same time, it is the ideal job" for many people who take it. Low wages often come part-and-parcel with a satisfying career, especially in the world of nonprofits. Organization officials report that it "has an annual [salary] increase system in place for domestic and international employees. Additional increases are based upon performance." First jobbers identify numerous perks; they tell us that "it's hard to beat getting paid to run around the African bush in a Land Rover and attend regional meetings in Zanzibar. But better than any of that is the chance to meet firsthand and talk to the people IRC assists and works with. These are people who have suffered through some of the worst oppression and privation one can possibly imagine, and yet are in many cases some of the most optimistic and inspiring people you will ever meet." They also appreciate that "there is flexibility within the organization" and that "it's not terribly formal. You have to wear your suit when you go to meetings at the United Nations, but you can wear jeans otherwise."

THE ROPES

Orientations at IRC are "held on a quarterly basis and bring together new staff from headquarters, regional resettlement offices across the United States, and from field offices around the world for three days in New York." The orientation "typically covers payroll and benefits, IRC policies and procedures, a general introduction to other IRC programs, security and safety procedures when working for IRC overseas, how to manage stress while working overseas, and other topics." International staff members "receive an orientation in-country upon arrival." Reports one staffer who worked in Guinea and Ethiopia, "When I arrived in Guinea, my supervisor immediately took me out into the field for a week to visit all of the refugee camps and meet the staff in three different field sites. My boss met me at the airport, helped me change money, and showed me my accommodations. In Ethiopia, my immediate supervisor actually met me at the airport at 2:00 AM when I arrived. I had a two-day orientation [at] headquarters and then flew to the field to visit two refugee camps and to meet my staff." Training is often on-the-job and handled by mentors. Writes one first jobber, "Although there was a steep learning curve, I didn't find this to be a problem and never felt like I did not know enough. You have to quickly absorb a lot of information about subjects as diverse as public health surveys, international social work, United States government grants and contracts, and United Nations peacekeeping operations."

DAY IN THE LIFE

The IRC calls on its first jobbers to perform a wide assortment of jobs, both at home and abroad. The tasks are enormously complex and often difficult, complicated by the variety of governments with which the IRC must work. That the IRC only operates in trouble spots makes the job more challenging still; so too does the organization's modest budget. Explains one program specialist, "Budgets at nonprofits are tight, and there's a lot of administrative work that needs to get done, so program specialists wind up bearing the burden of photocopying, making travel arrangements, scheduling meetings, and other not so intellectually rigorous tasks. At the same time, the nature of international assistance is that it is constantly overwhelming, but usually in a positive, up-to-your-eyeballs-and-loving-every-minute-of-it sort of way." First jobbers may find themselves a little overwhelmed at first, but eventually they hit their stride. Writes one, "Someone new to the world of international humanitarian assistance simply does not possess the knowledge and experience to weigh in on substantial issues. With time (and in particular by getting the chance to travel to the field and see firsthand how IRC assists refugees and partners with communities to help them recover from conflict), [we] develop into experts on their programs and their part of the world and are able to make substantive contributions to the organization." And of course, there's another payoff: as one first jobber puts it, "The work is rewarding and the people I work with are highly motivated, intelligent, compassionate, and cosmopolitan."

PEERS

IRC first jobbers in the United States tell us that "there's a lot of camaraderie and a solid after-hours social scene. Informal happy hours happen approximately once a month or so." Overseas, "All of us expatriates live together. Thus we work *and* live together, and we socialize all the time. As we are all living away from friends and family, we tend to largely socialize with each other outside of work. We often eat together, etc. In overseas work, I think expatriate staff spend a great deal of time together (which is also why personality and an ability to cope with overseas life is very important). Even if we are different, we are going through a similar experience and facing similar challenges." Another perk of the peer network is "making friends with colleagues around the world. After working at IRC, odds are you'll have friends [in every continent on] whose couches you can crash."

MOVING ON

The IRC tells us that "Domestically, most staff leave to pursue higher education and professional growth. For our international employees, much of our work takes place in high security areas, such as Afghanistan or the Congo. Therefore employees may leave to work in a more stable environment or to take a break from the rigors of overseas work." The average tenure of an overseas employee is two years; domestic employees tend to last longer.

ATTRITION

"Some people have real difficulty adjusting to the fast pace of the NGO [nongovernmental organization], the heavy workload, and the stress of living overseas," workers at the IRC tell us. "There are also a lot of frustrations in terms of logistics, working through the bureaucracy of overseas governments, dealing with donor limits and demands, and the challenge of working with and managing staff of different nationalities and cultures." These challenges, plus the challenge of living on a low wage, drive some first jobbers to other pursuits. Writes one employee, "I have no plans to leave at this point, although it is always tempting to go to the for-profit world and make more money. That said, I am very aware of the intangibles that I would be giving up here, and so I stick around."

J. E. T. PROGRAMME
Coordinator for International Relations and Assistant Language Teacher

THE BIG PICTURE

J. E. T.s—that's what participants in the Japanese Exchange and Teaching Programme are called—spend a year (or more) in Japan, primarily teaching English, although the program also offers some other community service jobs. The J. E. T. Programme is a great way to visit Japan and get immersed in Japanese culture on someone else's dime.

STATS

LOCATION(S) WHERE ENTRY-LEVEL EMPLOYEES WORK

Many locations within Japan

AVERAGE NUMBER HIRED OVER THE LAST TEN YEARS

Approximately 2,500 people are hired per year.

ENTRY-LEVEL POSITION(S) AVAILABLE

New hires work as assistant language teachers, coordinators for international relations, and sports exchange advisors.

AVERAGE HOURS WORKED PER WEEK

New hires work thirty-five hours every week.

PERCENTAGE OF ENTRY-LEVEL HIRES STILL WITH COMPANY AFTER THREE, FIVE, AND TEN YEARS

Not applicable. "The programme is for one year with the possibility of extending twice."

AVERAGE STARTING SALARY

New hires earn 3.6 million per year (calm down; that's yen, not dollars!). Exchange rates fluctuate daily, but use an online currency converter to see how much this is in United States dollars.

BENEFITS OFFERED

New hires receive Japanese national insurance, accident, and medical insurance.

CONTACT INFORMATION

Visit the website at www.jetprogramme.org.

GETTING HIRED

The application process is "run by Japanese embassies and consulates in forty countries, and differs slightly accordingly." Applications can be downloaded at Japan's Ministry of Foreign Affairs home page; the application is standard, and asks for education and employment background information, a statement of purpose essay, academic transcripts, and letters of reference. After reviewing applications, the Japanese government contacts likely candidates to schedule interviews. Writes one new hire, "I was interviewed by three people: a former J. E. T. employee, a university professor, and a Japanese consulate representative. It was a formal interview; all questions had been prepared by the interviewers and written down beforehand. Each interviewer asked three to four, mostly situational, questions. Some examples are: 'Since you are a vegetarian, what would you do if the principal at your school invited you over for dinner and offered you meat?' [and] 'Boys can be curious about female bodies. What would you say if one of your students asked for your bust-waist-hip measurements?'" Adds another, "I was intimidated when being interviewed by three people, but it wasn't bad. The interviewers were friendly. The application process is long, and you don't find out where you are placed until after you accept the position, which could be a drawback for some."

MONEY AND PERKS

J. E. T.s think you should know that "the terms of [their] contract are government policy and in no way flexible," so don't bother trying to wrangle a few extra yen during the interview. J. E. T.s mostly think they get a fair deal. Writes one, "I was supplied an apartment, was helped getting set up with a bank account and phone, etc., and was paid well." They also appreciate the fact that "J. E. T. is affiliated with both the Japanese and United States governments, so you know it isn't a back-door, monkey bars company." For the teachers, the best fringe benefit—besides the free trip to and from Japan—is the work schedule, which includes many vacation days.

THE ROPES

New J. E. T.s start out with "a couple of orientation sessions at the Japanese embassy in DC," then continue in Tokyo once they arrive. Writes one J. E. T., "The [Tokyo] orientation was a grueling three days in an overpriced hotel. It was a series of meetings and seminars relating to the J. E. T. Programme and teaching ideas." Adds another new J. E. T., "They told us things like 'Don't stick your chopsticks in your rice' and 'Never put sugar in green tea.' Yes, their orientation programs need some help. I know that most J. E. T.s (including me) were disappointed that we didn't get more practical information or teacher training." Afterward, "most training was on-the-job, learning the boundaries of what was and wasn't expected of me."

DAY IN THE LIFE

The vast majority of J. E. T.s serve as assistant language teachers. Here's how one describes her typical day in Japan: "Arrive at 8:20 AM. Sit through a five-minute morning meeting in Japanese. Drink green tea.

Begin reading my teaching materials or the text books to make a lesson plan. (I typically had two to three classes, fifty minutes each, a day.) Read a book or the newspaper. Eat lunch in the teachers' room. Go to the convenience store to buy chocolate. Continue making a lesson plan for the week. Talk to students in the hall. Drink more green tea. Leave by 4:00 PM." Another J. E. T. agrees that the workload is often surprisingly light: "Typically, I taught anywhere from one to three fifty-minute classes per day (out of an eight-hour work day). The rest of the time I [planned lessons], emailed, read, wrote, studied Japanese, spaced out, and observed. Teaching consisted of reading a one page passage out of the textbook that my kids would repeat and then write in their notebooks. About every two weeks I would plan a game or speaking activity." Despite occasional bouts with boredom, most J. E. T.s describe their experience as a valuable one. As one notes, "I worked with some incredible teachers and some mediocre ones. The best ones helped me with my Japanese language studies and answered questions I had about Japanese culture. I learned both what I wanted to aim for in my teaching career and what I wanted to avoid in terms of style of teaching."

PEERS

Peer relationships in J. E. T. depend largely on the assignment. As one newbie tells us, "I was the only J. E. T. in my town, so it was pretty much up to me to meet other J. E. T.s and make plans with them. There were other towns that had, like, thirteen J. E. T.s, and some of these people hung out exclusively with other J. E. T.s at western-type bars, clubs, and restaurants. I tried to hang out equally with other J. E. T.s and Japanese people." Offers another J. E. T., "I made friends, but the other J. E. T.s were all across the board. I definitely met some great people; I even met my boyfriend through the J. E. T. program. Without fellow J. E. T.s, life in Japan can get lonely;" as one teacher explains, "I felt isolated. There was the language barrier, as well as the fact that an outsider, especially a foreigner, is not really welcome into the larger group or expected to do real work or take on real responsibilities."

MOVING ON

The J. E. T. Programme is a one-year deal, although J. E. T.s can renew their contracts twice to extend their stays to three years. Most return home to attend graduate school or seek teaching jobs in the United States. Recalls one, "I left after one year. I had a great time and would recommend the program to anyone, but it was time for me to go. I felt that I had a good experience and staying any longer would have dragged it out to the point that it became unpleasant."

ATTRITION

Homesickness and loneliness are the chief causes of attrition, but there's a huge disincentive to leaving the program early: Participants are responsible for airfare home, plus other related expenses (rent and fees on a participant's apartment in Japan, for one) that quickly add up to a small fortune. If they fail to complete the contract for any but the most dire reasons (i.e., a death in the immediate family), they must pay all these costs.

JOHNS HOPKINS UNIVERSITY APPLIED PHYSICS LAB
Various Positions

THE BIG PICTURE

The Johns Hopkins University Applied Physics Laboratory does a ton of work for NASA and the Navy. It also performs research for other government agencies. There is no formal entry-level program, but there are plenty of jobs for those with highly developed technology and/or science skills.

STATS

LOCATION(S) WHERE ENTRY-LEVEL EMPLOYEES WORK

Laurel, MD

ENTRY-LEVEL POSITION(S) AVAILABLE

There are opportunities in many of APL's 130 labs and technical facilities.

AVERAGE HOURS WORKED PER WEEK

Entry-level hires work forty hours per week.

BENEFITS OFFERED

"APL's flexible benefits plan offers different health care options to meet the needs of staff members and their families. Covered services from designated providers generally require small co-payments; covered services received outside the designated provider network (opt-out benefits) are covered after a deductible amount is satisfied. Two dental insurance plans cover preventive, diagnostic, and restorative services for employees and their eligible dependents." Additional benefits include paid leave, flexible spending program, pension plan, continuing education funding, and scholarships.

CONTACT INFORMATION

Visit the website at www.jhuapl.edu/employment.

GETTING HIRED

One entry-level employee at APL tells us that the application process "is rather simple. I gave my resume to the recruiter at the college career fair, and I received an email a month later inviting me to interview. APL sends your resume to all departments, and you interview with all departments that have an interest in you. For the interviews, the tone was very casual, and I interviewed with four members of my current group. After all of my interviews were conducted, I received a job offer that afternoon." Many describe the hiring process as surprisingly pleasant. Offers one first jobber, "I had a great experience communicating with the lab prior to attending the interview. All accommodations were taken care of and everything was explained to me prior to flying out to interview." New employees recommend that you "ask intelligent questions that show you've taken the time to look around [the] website. Also, indicate a department you are interested in working in." Those who serve successful internships have an inside track on being hired.

MONEY AND PERKS

Salary, start date, and the nature of the job are "somewhat negotiable," new hires tell us. Writes one, "My group had some tasks in mind for me when they hired me, but they remain somewhat flexible as to which projects I get to work on (based on my preference). If I decide one day that I don't like what I'm doing at all, I'm of the impression that I can apply for a position in another group at APL, so there's also opportunity for lateral movement here." Workers praise the retirement plan; one employee says, "APL matches my donation to my retirement account two for one up to a fixed percentage of my salary. Other than that, an APL employee is entitled to discounts throughout Maryland. So another example of a fringe benefit of working here is that I get 12.5 percent off of my cell phone bill every month."

THE ROPES

"There are a few layers to the orientation process" at APL. "On the first day of work, there is an orientation process which lasts about half a day and provides information on the various employee benefit programs, goes over adherence to national security guidelines here at APL, and outlines some basic company policies. After that half-day session, you start working. There is an additional week-long orientation that is held twice a year." That training, called Professional Staff Orientation Program (PSOP), "lasts for one full week, and each day you learn about two departments at the lab, take tours of those departments' facilities, and meet people [who] you would have otherwise not been able to meet." Regarding an employees' tenure a new hire says, "When there is a need for some explanation of something specific to my job here, it's usually done by my supervisor or one of my more experienced coworkers. The only formal training I've had since coming here was a week-long class I took at Penn State University, which provided a good background for the field I'm working in."

DAY IN THE LIFE

APL has many divisions working on so many different projects. There is no typical day within a single division, much less within the entire enterprise, according to workers. All work is project-based; sometimes workers are assigned to several projects at a time. Here's how one employee describes his first assignment at APL: "When I was first hired, my responsibilities were to spend half my time researching a new technology that my group was considering implementing, and half my time becoming familiar with a project that was started by a former group member. Originally, I was supposed to continue work on the project where the former employee left off. Within that framework, a typical day for me included reading textbooks and journal papers for half the day and looking through and experimenting with existing Matlab code for the other half. The goal in looking through the Matlab code was first to assess the performance of the existing project, then to make a recommendation of whether or not we should move forward with the project and if so, then to suggest a methodology for moving forward with it. Within a few weeks, I stopped working on both projects and began working on a few different existing projects, but I was adding to and enhancing them as opposed to just analyzing them. Now I spend most of my day writing code using Matlab."

PEERS

Other than orientation, "there aren't many structured social activities for new employees," first jobbers tell us. "However, there is an active network of younger employees at APL called the Recent Graduate Network that gets together both at and outside of work. I've definitely made some friends and good acquaintances this way. The actual number of hours per week that we interact varies, but often times we'll do lunch during the week, and we'll go out to happy hours or clubs about once a week." Agrees another worker, "APL has great camaraderie! There's always a group doing something after-hours or somewhere to go with other employees. There are all kinds of sports and clubs at the lab [over two dozen, according to APL representatives]."

MOVING ON

The APL is a great place to build a career, and the folks we spoke with have no intention of leaving. Complaints are slight; "APL has a tendency to promote brilliant scientists to management [positions]," writes one employee wryly. "However, not all scientists have management skills." Writes another, "Most APL employees are pretty happy with their jobs, and I definitely fall into that category. People here like the relaxed atmosphere. You don't have dress up to come to work, and APL is very flexible in letting you schedule your forty hours per week. Some people work nine hours per day and take every other Friday off. APL also has a great employee benefits package." People who do leave most often move onto positions with other movers and shakers in the world of applied physics; other people return to academia.

ATTRITION

APL representatives say that "volunteer turnover [terminations excluding retirements, disability, and for-cause releases] is very low, particularly among the technical professional staff (less than 2 percent)."

KATZ MEDIA GROUP
Sales Assistant

THE BIG PICTURE

Katz Media, which includes the Katz Radio Group, the Katz Television Group, and Clear Channel Radio Sales, sells commercial time for more than 2,600 radio stations and 400 television stations across the country. If you love the media, advertising, and schmoozing, Katz Media could be the gateway to your dream career.

STATS

LOCATION(S) WHERE ENTRY-LEVEL EMPLOYEES WORK

21 regional offices

AVERAGE NUMBER OF APPLICATIONS EACH YEAR

Katz receives 5,000 applications every year.

AVERAGE NUMBER HIRED OVER THE LAST TEN YEARS

The company hires 300 people per year.

ENTRY-LEVEL POSITION(S) AVAILABLE

New hires work as sales assistants.

AVERAGE HOURS WORKED PER WEEK

New hires work forty hours per week.

AVERAGE STARTING SALARY

The starting salary for entry-level hires is $23,000 per year.

BENEFITS OFFERED

The company offers medical, dental, and life insurance, as well as short-term and long-term disability. Additional benefits include employee stock purchase plan, 401(k), tuition reimbursement, commuter check, and employee assistance program.

CONTACT INFORMATION

Anne Strafaci

Vice President of Recruitment

125 West 55th Street

New York, NY 10019

212-424-6110 (fax)

Email: anne.strafaci@katz-media.com

Getting Hired

Katz's on-campus recruiting consists of "interviewing on campus with a few area colleges that are close to our offices" and "attending many career fairs that usually consist of several colleges." A resume referral program is available for interested students from out-of-area colleges; the firm will "accept applications from anyone with a strong interest in media, strong background in client relations, and the personality to match." Here's how one successful hire describes the interview process: "I was interviewed initially by human resources. My interviews went very well, and the next step was to see where my specific skills could be put to use. A week later I was called in to interview with two different divisions. With each division I was interviewed by three different individuals who gave me a feel for what each department did and how I would fit into the scheme of things." Many successful candidates, we're told, have previously completed internships in the field of media buying.

Money and Perks

During their first year at Katz, sales assistants "could receive one to two pay increases, depending on performance and the department's budget. After that, there are yearly performance reviews" to determine raises. The firm engages in other "employee morale efforts," such as "an Instant Rewards Program (employees recognized with gift certificates for a job well done), on-site yoga classes (in New York), and on-site personal development seminars like financial planning, parenting, nutrition, etc." First jobbers appreciate that "there are many opportunities for upward mobility within the company." They also love the fact that "everyone, especially the managers, is aware of how intense days or even whole quarters can be. We are constantly taken out to lunches and dinners; group activities are planned; and having basketball, darts, and golf in the office makes working here so much fun."

The Ropes

Orientation at Katz is a half-day affair, and is "very informative." One employee recalls, "It basically gives you an overview of the company and the services that it provides to its clients. The orientation also goes over basic paperwork necessary for any new job. Additionally, the orientation allowed us to find out about the most important clients: the employees. Learning about the different perks and services available to employees definitely was the highlight of orientation." New hires subsequently "receive training on how to use the various computer systems specific to [their] industry. The computer information systems department holds weekly workshops to help new hires adjust to working with the new programs. [Employees] also [get] additional training from [their] supervisors and fellow sales assistants." Firm officials note that "there are a number of veteran employees who informally act as mentors to new employees." Explains one sales assistant, "We are constantly having assistant sales training classes taught by the account executives, and my own rep, whom I assist, is very helpful in showing me anything he can to help me in the job."

DAY IN THE LIFE

Sales assistants "are the backbone of Katz Media Group's sales teams because they assist account executives with the high-volume work of television, radio, or Internet sales," a representative from the firm tells us. As their title suggests, these entry-level employees "assist all the sales reps on a team. [They] input orders, send revisions, process 'make-goods,' request contracts, and interact with the stations and agencies via email and telephone." It's a job that requires newbies to stay on their toes; writes one newbie, "My most important job is to maintain my contracts and make sure that spots are running. If they are not running, I troubleshoot to fix the problem. My job entails a lot of troubleshooting and management of relationships!" At first, sales assistants have to run everything they do by their supervisors, but "as time goes on, you're given more responsibility and do not have to report to your sales rep for as many things." Another new hire says, "For me, a trust developed between us, as the reps saw what I was capable of and knew that my understanding of the business was growing." As they work their way up the corporate ladder, sales assistants appreciate that "high level people are very accessible; that is what makes [their] division at Katz a good working environment. [Their] execs are very visible, and this allows for a better rapport to be established between the execs and employees."

PEERS

Because "this industry is *very* social at all levels of employment, and entertaining clients is an important part of the job," Katz employees participate in a "huge after-work social scene." Their socializing, though, is more often with "reps, their assistants, and media buyers" than with other Katz first jobbers. A new hire writes, "All of us entry-level employees definitely get along very well, and there is a sense of friendship among us. We don't hesitate to help each other out and ask one another questions when they arise. We occasionally go out for happy hour together (maybe once a week), which is a great opportunity to get to know your coworkers on a more social level. All in all, it's nice to have other young people around you, which makes the transition into your first job an easier experience."

MOVING ON

Sales assistants generally stay in their position for one year, then either move up or move out. Some leave to work at "ad agencies, radio and television stations, and other sales-related companies." A first jobber here "take[s] it day by day," telling us that "as along as I enjoy what I am doing, I will stick with it. When the day comes that this gig or company is not fun, then I will make a change."

ATTRITION

People who leave before their first year is up—and that's about 30 percent of all first jobbers, according to Katz—usually "complain about the pay, but who is ever satisfied with their salary?" A few people find themselves assisting account executives with whom they are incompatible; employees who cannot get themselves reassigned usually leave the firm.

KPMG

Client Service Professionals

THE BIG PICTURE

KPMG is one of the "big four" in the assurance and tax services business (the other three are Deloitte Touche Tohmatsu, Ernst & Young LLP, and PricewaterhouseCoopers). Aspiring accountants can hone their skills at KPMG while preparing for their CPA exams, for which the company offers study materials and other support services.

STATS

LOCATION(S) WHERE ENTRY-LEVEL EMPLOYEES WORK

122 offices throughout the United States

AVERAGE NUMBER OF APPLICATIONS EACH YEAR

KPMG receives many applications; approximately 5,000 candidates reach the interview stage.

AVERAGE NUMBER HIRED OVER THE LAST TEN YEARS

KPMG hires approximately 1,500 people annually.

ENTRY-LEVEL POSITION(S) AVAILABLE

"Assurance associates [work] in our Business Measurement Process (Audit), Financial Advisory Services, and Risk Advisory Services practices. Tax associates [work] in our Federal Tax, State and Local Tax, International Executive Services, International Corporate Services, and Economic Consulting Services practices."

AVERAGE HOURS WORKED PER WEEK

New hires work fifty hours per week.

AVERAGE STARTING SALARY

"Average starting salaries for our new hires vary greatly by practice, degree, and geographic region."

BENEFITS OFFERED

Company benefits include a point-of-service health care plan with choice of network or non-network physicians; a number of medical plans, with no physician networks, that vary by deductible and coinsurance levels; HMOs (available in most locations); prescription drug program; dental plan; vision care; Vision One discount plan; short- and long-term disability; and life insurance. Additional benefits include twenty-five paid personal days accrued monthly for vacation, illness, or other absence; eligibility for the incentive compensation program; bonus for passing CPA, Bar, or Enrolled Agents Exam; free

MicroMash CPA Exam review software and discounts for CPA Exam review courses; flexible spending accounts of up to $3,000 pre-tax for non-reimbursed eligible medical expenses and up to $5,000 pre-tax for eligible dependent care expenses; 401(k) plan with KPMG match, including Merrill Lynch Benefits OnlineSM (assistance in preparation and management of retirement savings and financial investing); KPMG pension plan; paid time off for new parents; adoption reimbursement program; child care discounts; emergency backup dependent care program; METPAY auto and home insurance discount program; and mortgage assistance programs and financial assistance.

CONTACT INFORMATION

Visit the website at www.kpmgcampus.com.

GETTING HIRED

KPMG recruits on a number of college campuses across the country. In addition, "students from all schools can submit their resumes online at www.kpmgcampus.com." At many schools, "representatives from each of the big four firms make trips prior to accepting resumes for specific positions. Firms set up social events to meet potential interview candidates and have a presence at university-hosted career fairs." These events, our respondents say, offer the perfect opportunity to meet face-to-face with recruiters and hand out resumes. Next come on-campus interviews. Here's how one entry-level employee describes the experience: "The night before the interview, KPMG held a dinner, which gave candidates the opportunity to meet their interviewer, as well as other members of the firm. The tables were set up so that all the interviewees were seated with their interviewer for the next day. About seven interviewees, the interviewer, and two other KPMG employees sat at each table. The subsequent interview was relaxed and easy. A manager from the Boston office interviewed me. It was a conversation about the experiences that I had on my resume, my plans to continue my education, [and] my expectations of what the firm could offer me." Entry-level workers note that there are practice questions on the KPMG website to help you prepare for the interview. After the initial interview comes another round of interviews, similar in content, but this time at a KPMG office. The lucky few candidates who clear this hurdle receive job offers soon after.

MONEY AND PERKS

"The market generally sets salaries and KPMG is competitive with the other firms, but there is little negotiation," entry-level employees tell us, although one of our survey respondents note that "salary is negotiable if you have another competitive offer." Everyone agrees with the company line, namely that "salaries are commensurate with the level and competitive with the marketplace. Top performers have the opportunity to earn incentive compensation if the firm has met its revenue targets." Workers' favorite perks include five weeks' paid vacation ("KPMG believes in a good work/life balance; the firm wants its employees to work hard when they have to but to take time for themselves as well."). "Discounts with various companies, and the flexibility of the job itself" are also popular. Aspiring accountant types with a touch of wanderlust could be happy with KPMG: "One of the great aspects of KPMG is that it is an international organization, and the firm would rather keep you and make you happy than lose you. Therefore, it is relatively easy to move from one office to another, especially [at] the beginning of your career."

THE ROPES

Training at KPMG begins with a brief orientation ("new hires complete relevant paperwork and are provided a firm overview that helps them understand our business structure and core values"), followed by "local office training that provides them with information specific to their offices ([i.e.,] security badges and parking information). In addition, all professionals attend a five-to-ten day national training program soon after their start date, where they learn how to perform the client engagement responsibilities of a new associate." Reports one employee who recently completed the process, "You begin in your office, [where you focus for three days] on KPMG's policies and procedures and becoming more familiar with the office itself. It's a combination of self-study and instructor presentations. This is also the time period during which you will meet some people from your line of business and your performance managers; you will also receive your schedules. Then you have the opportunity to train with all the individuals in your same position nationwide. This year we went to Florida for ten days. These ten days consisted of eight days of class, a day of community service, and one free day. Classes consisted primarily of lecture and exercises reinforcing the lectures." Once back at their home offices, "all new hires are assigned a mentor. Often this is someone who graduated from the same school as the new hire. Our mentors volunteer to work with new hires and are excited to assist them in the transition process from student to full-time employee. In addition, each new hire is also assigned a performance manager who helps them set goals and measures them against their goals providing feedback throughout the year."

DAY IN THE LIFE

Everyone we interviewed at KPMG agrees that "there is no such thing as the typical day here, which keeps things interesting." One newbie reports, "My responsibilities at first ranged from administrative tasks to understanding business documentation, process analysis documentation, and basic audit test work. In my experience, the entry-level employee will audit the lower risk, less complex areas such as cash and investments." Naturally, responsibilities increase as employees gain experience. Explains another employee, "The first two years you work as an associate, then progress to [become] a senior associate where you are responsible for managing associates on the engagement. After about five years you are promoted to manager, where you have a number of clients and are responsible for developing the audit and managing the senior associate on all engagements." Despite what you may think, folks do more than crunch numbers. As one employee puts it, "People have the impression that accountants sit in front of a computer all day. While there is definitely some time [spent] sitting in front of the computer, there is also a great deal of people contact with frequent client interviews and meetings."

PEERS

Entry-level employees at KPMG enjoy "a significant amount of contact and camaraderie." One explains that "I started with at least fifty other people my age. Going away for training was a great way to get to know each other and to make friends. When work is less busy, I would say that I see KPMG friends after work at least every few weeks." Friendships develop easily because "KPMG does an excellent job of hiring outgoing people who are easy to talk to." The firm also works hard to promote unity among its workers. According to one worker, "There are numerous social events held by the firm and organized by first-year people. There are events almost every week."

MOVING ON

Many new hires stick around for the long haul, but KPMG concedes that some employees can be lured away. Notes a spokesperson from the company, "During their tenure with the firm, KPMG professionals develop a skill set that is in demand throughout the financial services industry. Private industry (in-house accounting and financial positions in all industries) and our competitors (other big four and smaller firms)" sometimes entice KPMG entry-level employees away with higher salaries or better opportunities.

ATTRITION

Not everyone can handle the heavy workload at KPMG. Common complaints are often "about the hours," writes one newbie, explaining why some of her colleagues quit. "I understand how an individual may feel this way, but I also feel one can make the hours work easily into a work/life balance, and long hours are not required all year."

BEST AND WORST

To read about some of KPMG's successful entry-level employees, surf over to www.kpmgcampus.com/campus/know/who/about.asp and click on the "Meet Some of Us" link.

THE LEAGUE OF AMERICAN THEATRES AND PRODUCERS
Administrative Assistant to the President

THE BIG PICTURE

Not everyone can be administrative assistant to the president of the League of American Theatres and Producers (LATP). In fact, only one person a year can enjoy the opportunity. That one lucky person spends a year assisting the head of the organization who promotes Broadway theater, produces the Tony Awards® and the National Broadway Theatre Awards, and supervises a myriad of business and charity enterprises associated with the theater. And, of course, if the president gets sick and can't be there on opening night, well, then, *you'll* just have to go out there and be president. (Well, not really.)

STATS

LOCATION(S) WHERE ENTRY-LEVEL EMPLOYEES WORK

New York, NY

AVERAGE NUMBER OF APPLICATIONS EACH YEAR

The LATP receives seventy-five to 100 applications each year.

AVERAGE NUMBER HIRED OVER THE LAST TEN YEARS

The LATP hires one person per year.

ENTRY-LEVEL POSITION(S) AVAILABLE

New hires work as administrative assistants to the president.

AVERAGE HOURS WORKED PER WEEK

New hires work fifty hours per week.

PERCENTAGE OF ENTRY-LEVEL HIRES STILL WITH THE COMPANY AFTER THREE, FIVE, AND TEN YEARS

After three years, 50 percent of all new hires remain with the company, and after five years, 25 percent remain with the company.

AVERAGE STARTING SALARY

New hires earn $22,000 per year.

BENEFITS OFFERED

The LATP offers medical (HMO or PPO), dental, and vision insurance. Additional benefits include possible theater tickets and Tony Awards® tickets.

P. Casterlin

The League of American Theatres and Producers, Inc.

226 West 47th Street

New York, NY 10036

GETTING HIRED

With only one position to fill, LATP obviously doesn't need to recruit on campuses. One former assistant discovered the job through an ad in *Playbill;* another learned about it while serving an internship in the theater industry. The application process is quite simple. According to the LATP, you "send your resume. We interview qualified candidates." That's about all there is to it, except, of course, that you'll be competing with a horde of people for a single position. Here's how one successful candidate describes the interview process: "I sent my resume in and crafted my cover letter to express my interest in the theater and my desire to learn about the industry. I was interviewed by the president's executive assistant, with whom I would be working side by side. The first interview was very casual and comfortable. We talked about my schooling and my past experiences and internships. They of course asked about my interest in theater. I then came in for a second interview with the president, which was a little more intimidating. My references were checked, and I was offered the job a few days later." Notes one former assistant, "During the interview, I was asked about my education and theater background and what I saw myself doing in five years. The president asked me which productions I liked and why. Coincidently, we both love one particular musical, and I think that definitely worked in my favor." The president, we're told, is "very nice."

MONEY AND PERKS

As you might expect for an exclusive, springboard opportunity like this one, very little in the job offer is negotiable. Writes one former administrative assistant, "The only thing that was negotiable was when I started. Everything else was set up already, including salary." Everyone we spoke with agrees that the best fringe benefit is "getting the opportunity to see almost all the Broadway shows of the current season at no cost and, in addition, to meet the industry's top people." Writes one, "Out of a five-day work week, I am seeing four plays free this week. I see an average of two plays a week."

THE ROPES

The president's assistant is trained by his or her predecessor; explains one who has held the job, "I had an overlap period with the person I replaced. We were working together for about two weeks, which I believe to be rare for the position." Usually, the overlap period is one week. "We went over the important things together, and since then I have done some adjusting on my own. I have been working directly with my boss from day one." At first, "there are a lot of names to remember and people to meet," warns another former administrative assistant. "I learned by working with the executive assistant and writing everything down. That was very important!"

DAY IN THE LIFE

"It is hard to describe a typical day because in this job each day was different," writes one former president's assistant. "Usually we met in the morning to look at the day's schedule and worked from there. There was a lot of scheduling and travel arrangements and phone calls coming in constantly. Being in the president's office you are often interfacing with the industry's top people, whether it be producers, executives, or actors." It's an important job, those who do it tell us, even if it isn't always glamorous. As one explains, "Keeping the president organized and happy is very important to the structure of the company, so I think I mattered. The work I was doing certainly wasn't like performing brain surgery, but I felt like my contributions were important and appreciated, even if the actual activities were somewhat mundane." On the plus side, the president's assistant interacts with the industry's movers and shakers all the time. "One of the best things about this job," writes one, "is that nearly all of the time that I am not spending sitting at my desk working is spent interacting with high-level people. On a daily basis, I am meeting the people who are shaping this industry."

PEERS

Because the training program LATP offers has a population of one, "There is not such a big social scene. Working for the 'boss' often isolates you. During the workday I would interact, but not as much after work." Those who work here share a passion for the theater, though, and that invariably creates some sense of community; as one former administrative assistant tells us, "Younger staff members definitely hang out and have lunch or see shows together, and there is certainly camaraderie within each department as well. However, there isn't a big after-hours social scene." All who have worked here would agree that "the office has a nice air to it" and that coworkers are a friendly, helpful bunch.

MOVING ON

The administrative assistant position at the LATP is a one-year-only job, and some people "usually go to other industry jobs," while other people wind up in "arts positions or in other fields." Some find other jobs within the organization and make a career at the LATP; one of the former administrative assistants we spoke with has moved on to another department and has been with the company for over seven years.

BEST AND WORST

The best administrative assistant is one who "learns quickly, excels at work, asks for more responsibilities, and successfully completes them, resulting in a promotion to another department when the year" is over. The worst was one who "accepted the job with unreasonable expectations and was disappointed."

LIFESCAN

Associate Marketing Manager, Associate Financial Analyst

THE BIG PICTURE

LifeScan, a Johnson and Johnson company, produces diabetes-monitoring equipment for home use. According to the company's website, new hires can "explore [their] entrepreneurial drive in a small-company environment that encourages personal and professional growth. At the same time, [they] discover the stability and resources of an international health care company developing life-enhancing technology."

STATS

LOCATION(S) WHERE ENTRY-LEVEL EMPLOYEES WORK

Milpitas, CA

AVERAGE NUMBER OF APPLICATIONS EACH YEAR

Lifescan receives sixty applications per year.

AVERAGE NUMBER HIRED OVER THE LAST TEN YEARS

The company hires eleven people per year.

ENTRY-LEVEL POSITION(S) AVAILABLE

Entry-level hires work as associate marketing managers and associate financial analysts.

AVERAGE HOURS WORKED PER WEEK

New hires work forty hours per week.

AVERAGE STARTING SALARY

Undergraduates earn from $66,000 to $89,000, while employees who have their MBAs earn from $77,000 to $103,000.

BENEFITS OFFERED

On the health care front, the company offers medical, dental, and vision insurance. Additional benefits include life insurance, tuition reimbursement, 401(k), on-site company store (headquarters), and on-site workout facility (headquarters).

CONTACT INFORMATION

Visit the website at www.LifeScanCareers.com.

GETTING HIRED

LifeScan accepts applications on its website; company officials add, "We have our core schools that we recruit from, but we also accept students from other colleges and universities." The company's recruiters seek "customer market focus, interdependent partnership, mastering complexity, and creativity" in potential hires. One successful applicant describes the vetting process this way: "I was interviewed by different levels of people: the associate marketing managers, marketing managers, and directors. The interview was a mixture of behavioral and case questions. Some questions focused specifically on the competencies required for the position. After two or three weeks, I received an offer from the company. LifeScan hosted an event in January for people who received an offer. The purpose of the event was to convince us to accept the job." Applicants with prior experience in marketing and/or financial analysis have a leg up.

MONEY AND PERKS

Starting date is negotiable at LifeScan, first jobbers tell us. Job description and salary are not, although some first jobbers are able to negotiate their signing bonuses; company representatives say, "Salaries are determined based [on] the economy and internal equity." Top perks include "access to an on-site company store, where Johnson & Johnson products are sold at an employee discount, [and] a free on-site health club facility."

THE ROPES

LifeScan newbies begin their jobs with their eyes wide open, they tell us. "I knew about the job before I started. The team leader for recruiting communicated a general description of the job to me. Around June, I discovered the area that I was going to be working in. I also received a call from my manager a week before I started my position. I didn't need to know more beforehand." Orientation "is very generic to company goals and regulatory requirements. It lasts one to two days, depending on your position." Subsequent training varies according to function; some first jobbers continue with formal training "given by various marketing managers, finance, operations, etc.," while others simply learn through "on-the-job training by our manager."

DAY IN THE LIFE

LifeScan first jobbers handle the nitty-gritty tasks of keeping LifeScan afloat: developing budgets, assisting with sales campaigns, and collaborating on advertising campaigns to expand the company's presence around the world. The company expects many of its employees, as "the organization is very lean." "There's no time to be bored, and sometimes it's pretty overwhelming, depending on the timing within the month," one new hire tells us. People who show promise are quickly handed "even more responsibility to cover more areas." Fortunately, "impressive lower-level managers" are there to offer guidance and support. Although the bare-bones staffing means that [all] workers [have] at least as much work as [they] can handle—which, employees admit, is often stressful—the upside of the situation is that low-level staffers have relatively good access to higher-ups. Writes one first jobber, "I feel that I have exposure to senior management. I sit in on a meeting once a month with senior management—vice president of marketing, vice president of marketing and sales, directors of various areas of marketing. Also, the associate marketing managers have lunch with the vice president of marketing."

PEERS

"There is a lot of contact" among LifeScan first jobbers, especially among the assistant marketing managers, who tell us they frequently enjoy "AMM Happy Hours." "We interact every day of the week at work, and probably go out together after work once or twice a month," explains one newbie. Friendships are easily forged among the workforce at LifeScan.

MOVING ON

"There is no one particular reason" that first jobbers leave LifeScan, company officials report, listing "better opportunities, more money [offered elsewhere], going back to school, and relocation" as the most common reasons. The first jobbers we spoke with report that some coworkers bristle under the heavy workload required of them; it's enough to make some people move on. Even so, most people we spoke with are highly satisfied both with their jobs and their prospects for advancement.

LOCKHEED MARTIN
Leadership Development Programs

THE BIG PICTURE

Lockheed Martin, an advanced technology company that does the lion's share of its business with the Defense Department, offers Leadership Development Programs (LDP) in communications, engineering, finance, human resources, information systems, and operations. All of these programs incorporate job rotations, technical training, and leadership development conferences to fast-track college graduates into management positions with the company.

STATS

LOCATION(S) WHERE ENTRY-LEVEL EMPLOYEES WORK

Lockheed has locations in nearly every state in the United States.

AVERAGE NUMBER OF APPLICATIONS EACH YEAR

Lockheed Martin receives 1.2 million applications for [positions in] the entire company; specific numbers for Leadership Development Programs are not available.

AVERAGE NUMBER HIRED OVER THE LAST TEN YEARS

"In the past six years, we've hired an average of 2,200 [people] per year."

ENTRY-LEVEL POSITION(S) AVAILABLE

There were approximately 2,800 available positions in 2003.

AVERAGE HOURS WORKED PER WEEK

New hires work forty hours per week.

PERCENTAGE OF ENTRY-LEVEL HIRES STILL WITH THE COMPANY AFTER THREE, FIVE, AND TEN YEARS

The percentage of employees who remain with the company after three, five, and ten years are 84 percent, 76 percent, and 66 percent, respectively.

BENEFITS OFFERED

The company offers health, dental, and vision insurance. Additional benefits include a retirement plan.

CONTACT INFORMATION

Submit your resume at http://lmpeople.external.lmco.com/careers/secure/resume/resume_check.asp.

GETTING HIRED

Lockheed recruits on select campuses; the company accepts applications from all college students through its website. In examining candidates, Lockheed "focuses on senior projects, work experience, and skills that are job related." Interviews are "extremely friendly and somewhat casual/candid." That doesn't mean candidates don't get a good going over; most of the first jobbers we spoke with tell us they were interviewed numerous times before the company reached a decision. Writes one, "Five managers, in fifteen to thirty minute increments, interviewed me. A few asked technical questions. They told me about their positions/departments and life within Lockheed, such as that it is family friendly. Another thing that was discussed was the typical 'how do you work in groups?' type questions."

MONEY AND PERKS

The salaries of LDP participants are "based on certain variables such as education level (bachelor's or master's) and previous work experience. Within that framework, salary is written in stone." First jobbers praise the company's tuition reimbursement program, telling us "it's 100 percent, and it's easy to get your reimbursement for tuition and books." They also like that employees "accrue vacation days, and if you don't have enough you can actually debit them and make them up later." One participant says, "[I enjoy] moving every six months. It was so great to have the opportunity to live in four cool cities in two years. The company moved me each time."

THE ROPES

Lockheed's Leadership Development Program runs two to three years (depending on the department), with participants rotating jobs every six months. In each rotation, "You start off slow (I took a few days to read any manuals and Lockheed documents I could find, and I asked my manager if there was anything he might recommend to shorten my learning curve), try to follow the format of what was done previously (when available), and ask lots of questions!" Some training is conducted in person by managers, but much of it occurs online; explains one LDP, "You can always take free, online training classes from a list of several hundred at different levels (and they don't have to be job-applicable!), or your department sponsors you for further training at one of our many computer labs or external computer classes." All LDP participants must attend Leadership Development Conferences, which stress teamwork, problem-solving strategies, communication skills, and familiarity with Lockheed's corporate culture, values, and goals.

DAY IN THE LIFE

An LDP participant's typical day depends on his or her program and placement, of course. Explains one participant in finance, "My typical day has changed drastically with each rotation. In the Financial Analysis Department, I worked on financial models dealing with sensitivity and impact. I reported to both the director and vice president of financial planning. I updated charts and aided in financial statements management. In the tax department, I worked on federal tax packages for our three biggest sites (spending the day on the phone with our sites to make sure that everything [was] accounted for properly and using the previous year as my model). In billing and collections, I checked my computer for invoices that are declared billable, [spoke] with government payment offices to clear up any discrepanc[ies] with contract payment reconciliation issues, and deal[t] with our contract administrators to make sure that the billings [were] correctly done."

Peers

"LDP participants tend to group together at each site, both formally and informally," program participants tell us. "At some sites we had an LDP council where we planned community service activities as well as happy hours, etc. At other sites, it was more informal gatherings. At each site my group of friends was made up of LDP participants; there is a real sense of camaraderie between us since all of us were in the same situation." There is "a big after-hour[s] social scene, with a relatively large group [who] goes out a few times a week" at most sites. These first jobbers have a lot in common with each other, we're told; writes one, "It's easy to make friends. LDP participants tend to have outgoing personalities since all of us were chosen in part because of our leadership ability."

Moving On

Leadership trainees at Lockheed generally enjoy the "great exposure and diverse assignments that they have" at the company, and most plan to stay at Lockheed for a long time. A few people complain about the difficulty of finding suitable rotations, and some others feel that salary and relocation packages could be more generous. Those who are unhappy at the company sometimes return to school to study business, technology, or science.

MERCK
Various Positions

The Big Picture

Big pharmaceuticals is big business, and Merck is one of the biggest pharmaceuticals there is: Vioxx, Zocor, Fosamax, and Singulair are just a few of the drugs this giant corporation produces. Here's a place where you can parlay a degree in the sciences or engineering into a fulfilling and lucrative career. There are also plenty of opportunities to sell drugs.

Stats

Location(s) Where Entry-level Employees Work

Engineering and science positions are available in New Jersey, Pennsylvania, California, Georgia, North Carolina, Virginia, and Washington; sales positions are available nationwide.

Average Number Hired over the Last ten Years

Merck hires 200 entry-level employees per year.

Average Hours Worked Per Week

New hires work forty hours per week.

Benefits Offered

Health care benefits include dental, short- and long-term disability, long-term care, and on-site health services. Additional benefits include 401(k), pension, mentoring program, and flexible work arrangements. On-site services include health services, fitness center, dry cleaning, credit union, and child care.

Contact Information

Visit the website at www.merck.com/careers.

Getting Hired

Merck targets schools that "meet its hiring requirements based upon [its] business needs (i.e., science, engineering, information technology, etc.)," but through its website the company accepts applications from all college graduates. Many of the first jobbers we spoke with had an "in" at Merck: Some people had previously served summer internships, and others made connections through their college professors. One newbie we spoke with who didn't take either of these routes presented a strong background in her chosen field. Here's how she puts it: "Marketing of vaccines has a public health emphasis, so my joint degree in business and public health made me a perfect fit (for the available job).

To prepare, I visited Merck's website and learned all about their products. I made sure to understand how I was differentiated compared to other candidates based on my public health background, and I communicated that in my resume and interviews. The interviews were very conversational. There were a few case questions [behavior-based] and many questions requesting that I give examples from past experience."

MONEY AND PERKS

Starting salary at Merck is somewhat negotiable, depending on the skills and background a new hire brings to the company. Advanced academic work and previous work experience in the field should provide some leverage in these negotiations. The start date, all our survey respondents agree, is highly negotiable. The coolest fringe benefit, according to newbies, is the flex-time arrangement: "They don't care when you do it—as long as the work is getting done; I could decide to not work every Wednesday if I wanted to. It comes [down to the fact] that they completely trust everyone to perform and deliver."

THE ROPES

Merck's new hires waste little time getting to work. Reports one, "The orientation was very quick. I had an administrative orientation on the first day, but was then immediately introduced to my supervisor and the research group. Within one week I was running experiments." Afterward, training occurs primarily on the job. Explains one scientist, "I got basic safety training from our safety officer and then received training on laboratory techniques from a colleague at my level. This colleague was referred to as my buddy. The buddy-system was very effective; initially we did all [the] experiments together to ensure that my techniques met Merck standards. My supervisor also provided some basic analysis training." In some areas, formal training sessions are also part of the indoctrination process.

DAY IN THE LIFE

Merck is a huge company; while primarily engaged in research, the company requires a substantial support network to handle human resources, payroll, sales, and other essential functions. For employees in the glamorous research field, every day is an adventure: "Given the proprietary nature of our job, it's difficult for me to provide an example [of what I do]. However, my responsibility includes developing a portion of a manufacturing process that would be used in producing an HIV vaccine. The work was challenging, and I did not necessarily work under another engineer—it was my primary responsibility, and I was expected to drive the development. Working at Merck Research is like trying to take a drink of water from a fire hydrant—you need to suck up as much as you can!" Employees in the less glamorous areas—we spoke with one person in payroll—also find their work challenging and fulfilling; our respondent says, "A former compensation analyst was transitioning into a new role approximately three months after I came on board. I slowly became a point of contact for people in the division concerning compensation-related matters. I was also given more projects with more complexity and became more challenged in my analytical and leadership abilities. My manager began to give me increased autonomy, meaning he would give me a project and expect me to deliver with minimal supervision."

PEERS

Many Merck entry-level employees tell us that the company supports "a large social scene because so many of [the new hires] are so young. There is a large group of people [who] are less than thirty years old. There is a great sense of camaraderie, and these people have evolved into true friends. [They] routinely hang out together; [they] feel like [they are] back in school, and all of [them] are in the same lab." Writes one first jobber, "Many of us were new to the area where we work; therefore we tended to socialize after work to help one another become acclimated. The great thing is that I got to meet people who like to do a variety of things and are very open-minded to my suggestions and those of others."

MOVING ON

Merck offers internships and co-op assignments, but it does not have a first job program per se. People who come on board do so expecting to start and build careers at Merck or with a related business.

BEST AND WORST

When asked about the best example of an entry-level hire, company representatives said, "Roy Vagelos started as an intern and became our chief executive officer."

MONITOR GROUP
Various Positions

THE BIG PICTURE

The Monitor Group is a big and prestigious consulting firm. Undergraduate group consultants learn on-the-job, performing nuts-and-bolts analysis under the guidance of their mentor/supervisors. Successful hires find themselves advising businesses on increasingly important matters as their talents and knowledge develop.

STATS

LOCATION(S) WHERE ENTRY-LEVEL EMPLOYEES WORK

"In North America, we [recruit] for positions in Cambridge, MA; New York, NY; Chicago, IL; Los Angeles, CA; and San Francisco, CA. Those interested in international positions should apply through the normal process in North America, and we will coordinate with other offices on their behalf. We have global recruiting standards, so if a candidate qualifies for an offer and meets local language requirements, we will determine whether or not there are available positions in the offices in which they are interested."

AVERAGE NUMBER HIRED OVER THE LAST TEN YEARS

The Monitor Group hires about forty people per year.

ENTRY-LEVEL POSITION(S) AVAILABLE

Entry-level positions change annually according to our growth forecasts and business needs.

AVERAGE HOURS WORKED PER WEEK

New hires work sixty-five hours, with a lot of variation and unpredictability. On some weeks employees may work as little as fifty hours, while on other weeks, they will work as much as eighty-five or ninety.

PERCENTAGE OF ENTRY-LEVEL HIRES STILL WITH THE COMPANY AFTER THREE, FIVE, AND TEN YEARS

"We don't track this data specifically. Since there are multiple different career paths depending on one's interests and development goals, many undergrads stay longer than expected because they gain the opportunity to try different types of consulting domains or focus on areas that are of greater interest. Advancement into management positions is a function of skill, not degree or tenure."

AVERAGE STARTING SALARY

The starting salary is "competitive within [the] industry," which tends to be roughly $50,000 per year.

BENEFITS OFFERED

Medical benefits are "competitive within [the] industry," and additional benefits include dental, 401(k) plan, and a generous paid time off program.

CONTACT INFORMATION

Amanda Waterbury

617-252-2588

GETTING HIRED

Monitor recruits its fledgling consultants on college campuses, primarily in Ivy League campuses. Students attending other schools are welcome to submit applications online but must be prepared to interview at a Monitor office, if called. And that's a big "if." As one entry-level employee explains, "Consulting is a very competitive industry to get into, and Monitor is one of the top-tier firms in terms of appeal to college students and prestige." Notes another entry-level employee, "Getting the interview is the real major hurdle in the application process. Resume screening is notoriously tough, and there just aren't that many slots available—ten to twelve, tops. To get an interview, you must have demonstrated some meaningful work experience and/or superior academic achievement. Your resume and cover letter must tell a very compelling story." The lucky few who pass the gatekeepers' muster enjoy a "great interview process, very casual and also candid. It was more of a conversation than an interview. The interviewers immediately set the tone for Monitor as welcoming." Successful applicants go through several rounds of interviews; the first includes a case exercise, while later rounds put prospective hires through their paces in group exercises and "a client scenario role play exercise."

MONEY AND PERKS

As is the case at most entry-level gigs, you won't get rich in your first year at Monitor. Newbies gripe a little more about the pay than do their peers in similar programs because of the long hours, but they also understand that they're receiving invaluable training that will serve them throughout the rest of their more lucrative careers. Go-getters can earn quick raises; "salary increases are based on performance and are not linked to tenure. We are flexible in our ability to award strong performers," firm officials write. Perks include "support to those interested in returning to graduate schools for MBA degrees, paid dinners, [cab] rides home, free drinks, (often) food in the office, off-site corporate retreats, [and] one to two weeks off around Christmas in addition to vacation time."

THE ROPES

Orientation for Monitor new hires involves "a weeklong process of all-day sessions covering subjects ranging from Excel to filing for expense reimbursements to finding the bathroom. I was assigned to my first case team at the end of the first week." Firm officials point out that its orientation program "is designed to familiarize new hires with overall firm history, strategy, values, and expectations. It is also intended to facilitate networking and expose new consultants to as many different facets of Monitor and people within the firm as possible." Skills training necessarily plays a small role in orientation. As one intern explains, "Monitor had great training, but mostly I learned on the job. There really is no other way in consulting because each case and each firm is unique." Work experience is supplemented by seminar-like "modules of learning" that "focus on a given discipline, i.e., corporate finance, enterprise economics, etc." Modules "are taught by subject area experts that work at the firm. Many former Harvard Business School professors lead training seminars."

DAY IN THE LIFE

Monitor trainees spend their days performing "basic analysis, such as answering basic business questions. [Some examples are] 'What organizational structure do I feel would best allow our client to achieve their strategy?' We do the analysis (including research, interviews, group brainstorming, etc.), synthesize data, make recommendations, and support them." Explains one consultant, "A typical day would involve a couple of hours on the phone discussing problems with a client, a couple of hours with my case team discussing various ideas and hypothesizing solutions, several hours performing analysis on data (Excel), and some hours organizing findings and recommendations into a Microsoft PowerPoint® presentation." It's hardly grunt work, say the trainees; notes one trainee, "What I do matters a lot. Without me, my case teams would be unable to complete important analyses and deliver [impacting] and meaningful work to our clients." The work is "demanding, occasionally overwhelming, but never boring," and extremely educational; as one consultant puts it, "I have learned an incredible amount. For the most part Monitor bosses are a good combination of demanding and understanding." Agrees another consultant, "Some [of my bosses] are great coaches who are willing to take you under their wing and teach you and mentor you a great deal." As an added bonus, this program affords "a lot of interaction with higher-level people. The leaders on my team are very open to talking with me and make an honest effort to involve me and hear my opinions. Not only am I allowed to sit in on important meetings, [but also] I am encouraged to do so. Professional development is a priority here."

PEERS

Newbies at Monitor "are all good friends" who tell us that "the intensity of this job pulls people together. Everyone [shares] common experiences." One young consultant offers, "Some of my best friends are from the company. We hang out after work and on the weekends on a very frequent basis. I interact with friends from work anywhere from six to twenty hours a week (entire days of the weekend at times) outside of work." As work commitments increase, the social scene subsides a bit. "We went out a lot together at first, though that has waned as we've all become busier," comments another employee. Everyone seems impressed with their peers. "The people at Monitor are among the most intelligent and intellectual I've ever met," says one typical trainee.

Moving On

According to consulting firm officials, "most people tend to leave Monitor to seek other opportunities after having been with the firm for three or four years. However, a growing number are finding interesting opportunities within the firm [that allow them to] have longer-term careers in areas that are of particular interest to them." More than a few consultants eventually leave Monitor to pursue their MBAs. "That's essentially the standard path," reports one consultant.

Attrition

Graduate study, opportunities outside the field of consulting, and a mismatch between the company and the employee are the most common reasons employees leave Monitor's training program early. Few people leave to pursue other consulting opportunities, firm officials report.

Best and Worst

Firm officials tell us that "the type of person who is most successful is the person who asks lots of questions, is curious about the work they are doing and how it fits into the bigger picture, is eager for constructive feedback to improve [his or her] performance, and uses their organizational and analytical abilities to produce high-quality outputs." Less successful first jobbers "tend to be the ones who do not recognize the level of commitment that consulting requires. They tend to have less valuable experiences because of a misalignment in their expectations and usually are not open to the valuable feedback they receive about how to improve their performance."

MONSTER
Customer Service

THE BIG PICTURE

The world of employment agencies meets modern times at Monster, a website that lists available jobs across the country. The company hires college grads for its customer service division, meaning "phone experience in a call-center type of environment" and the ability to be comfortable in such a work environment "[are] important qualit[ies]." Entry-level employees like the fact that the company offers "strong opportunities for advancement."

STATS

LOCATION(S) WHERE ENTRY-LEVEL EMPLOYEES WORK

Maynard, MA and Indianapolis, IN

ENTRY-LEVEL POSITION(S) AVAILABLE

New hires work as customer service representatives.

AVERAGE HOURS WORKED PER WEEK

Employees work forty hours per week.

BENEFITS OFFERED

The company offers medical, dental, and vision insurance. Additional benefits include 401(k) and life insurance.

CONTACT INFORMATION

Go to www.monster.com and search for "monsterjobs."

GETTING HIRED

To apply for a job at Monster, simply post your resume on www.monster.com. It's very simple. When the company is looking for new hires, it scours posted resumes for likely candidates. "I placed my resume on Monster and a recruiter from the company called me that day," reports one first jobber. "She explained the position to me very thoroughly and it sounded like something I would be interested in. Plus, I knew that Monster was a great company!" Candidates go through several stages of interviews; explains one, "My first interview was with a member of the human resources department and was more informative than the second interview, which focused on my skills and explored whether I was a good match for Monster. The first visit entailed a tour of the facility that immediately caught my attention due to its creative layout and relaxed atmosphere. The walls are painted all sorts of funky colors and while people work very hard here, I could tell right away that Monster is a fun place to work. I also got a free lunch! The second interview was with the two bosses of the department and focused more on my work experience and whether I would be a good match for Monster and the Client Relations department. A few days after my second interview I received a phone call with an offer." Sometimes the company has interviewees "shadow" current employees; writes one new hire, "For my second interview, I job shadowed an employee of the department and then spoke with another manager. I really liked the fact that I was able to listen to a few calls during the interview process."

MONEY AND PERKS

Entry-level employees agree that the biggest perk of working for Monster is the "fun working environment." Workers enjoy, among other things, "free drinks, a den where you can relax for an hour on your break, [and] a gym on the floor where I work." Note company representatives, "Monster still has that dot-com feel, which is enticing to many people. Candidates walk into Monster and are greeted by a huge monster in the lobby and purple carpets. There is also a den that houses a ping-pong table and pool table. In the Monster kitchen, there is free soda and coffee throughout the day. The Monster motto is you work hard but you also play hard!"

THE ROPES

Monster uses a buddy system to help new hires adapt to the Monster way of doing things: "When an offer is extended to a candidate, they are immediately assigned a buddy by their future supervisor. A buddy is responsible for showing a new hire around their first week and getting them acclimated to the company." One first jobber recalls, "On my first day I was greeted by a buddy who was assigned to show me around and help me with any questions that I might have. I got a tour of Monster and was introduced to everyone in my department. I still went to my buddy with questions for weeks after that." Newbies also undergo "a new hire training class that lasts one week and is held once a month." There is a "great deal" of subsequent training; "I sat with almost everyone in customer service and listened to them either take or make calls. These sessions were very beneficial and all the staff members did a fine job teaching me all about Monster's products and services," says one employee regarding the training process.

DAY IN THE LIFE

For most new hires, a typical day at Monster consists of "answering inbound calls from Monster customers and making outbound calls to Monster customers." Other possible assignments include "posting jobs for employers, doing contract set-ups for sales reps/employers, and answering emails from customers and sales reps." What most first jobbers find appealing about the job is not necessarily these assignments, but rather the "enjoyable working environment" and the "opportunities to advance." They also love the close contact they enjoy with company higher-ups. Writes one employee, "We definitely have contact with high-level people, and we sit on important meetings at least once a month. They always encourage this." Those meetings "update all employees on Monster's upcoming programs, goals, etc. These meetings are very good if one wishes to learn about the company's vision for the future. I have interacted with higher level employees at Monster quite frequently. Everyone gets along very well."

PEERS

Monster's buddy system helps foster strong bonds between entry-level and more senior employees. Among the first jobbers themselves, "There is a decent amount of camaraderie because you are training with them and going to orientation, etc." Notes one, "There is a lot of contact with other first jobbers here—a lot of things to relate to, but at the same time we do not alienate other employees." New hires appreciate that "everyone seems pretty cool, nice, and laid back," and tell us that "there is an after-hours social scene, although not everyone takes part."

MOVING ON

Monster is a relatively new company; it hasn't been around long enough for lots of employees to "move on." The company tells us, "We have a fairly low percentage of first jobbers who stay less than twelve months. A lot of our employees have been here for a number of years." For the few people who do leave, at least they know where to go to look for their next jobs.

NATIONAL CANCER INSTITUTE
Various Positions

THE BIG PICTURE

Come to National Cancer Institute (NCI) and help search for the cancer cure.

STATS

LOCATION(S) WHERE ENTRY-LEVEL EMPLOYEES WORK

Bethesda, MD and Frederick, MD

AVERAGE NUMBER OF APPLICATIONS EACH YEAR

"NCI has approximately 100 permanent, full-time vacancies per year. The number of applicants for each opening can range from a handful to as many as 300, depending on the position. As many as 1,000 students apply for summer internships annually; as many as 400 students apply for one-year internships annually."

AVERAGE NUMBER HIRED OVER THE LAST TEN YEARS

"[We hire] approximately 600 positions total per year across all levels of the organization, including permanent, full-time federal employees; internships (summer and one-year); and post-doctoral fellows. Currently, this number is lower as parts of the federal government are under a hiring freeze. As a result, employment opportunities are being created at other companies (contractors) that would afford an individual an opportunity to complete work [that is] related to our mission and within our offices."

ENTRY-LEVEL POSITION(S) AVAILABLE

"A limited number of permanent, full-time federal positions are available as we are under a [hiring] freeze at [the time of this writing]. We continue to hire entry-level summer interns (about 250 per year) and entry-level one-year interns (about 100 per year). The following are the [branches and respective areas where] entry-level candidates [can typically find positions]:

Sciences: Biology (biomedical, biophysics, biostatistics, cancer biology, cellular, computational, developmental, etc), chemistry (analytical, inorganic, medicinal, organic), cytology, epidemiology, genetics (drosophila, functional genomics, molecular), hematology, immunology, mathematics/statistics, oncology, pathology, pharmacology

Administration/management: Administrative officer, budget, contracts, grants administration, management/program analysis, project management, public health/affairs, writing/editing.

AVERAGE HOURS WORKED PER WEEK

"Most [entry-level employees] work a forty-hour week. Some extra time may be expected in the lab environment."

PERCENTAGE OF ENTRY-LEVEL HIRES STILL WITH THE COMPANY AFTER THREE, FIVE, AND TEN YEARS:

After three, five, and ten years, the amount of entry-level hires who remain with the company are 85 percent, 75 percent, and 44 percent, respectively.

AVERAGE STARTING SALARY

New hires who work in permanent, full-time administration/management positions earn from $26,000 to $40,000 (depending on education and experience). Science interns earn from $21,000 to $35,000 (also depending on education and experience).

BENEFITS OFFERED

"[The company] offer[s] both health and life insurance benefits and long-term care insurance to permanent full-time employees." Additional benefits for "permanent, full-time positions [include] vacation leave, sick leave, ten paid federal holidays, a wide range of retirement benefits, flexible spending accounts, Transhare (free on-site parking or mass transit subsidies), on-site child care programs, referral services (child care, elder care, legal, financial, housing). [Additional benefits for] science internships [include] ten paid federal holidays, Transhare, on-site child care, [and] referral services."

CONTACT INFORMATION

Katie Fontaine

fontainem@mail.nih.gov

To apply for a summer internship, you complete an online application at: http://generalemployment.nci.nih.gov/.

To submit a resume for hiring managers to review, go to the same website.

To review vacancy announcements for federal positions, go to http://reports.cit.nih.gov/jobsnih/advacsearch.asp and select "National Cancer Institute" in the second drop down window.

GETTING HIRED

"Each scientific division and program area determines its employment needs individually" at NCI. NCI recruits at select schools but does not interview on campus. It accepts online applications "for summer science internships and maintains a resume database for permanent full-time positions, one-year internships, and post-doctoral fellowships." Many first jobbers learn about open positions from professors and research partners. For science positions, "a typical application process involves many steps. Candidates first have to fill out an application online and then submit it. If the candidate qualifies for the position, they will have to go to at least one of three possible interviews, which would include supervisors, administrative officers, and lab managers. After this step is accomplished, the selected candidate will then get an offer letter, which includes a date for an orientation they have to attend, and they will have to fill out a large folder of papers and attend a half-day seminar. So to make a long story short, the application process can take up to three months to complete, if not longer." Examples of typical interview questions include: "Tell us about a project or activity where you played a leadership role, and describe your contribution. Describe a challenging experience and how you handled it. Describe a situation or attitude that you would find difficult to work with. What is your approach when presented with [a] new procedure or a problem?"

MONEY AND PERKS

NCI reports that "each employee may be eligible for a raise each year. Permanent federal employees typically get a 3.6 percent raise from Congress and are eligible for a step increase each year. Additionally, permanent employees become eligible for promotions based on performance and employer needs that can result in a substantial raise of $3,000 to $7,000 during one year." Adds one current entry-level employee, "If you have a previous job before coming [here], your salary might be negotiable, but in most cases you are given a set series and grade, and you have to excel from there." One employee says, "[Top perks include] a flex schedule that allows you to have a compressed work schedule. And don't let me forget the health benefits and holidays. [Those are] the best!" Newbies also love the fact that "being housed in one of the greatest research institutions in the world means [they have] access [to] fantastic conferences and lectures!"

THE ROPES

NCI hires for numerous positions in a wide variety of areas, so specific training regimens vary widely. For all employees, the institution has "a half-day orientation that introduces employees to the agency and the resources available to employees." Officials also point out that "in scientific divisions, mentoring is a longstanding tradition for all employees. Throughout NCI, new hires work under senior managers and should have multiple resources and at least one staff member who is knowledgeable and available to answer questions and address concerns." Most divisions and program areas "have their own orientation process as well." Because most post-doc fellows "are from foreign countries, visa and immigration training is given."

DAY IN THE LIFE

NCI representatives state, "Our array of positions makes [describing a typical day] impossible; however, each position and its responsibilities should be comprehensively explained and on-going guidance provided [by the new hire's supervisor]."

PEERS

One newbie says, "We have a great sense of camaraderie! At NCI, I have gotten along well with other fellows. I spend one-on-one time with other interns about once a week. There's a happy hour once every couple of weeks, but we mostly communicate with each other on-the-job during lunch or on a work break." In most divisions, there isn't much of an after-hours scene, since "many of the employees here have families and live" far apart. Our survey respondents all agree that one major asset of working at NCI is "being around people who are driven by the mission to help others; [they are] truly honored to be associated with [the agency] professionally and [personally]."

MOVING ON

Many first jobbers leave NCI to return to school; writes one typical newcomer, "I plan to go back to school for a master's degree in nutrition (probably with a focus on health communications)." Other people find related work in the medical field, while employees in administration move onto other, better opportunities within the federal government. NCI does not track data on exiting first jobbers.

BEST AND WORST

The most successful first jobbers at NCI are "individuals who have a desire to work in public service and who have a passion about the mission of the National Cancer Institute, to eliminate suffering and death caused by cancer. NCI culture rewards collaboration, teamwork, commitment, and an ability to provide leadership within the system. Because NCI is part of a much larger system (one of twenty-seven institutes at the National Institutes of Health, which is one of many operating divisions within the Department of Health and Human Services), ideas, programs, and decisions do not occur overnight. [NCI] is not the best employer for individuals looking to make lots of money quick or [to] be the one individual in the spotlight. While each person is expected to fully contribute and [be] recognized for excellence, there are few individual spotlight moments on the road to curing cancer."

NPR
Departmental Assistant

THE BIG PICTURE

Welcome to the world of talk radio, music, oddly informative quiz shows, and auto mechanics who think they're funnier than they really are. Take the job that will drive your conservative parents nuts; in the process, you'll join what is arguably the nation's best broadcast news organization.

STATS

LOCATION(S) WHERE ENTRY-LEVEL EMPLOYEES WORK

Most positions are in Washington, DC. A few are available at NPR's West Coast facility in Culver City, CA.

AVERAGE NUMBER OF APPLICATIONS EACH YEAR

NPR receives 1,500 applications every year.

AVERAGE NUMBER HIRED OVER THE LAST TEN YEARS

NPR hires 150 people per year.

ENTRY-LEVEL POSITION(S) AVAILABLE

Entry-level hires work as production assistants, editorial assistants, research assistants, development assistants, and administrative assistants.

AVERAGE HOURS WORKED PER WEEK

Weekly hours vary by position, but employees work at least forty hours per week.

AVERAGE STARTING SALARY

Production and editorial assistants earn $43,000; research assistants earn $37,000; administrative assistants earn $32,000.

BENEFITS OFFERED

In terms of health care coverage, NPR has a cafeteria-style benefits program where employees customize their benefits selection. NPR offers three medical plans, two dental plans, and a vision care plan. Additional benefits include supplemental life insurance and other optional items. In addition, all employees receive life insurance and long-term disability. New employees receive three weeks of annual leave per year. (After three years, employees receive four weeks of annual leave.) Employees also receive two days of personal leave, three days of bereavement leave, and ten days of sick leave each year. NPR also has ten paid holidays per year. NPR has a 403(b) retirement savings plan.

National Public Radio

Human Resources Department

635 Massachusetts Ave., NW

Washington, DC 20001

Fax: 202-513-3047

Email: employment@npr.org

GETTING HIRED

The best way to get a job at NPR, it seems, is for interested candidates to obtain internships during their college careers so they can make the contacts necessary to get full-time positions when they open. Many of the employees we spoke with got their jobs this way. NPR posts open positions on its website, and anyone may apply for one; the organization seeks individuals "with journalism and/or media backgrounds and experience. Experience working in and/or knowledge of public radio and the public radio system are preferred." One successful hire says, "The application process was long. I interviewed with a manager and then a vice president. The interviews were professional and conversational. The interviewers mainly focused on why I wanted to work for NPR. It was important that I had a passion for the mission of the organization."

MONEY AND PERKS

Starting salaries at NPR are fixed by job. "Over the first few years salaries increase based on cost of living adjustments and merit," NPR officials tell us. The best perks, according to first jobbers, include free CDs and books, meeting on-air hosts, frequent travel, and doing a job that they love. Explains one, "I am challenged and respected by my coworkers, who I get along extremely well with. The people here are great [and] they generally want to be here doing what they are doing. NPR can be [a] very meaningful place to work. On a more superficial, image-only level, when I tell people I work at NPR they always say, 'Oh, I love NPR!'"

THE ROPES

Orientation at NPR is a brief affair—it's a little more than "several sessions regarding general employment practices at NPR (i.e., completing new hire forms, benefits, and IT orientations, etc.). Additional orientations (some optional) can be scheduled to further acquaint the new employee with employment at NPR." After that, most employees receive on-the-job training. Explained a producer for *Day to Day,* "I was pretty much thrown in the fire; we were in the piloting process of a brand new show and there wasn't very much time to sit down and learn everything before I started. I sort of learned as I went along. I did receive some training on digital editing software; the other producers helped me with that."

DAY IN THE LIFE

Depending on the area in which you wind up, a typical day at NPR could include "pitching stories, editing sound, writing host leads and questions for interviews; assisting in the overall management of cultivation events and fundraising (a typical day includes menu planning, creating travel and event agendas, writing donor letters, designing invitations, and participating in conference calls with event hosts); compiling submissions to award competition and just helping out on a variety of projects." There are a lot of different jobs to be done; read thorough descriptions at the job posting section of NPR's website.

PEERS

The entry-level employees we spoke with at NPR work in areas that lack other first jobbers or have very few of them. They described a comfortable, amiable work environment. Writes one, "I am lucky that although I am the only person in my department in my first year of working, I fit in well here for many other reasons." They also express admiration for their coworkers, telling us that they were "amazing; they are intelligent, interesting, genuine, and likeable."

MOVING ON

Low pay is the chief complaint of people who eventually leave NPR. Those who go usually do so to pursue other, more profitable positions in broadcast journalism.

NY CARES
Various Positions

THE BIG PICTURE

NY Cares coordinates volunteers for a variety of philanthropic activities. The organization helps "tutor children, feed the hungry, assist people living with HIV/AIDS, revitalize gardens, take homeless children on cultural and recreational outings, visit the elderly, and engage in many other hands-on activities." First jobbers tell us why they find the organization so attractive; "NY Cares' reputation and professionalism precedes it; [we] also believe in their work"

STATS

LOCATION(S) WHERE ENTRY-LEVEL EMPLOYEES WORK

New York, NY

AVERAGE NUMBER OF APPLICATIONS EACH YEAR

NY Cares receives from 300 to 400 applications each year, sometimes more.

AVERAGE NUMBER HIRED OVER THE LAST TEN YEARS

The organization hires four to five people per year.

ENTRY-LEVEL POSITION(S) AVAILABLE

New hires work as annual events managers, program managers, corporate relations managers.

AVERAGE HOURS WORKED PER WEEK

Employees work forty hours per week, including some nights and weekends.

PERCENTAGE OF ENTRY-LEVEL HIRES STILL WITH THE COMPANY AFTER THREE, FIVE, AND TEN YEARS

After three and five years, 30 percent and 10 percent of all entry-level hires remain with the organization, respectively.

AVERAGE STARTING SALARY

New hires earn approximately $31,000 per year.

BENEFITS OFFERED

As far as medical benefits go, individuals are fully covered by a point of service plan. Additional benefits include flexible spending accounts for qualified transportation expenses, a tax deferred annuity (403(b) plan), vacation and sick days, and ten paid holidays per year.

Human Resources Department

NY Cares, Inc.

214 West 29th Street, 5th Floor

New York, NY 10001

Positions are also listed on www.nycares.org.

GETTING HIRED

With so few positions to offer each year, NY Cares has no need to recruit on campus. Instead, the organization simply "posts job openings on certain websites specializing in nonprofit positions (i.e., www.Idealist.org) where [they] invite interested applicants to send their resumes." Any kind of "in" is valuable. Some people find full-time employment by applying for full-time positions after interning, while others are tipped off by friends who work for the organization. Here's how one worker describes the vetting process: "It was an extended affair (because there were no openings at the time I applied). First, I had an informational interview and spoke with a few former employees who helped me network to find some temporary work. The NY Cares staff and alums were very well-connected and had good suggestions for organizations that fit my interests and skills. About a month after my initial conversation, there were job openings in the Program Department at NY Cares, and I was interviewed for two positions simultaneously. The director of human resources and program director interviewed me first, and then I had a second conversation with staff members currently holding the project manager positions. I had follow-up conversations over the phone with the directors to discuss whether I had a strong preference for one position over the other."

MONEY AND PERKS

At NY Cares, "Management determines the maximum annual increase in salaries for all employees. The individual's supervisor determines the actual increase based on [his or her] performance." First jobbers tell us that starting salaries are "somewhat negotiable," although those coming in with little more than a bachelor's degree should expect to be paid an amount near the bottom of the pay scale. The best perks about working at NY Cares, newbies tell us, are "the social atmosphere and the friendships."

THE ROPES

Most of the training at NY Cares happens on the job. Preliminary orientation lasts a day or two and consists primarily of "meeting with various staff members, including the finance and operations officer, office coordinator, and other members of their department to understand office procedures and job specifics." After that, it's time to work. Fortunately, there's lots of mentoring for new hires. Recalls a newbie, "I was constantly in touch with my boss. She really helped me to get oriented and come along."

Adds another newbie, "NY Cares really had a commitment to sending me to workshops and trainings. This helped a lot. In looking back, I am grateful that I came to a place that really had such a nurturing environment."

DAY IN THE LIFE

Starting positions at NY Cares fall into three categories. The organization describes each position this way: "Program managers work directly with agencies to design meaningful volunteer projects. Our annual events staff runs four different events: a coat drive, a holiday gift exchange for needy children, and two citywide volunteering events in the public schools and parks. The staff is responsible for a multitude of tasks relating to the particular events' execution. Our corporate relations managers are responsible for maintaining the relationships with our corporate donors, mainly through enlisting their support for our annual events and other service projects." First jobbers find themselves handling a tremendous amount of responsibility early on in their tenures, and most find it gratifying. As one former employee explains, "One of the great things about NY Cares is that it is a relatively small organization; roughly thirty-six people were on staff when I was there. Everyone was close, and the executive director always had me [sit] in on important meetings. I was also expected to give my viewpoint."

PEERS

The environment at NY Cares, workers tell us, "is incredibly friendly." As one employee describes it, "the social scene is such an integral part of the culture here; we work hard all day and then socialize in the evening. Many of us go to local bars regularly to play pool and drink beer after work; many people date colleagues. We eat lunch (the younger staff) together all the time." Another approvingly adds, "The culture of NY Cares is one where there's an accepting spirit. It is full of smart, energetic, idealistic, and committed people—how could you not make friends in that environment?"

MOVING ON

Most people who leave this small organization do so because "it does not have a great amount of opportunity for advancement. While you can take on additional projects and responsibilities, there aren't many opportunities for promotions." Mostly they find jobs with other nonprofit organizations, although some proceed to graduate school. The average tenure of a first jobber is two years, organization representatives report.

ATTRITION

NY Cares does not offer a fixed-term first job program, so there is no attrition per se. Employees most often leave, as noted above, because the chances for career advancement are minimal. Some people say they leave because the pay is too low, especially given the cost of living in New York City.

NYC TEACHING FELLOWS
Fellow

THE BIG PICTURE

If you like the idea of "leaving corporate America" for the opportunity to make a difference and help shape the lives of young people, the NYC Teaching Fellows program may be just the thing for you. A two-year commitment to the program puts you in front of one classroom and makes you a student in another, so you can earn your master's degree in education.

STATS

LOCATION(S) WHERE ENTRY-LEVEL EMPLOYEES WORK

New York, NY

AVERAGE NUMBER OF APPLICATIONS EACH YEAR

The NYC Teaching Fellows receives 20,000 applications each year.

AVERAGE NUMBER HIRED OVER THE LAST TEN YEARS

The organization hires 2,700 people each year.

ENTRY-LEVEL POSITION(S) AVAILABLE

New hires work as teaching fellows.

AVERAGE HOURS WORKED PER WEEK

Fellows work forty hours per week.

AVERAGE STARTING SALARY

Fellows who have bachelor's degrees earn $39,000; for fellows with additional course work the salary can be higher. For more information, visit www.teachny.com/salary_calc.asp.

BENEFITS OFFERED

Fellows have a choice of health insurance plans, including medical, dental, prescription, optical, and hearing. Additional benefits include a subsidized master's degree, disability insurance, mortgage programs, special discounts, a pension plan, TransitChecks, and flexible spending accounts.

CONTACT INFORMATION

Apply at www.nycteachingfellows.org/how/index.html.

GETTING HIRED

Teaching fellows tell us that "the fellows have a reputation for being very selective. The process of applying is more rigorous than graduate school applications." Applications are accepted online; they require "basic" essays that "require thoughtful answers outside of the typical 'I want to be a teacher because I love children.'" Those who make the first cut are called for an all-day interview session. Reports one fellow, "The interview started in a group format. I had to prepare a five minute lesson (which, by the way, is not much time at all!). All of us were nervous, and the best thing I can recommend to anyone going through the process is to make friends with the other interviewees before the process begins. This puts everyone at ease, and, more likely than not, these are not the people you will be competing with, since there are many subjects areas for which qualified teachers are sought." The next part of the process is a one-on-one interview, which "consists of pre-written questions. The questions are read, and then the responses are written down word for word. The questions are mostly what-if situations; 'If you were teaching and blank happened, what would you do?' The woman who interviewed me was helpful, kind, and patient. She made me feel comfortable. She explained that later that evening she would meet with another group to review the results of the interviews and then make her recommendations. After spending the entire day (six hours) interviewing, I was told that I would have an answer within the month. I was accepted into the program 5 weeks later."

MONEY AND PERKS

Teaching fellows belong to the teachers' union, so their salaries are determined by the union contract. Because of the program's prescribed training program, starting dates are also nonnegotiable. Regarding placement, "The NYC Teaching Fellows program places teachers in high-need areas. We were given an opportunity to state our preferred borough and region, but the point of the program is to assist schools and children [with] the greatest need; the needs of the program come first. The desired subject/grade level was also needs-based, but we were given a chance to state our preference." Union membership ensures a solid benefits package. Teaching fellows are also eligible for a subsidized master's degree in education; in 2003, teachers were required to cover $2,000 in master's-related expenses, with the city picking up the rest of the tab. Other fringe benefits of the job include "great vacations." Writes one teacher, "I hate it when people say the best part about being a teacher is the summers off! This is the most demanding and difficult job I have ever held. If we didn't have vacations, I would burn out within a year. Besides, the next two summers of my life will be spent in graduate school classes!"

THE ROPES

Pre-service training, a six-week program that begins in the middle of June, is required of all fellows. Referred to by many as "summer boot camp," it is "consuming, exhausting, and demanding" but ultimately "a very positive experience." Here's how one fellow describes it: "It takes place in the college where you will be doing your graduate work (you need to get a master's degree to become a teacher). You get both academic classes and the 'straight dope' from actual New York City teachers called 'fellow advisors' who give you the low down on what to expect in the classroom. My fellow advisor was cool, and I was very impressed with that aspect of the program. Halfway through the summer, we were placed in a school in our district to assist another teacher teaching summer school. We assistant-taught in the mornings, then went to grad school in the afternoons." Although teachers are usually required to hold a degree in their area of specialization, New York makes an exception for math teachers (because they are in such short supply). A rigorous math immersion program, in addition to the above-mentioned training, is required of prospective math teachers who do not qualify to teach under the standard guidelines.

Day in the Life

Teaching is a demanding job, and the fellows we spoke with describe filled-to-bursting work days. According to one fellow, "My days typically started at 5:30 AM at home doing planning and correcting papers and homework. At school by 7:30 AM. Teach until 3:00 PM or 4:00 PM, depending on the day. Three days a week at college until 7:00 PM. Home by 8:30 PM. Planning, paperwork, studying, etc. until 10:00 PM." Lather, rinse, repeat—no wonder teachers are so effusive about their summer vacations! There's also once-a-month after-school faculty meetings, professional development sessions, and occasional teacher-parent meetings. It's a grind for sure, albeit a fulfilling one for the right individual. The job doesn't evolve over time, but the teachers do; explains one, "My job has not changed, but I have. I started the school year clueless as to how to reach and teach the children. I believe I have grown as an individual and a teacher through this experience, and not," she adds pointedly, "through my college courses."

Peers

Between teaching, grading assignments, and studying for a master's degree, most fellows have precious little time to hang with peers. "There was more camaraderie with my NYC Teaching Fellows classmates this summer," explains one teacher. "I find it difficult to maintain an active social life while teaching and attending college simultaneously. I keep close phone contact with several classmates, and we have a mass email system set up for our group, which we use regularly." Most understandably admire their peers, since they know exactly how heavy a load they are shouldering. Writes one, "I like most of my fellow fellows and genuinely admire many. They are mostly committed and intelligent people. It is unfortunate that the program is so designed that making friends is not really possible."

Moving on

The program is designed to generate career teachers; the master's degree in education is a huge incentive to remain in the school system, since it translates roughly into a 10 percent pay hike. Thus, many of those who complete the program continue to teach in the city school system. Other people move elsewhere in the state and continue teaching. More than a few teachers, however, get burned out by the demands of the job and seek employment outside the education world.

ATTRITION

Teachers who leave the program early receive no tuition compensation for their master's work, so the incentives to tough it out, regardless of how difficult it may be, are great. Even people who complain most bitterly about incompetent administrators, unreasonable demands and standards, the challenges of teaching in the city school system, and the superfluity of some graduate courses in education tell us they planned to remain in the program to the end.

NEWELL RUBBERMAID
Phoenix Representative Program

THE BIG PICTURE

Participants in Phoenix Representatives Program serve as liaisons between Newell Rubbermaid—which produces kitchen storage containers, high-end cookware, and home-improvement tools—and the stores that sell its products. It's a great job for a well-organized schmoozer who loves to travel.

STATS

LOCATION(S) WHERE ENTRY-LEVEL EMPLOYEES WORK

"Nationwide. We have reps in cities across the United States."

AVERAGE NUMBER OF APPLICATIONS EACH YEAR

The company receives over 10,000 applications per year.

AVERAGE NUMBER HIRED OVER THE LAST TEN YEARS

Newell Rubbermaid hires about 450 people per year.

ENTRY-LEVEL POSITION(S) AVAILABLE

Entry-level hires in Phoenix work as field sales and marketing representatives for the following Newell Rubbermaid divisions: Sharpie, Calphalon, and many other household names.

AVERAGE HOURS WORKED PER WEEK

The amount of hours entry-level employees work varies per week. During store openings, employees will work longer hours. Representatives work the hours necessary to accomplish their goals.

PERCENTAGE OF ENTRY-LEVEL HIRES STILL WITH THE COMPANY AFTER THREE, FIVE, AND TEN YEARS

Approximately 80 percent of all entry-level hires remain with the company after two years, which is as far back as the Phoenix Representative Program goes.

AVERAGE STARTING SALARY

All entry-level hires earn $37,000, regardless of the position.

BENEFITS OFFERED

In terms of health care coverage, the company offers medical, prescription, vision, and dental insurance. Other benefits include life insurance, a company-matched 401(k) plan, employee counseling, and a company-branded vehicle.

CONTACT INFORMATION

Students can apply online through www.newellrubbermaid.com/campusrecruiting.

GETTING HIRED

Successful hires in the Phoenix Representative Program have many gatekeepers to impress; the application process includes three separate interview sessions, the third of which is a three-parter. Explains one who made it all the way through, "The first [interview] was held on campus (at Eastern Illinois University) and was essentially a screening interview. I was asked about my involvement in college, career goals, and overall interests. An alumna conducted this interview. My second interview was also on campus and was with a different alumna of Eastern Illinois University. During this interview I was asked how I would react in different situations; it was a much more in-depth interview and covered a significant amount of information. The third [interview consists] of three rounds of interviews with different employees of different divisions. Here they asked about my relocation preferences, what I knew about the company, and why I thought I would be a [good] match. I received my offer letter about five days later in the mail." Undergraduates may also apply online; typically, those culled from this batch have their first two interviews with Newell Rubbermaid field representatives. According to company officials, "The biggest quality Newell Rubbermaid looks for is demonstrated leadership. We need leaders at all levels in our organization, and we want to recruit only those applicants who have shown that they are leaders. We also look for applicants who are team players, driven, and goal-oriented."

MONEY AND PERKS

All Phoenix Representative Program hires start at the same salary; explains one, "The job offer was negotiable in terms of when I started but not where I was going to be positioned or salary." The company "conducts reviews and [awards] merit raises once a year. Promotions result in a 10 percent salary increase with bonus potential or a 15 percent raise and no bonus potential." Regarding the job's perks, employees say, "The best is our company vehicle," which is branded (decorated with the logo of whichever product the representative promotes). "It saves you so much money [when you don't have] a car payment and insurance payment every month," explains one field representative. Additionally, "the freedom in this job is incredible. Every Phoenix employee in the field is in charge of maintaining his or her own territory, and this work is not done the same by any two employees."

THE ROPES

Phoenix training differs depending on the division in which the hire is placed. Some trainees start their tenures at one- or two-week orientation trainings. Other trainees work in the field for a while with a mentor before attending formal training sessions. According to company officials, "Our new hire orientation classes cover a variety of topics. The sessions start with corporate information, including a strategy talk from the chief executive officer, an event marketing overview, professional presence, human resources benefits and policies, career paths, who's who at Newell Rubbermaid, and world-class marketing to name a few. We then go into sales process training, which covers the steps in our sales process and role-playing for practice. The sessions conclude with division-specific breakouts to cover product knowledge and hands-on demonstrations." Trainees in all divisions agree that the formal orientation "consists mainly of product knowledge." Reports one Calphalon representative, "We cooked with our products to see the differences between them and also to learn how to do [the] demos that we perform at store level."

A Day in the Life

Once established in their jobs, Phoenix hires "work in the field on a daily basis [and are] responsible for all of Newell Rubbermaid's product lines in their stores." They "merchandise our products, sell orders, obtain extra shelf and endcap space [end-of-the-aisle display], plan and execute special store events such as grand openings or sales events." An average day, writes one Sanford pen representative, "would be to greet the managers and employees, give them a sample pen and train them about the benefits of the pen, then complete a store walk-through and write down any Sanford product placement or competitors' placement. I would also look for possible product placement and cross-merchandising opportunities. Then, I would make sure that any promotional displays from corporate were placed on the floor, labeled, and filled. Finally, I would go to the pen aisle and make sure that our products were correctly placed in the Plan-O-Gram [display], down stock the pens to make-sure that the pen isle is full, and label any spots that do not have a label. Then I would go to my home office and enter my daily activities and any expenses that need to be reported to corporate." As far as access to higher-ups goes, "there are no barriers at Newell Rubbermaid. Each employee has direct contact with every other employee in the company, regardless of rank. I have the cell phone number of the president of my division and have used it several times. All calls were received with enthusiasm and were valued for what they had to offer."

Peers

Unlike many other entry-level positions profiled in this book, Phoenix representatives have little face-to-face contact with each other after initial training. That's because most of their work is done in the field on their own. Notes one, "I have formed very close relationships with many of my peers at work, but we do not always get to spend a ton of face time working together because many of us live in different states. We do communicate by phone, Audix, and email very frequently." Agrees another, "Aside from direct contact, we all leave 'successes' on voicemail. The success stories help others to hear what other people are doing in the field to generate sales." When they do get together, Phoenix representatives enjoy each other's company; as one tells us, "I invite coworkers to my home, [and] my other friends always comment that I am lucky to have a network of young coworkers [who] are so outgoing and fun. They are jealous that we have so many great people in the company."

Moving on

Because the Phoenix Representative Program is relatively new, Newell Rubbermaid officials report that data on trainees who choose to move on is insufficient. So far, most new hires have stayed happily within the fold. "Based on anecdotal evidence, we most often lose people to pharmaceutical sales positions."

Attrition

According to a company representative, "By far, the most common reason people resign from the Phoenix Program is because of location. We ask these individuals to be very flexible in their first few years of employment [because] when they get promoted they will most likely be asked to move. In many cases, they aren't able to leave the city they are in for personal reasons and instead resign from Newell Rubbermaid. After that, the reasons given are too [few] to track."

Best and Worst

Great Phoenix representatives "are defined as such by their sales numbers, improved year[ly] store numbers, innovative merchandising ideas, and leadership." Bad representatives are "coached out of the organization."

NORTHROP GRUMMAN
Integrated Systems
and other Entry-level Positions

THE BIG PICTURE

Air defense systems, such as the unmanned Global Hawk, and airframe subsystems for surveillance, battle management, and warfare are the order of the day at Northrop Grumman's Integrated Systems sector. Tech-savvy job seekers could well find a happy home at Northrop Grumman, which offers a generous benefits package and job security.

STATS

LOCATION(S) WHERE ENTRY-LEVEL EMPLOYEES WORK

All over the country

AVERAGE NUMBER OF APPLICATIONS EACH YEAR

Northrop Grumman receives thousands of applications every year.

AVERAGE NUMBER HIRED OVER THE LAST TEN YEARS

"Prior to 2001, Northrop Grumman's Integrated Systems did very little college hiring. Over the last two years we have been hiring about 250 full-time college students and seventy-five interns."

AVERAGE HOURS WORKED PER WEEK

New hires work forty to fifty hours per week.

PERCENTAGE OF ENTRY-LEVEL HIRES STILL WITH THE COMPANY AFTER THREE, FIVE, AND TEN YEARS

"Over the last three years we have averaged a 4 percent attrition rate with our entry-level hires."

AVERAGE STARTING SALARY

"Salaries [are] based on co-op/intern experience, GPA, major, research work, and leadership and club participation."

BENEFITS OFFERED

All benefits begin on the first day of work. Benefits include health insurance coverage, 401(k), pension, results sharing, education reimbursement, pet insurance, gyms, clubs, organizations, and volunteer opportunities.

CONTACT INFORMATION

Visit the website at www.definingthefuture.com.

GETTING HIRED

Northrop Grumman recruiters visit select colleges that it determines to "have the necessary programs, research, etc., that will help meet our needs." Students from other schools "can apply by going online at www.definingthefuture.com and applying for a position through our college website." The company attends "career fairs, on-campus student events, information sessions, and other [places that have] opportunities for involvement with students and faculty. All of the resumes that come from these events are sourced against openings. When [Northrop Grumman] find[s] a match, [they] bring that student in-house for an interview." According to company officials, interviewers "use a combination of behavioral and technical interviewing questions. We are trying to see if candidates would be a [good] fit for the group, [if they have] interest in the position, [and] if their background and qualifications meet the job requirements." Successful hires tell us the interview process is "friendly and comfortable." Explains one, "I was a little overwhelmed with all the information that I was given about the company. The interviewer informed me of the direction the defense industry was taking and how this was going to be a great opportunity for me. I was very excited about possibly getting a job at [Northrop Grumman Corporation] but nervous at the same time because I didn't have any background in the defense industry. A week after the interview, I received a job offer."

MONEY AND PERKS

The first jobbers we spoke with tell us that their start date was negotiable. Some new hires tell us that salary is negotiable, while others say that the job offer carries with it a specific, nonnegotiable salary. Salaries increase as a result of "a performance review every year, as well as an equity adjustment review for the first three years." An employee describes the one top perk of the job: "frequently being able to see the flights of the plane I'm working on. It makes all of the hard work seem much more substantial and meaningful when you actually see the results." One newbie cites "going to a very important conference free and getting to be involved in organizations that mean a lot to me and have my company support it" as other extras that nicely round out professional life at Northrop Grumman.

THE ROPES

Employees say that orientation at Northrop Grumman focuses on "the nature of work for this company, which is very delicate; there was a lot of emphasis on security issues, which is natural" given the fact that much of Northrop's business comes from the United States and foreign militaries. Beyond that, orientation "is about the company in general, the business areas, how the company works, ethics, pay, benefits, savings plans, vacation time, commuter services, gym facilities, etc." The program lasts a full day; a second day of orientation "is conducted by the actual projects and can run from one hour to all day." Subsequent training occurs primarily on the job, "provided by other engineers, managers, etc." There is some training offered "through human resources for presentations and business writing. There is also ethics training available online."

DAY IN THE LIFE

Northrop Grumman hires entry-level employees for many different positions; most positions, judging from our respondents' surveys, are "challenging, detailed oriented, and sometimes a little stressful." Because there is so much to do, a first jobber can gain a broad range of work experience relatively quickly. Writes one engineer who works in unmanned systems, "My job has actually not stayed the same for more than a few months at a time. It has been constantly changing. This I attribute to the people I have worked for, who have made certain that I had very diverse experiences. I have gone from testing production parts, to design qualification, to working in the factory, to laying the groundwork for new designs, to managing spending time at the factory, to running my own little test and integration projects. The common thread between all of these various experiences is that I have gotten to work with really wonderful teams and that my manager always sought out new challenges for me."

PEERS

First jobbers tell us, "There is quite a bit of camaraderie among new hires at work. We have all formed good friendships and enjoy spending time together outside of work." Some tell us that "there is a good after-hours social scene as well as a lot of weekend activity," while others think that "there's really no after-hours scene." In a company as large as Northrop Grumman, the amount of peer networking first jobbers enjoy depends largely on their assignment. Regardless of the degree of contact outside the office, most agree that their peers are "smart and ambitious." It is a diverse workforce, a fact that appeals to many. Writes one newbie, "It is always nice to meet new people who have had experiences different [from] your own [because it allows you] to gain a new perspective on the world."

MOVING ON

When first jobbers leave "some [go] to work in other sectors of Northrop Grumman Corporation, some go back to graduate school, [and others] leave the defense industry as a whole."

ATTRITION

More than 95 percent of new hires last more than a year with Northrop Grumman; the few who leave often complain that the company is "too political and too bureaucratic." First jobbers tell us that the quality of one's first assignment is pretty much the luck of the draw; says one, "People who are less fulfilled than [me] usually cite feeling isolated, bad management, and excessive bureaucracy as primary criticisms. I feel like these are all very real problems at the company, but I have been particularly lucky in terms of not having to deal with it too much."

OGILVY

Assistant Account Executive and OgilvyOne Associate

THE BIG PICTURE

First jobbers at Ogilvy and Mather, "one of the most prestigious firms on Madison Avenue," enjoy "the opportunity to work on blue-chip clients." Notes one newbie, "It's fun to watch television with your friends and have every third or fourth commercial be an Ogilvy-created advertisement." Employees say they also benefit from "a training program that demonstrates Ogilvy's investment in its people . . . even contacts who had started at Ogilvy and moved to other agencies declared the excellence of training programs at Ogilvy and Mather. It didn't make sense to start anywhere else."

STATS

LOCATION(S) WHERE ENTRY-LEVEL EMPLOYEES WORK

Headquarters in New York, NY; about 450 offices are located worldwide. Regional offices hire on-site.

AVERAGE NUMBER OF APPLICATIONS EACH YEAR

Ogilvy receives 5,000 applications each year.

AVERAGE NUMBER HIRED OVER THE LAST TEN YEARS

The company hires seventy people every year.

ENTRY-LEVEL POSITION(S) AVAILABLE

New hires work as assistant account executives and OgilvyOne associates.

AVERAGE HOURS WORKED PER WEEK

New hires work forty hours per week.

AVERAGE STARTING SALARY

Employees earn a little over $32,000 per year.

BENEFITS OFFERED

The company offers "full medical" coverage. Additional benefits include company vesting, dental benefits, WPP stock ownership, life insurance, 401(k), and long-term disability.

CONTACT INFORMATION

Job Hotline:

212-237-5627

Getting Hired

Ogilvy "accepts and welcomes students from all schools, disciplines, and majors. All candidates can call the Ogilvy job hotline or, if applicable, their campus' career services office. Human resources representatives from Ogilvy travel across the country to different schools, promoting Ogilvy's entry-level positions and training programs." Successful applicants generally "are driven by a desire to succeed, show leadership skills, and have a passion for advertising, which can be demonstrated through prior work experience, classes, and activities." They are also the kind of people who demonstrate an ability to "work hard and have high energy; [and] are flexible yet detail-oriented." According to one first jobber, "Ogilvy has two different rounds of interviews. The first round is with a human resources representative. If they like you and feel you will be a good fit with the culture of Ogilvy, then [they bring you] back for second-round interviews with the teams you will be working with." During the interviews, recalls one assistant account executive, "I was asked questions about why I was interested in advertising, what my favorite ads were and why, and, the most intriguing question: If I had a full page ad in the *New York Times* to sell myself to Ogilvy, what would it say?" The process can be arduous; "In my case," offers one successful applicant, "it took three months and probably a total of twelve different interviews." One entry-level employee offers the following advice: "Before applying for any position at Ogilvy, I strongly recommend you read David Ogilvy's book, *Ogilvy on Advertising*. The book has many useful insights about the agency and how to get a job here."

Money and Perks

"Most assistant account executives are paid the same amount of money" at Ogilvy, and it's not much, but that's fine with most first jobbers because the job is a foot in the door at a preeminent ad agency. Salaries increase "based on performance; Ogilvy is a meritocracy." The best fringe benefit, some employees tell us, is "lots of free products. Ogilvy has tons of well-known clients and well-known products. If you work on Kraft Foods, it's a good bet you'll get a lot of food free or at a severely discounted price. If you work on Miller Lite, getting free beer shouldn't be a problem. The same goes for many of our other clients as well." Others love the half-days on Fridays in the summer and the paid Christmas week vacation.

The Ropes

"Ogilvy's heritage in training is immense, stemming back to the days when David Ogilvy ran the agency," company officials note, adding that "it is what differentiates [us] from any other agency." In the account management training program (AMTP), "between thirty and forty-five of the participants spend three-and-a-half months learning the ins and outs of the business. They spend five to eight hours a week in seminars hosted by senior management specialists. The assistant account executives and associates apply their learning from each of the seminars to the most important component of AMTP, the client case study." The client case study is the mother of all senior projects, undertaken with a real Ogilvy client; in it, "the trainees are grouped into competing 'agencies' to pitch against each other in the final presentations. The clients truly value this initiative and in the past have implemented some of the presented solutions and ideas into their brand strategies." Notes one graduate of the program, "During the project, your team is assigned a coach who is typically a very senior executive. My team's coach was the president of the New York office. It was fascinating to learn and discuss ideas with the head of Ogilvy's flagship office. It really shows how important this training program is to Ogilvy and its leadership." Indeed, first jobbers tell us that they love how Ogilvy "always puts training ahead of [their] daily responsibilities. The company's focus [is] on investing in long-term solutions as opposed to short-term fixes."

DAY IN THE LIFE

Cautions one entry-level employee, "As anyone who works in advertising will tell you, there is no typical day. Chaos is the norm at any advertising agency, and Ogilvy is no exception. Things change at the drop of a hat." That's why "it takes a certain disposition to work in advertising. Your ability to manage the chaos is one of the marks of a good account manager. I never get bored working at Ogilvy. Every day there is a new problem to solve and a new challenging experience to grab hold of." Interaction with top executives is often a part of a first jobber's day; writes one, "I spend an immense amount of time with high-level people at Ogilvy. I am invited to virtually every important meeting for my account (except for the most senior meetings, naturally), and I feel totally comfortable strolling into the office of an executive creative director or client services director [to] bring up an issue. This place has very few ageists and very few people who care a lot about titles." The job is tough; as one assistant account executive tells us, "There are times when things are just overwhelming. In these economic times, there are fewer people to do the same amount of work. But if you are diligent in managing your time and using it effectively, there is more than enough time to get the job done. Advertising is an industry where you have to put in the hours to get the results. It's certainly not a nine-to-five job."

PEERS

First jobbers at Ogilvy usually grow close during the intensive AMTP period. "For the first three months on the job, I had lunch with my entry-level companions every day. We went out at night, introduced each other to other entry-level employees, etc. There is quite a lot of camaraderie here, especially amongst the associates because all of us experience similar things," notes one entry-level employee. Adds another newbie, "Making friends was very easy. All of us share similar types of personalities, and all of us get along very well. Those that interviewed us made sure that all of us would fit within the Ogilvy culture, and those that do shouldn't have any problem getting along."

MOVING ON

When first jobbers leave the firm, it is most often to go back to school, to pursue another opportunity in advertising, or to switch careers entirely.

ATTRITION

Very few people—less than 1 percent, according to Ogilvy—drop out of AMTP. Those associates who don't like it "criticize its rotational nature. They feel that it's a negative to spend three to four months learning an aspect of the business only to be moved off and have to begin from square one somewhere else. Those who praise the program, ironically, also focus on the rotations. The reality is that this program is not designed to create superstars in the short-term; it's designed to cultivate Ogilvy's next generation of leaders in the long-term."

PEACE CORPS
Volunteer

THE BIG PICTURE

Travel the world and see developing countries without having to carry a machine gun. Help people help themselves. Broaden your horizons. The Peace Corps: the perfect job for the globe-trotting idealist in each of us. It is important to keep in mind that in this job you'll be placed somewhere in the developing world, where political and military situations can be uncertain. This is probably the most (potentially) physically dangerous job profiled in the book.

STATS

LOCATION(S) WHERE ENTRY-LEVEL EMPLOYEES WORK

Peace Corps volunteers work "in more than seventy developing countries in Africa, Asia, the Caribbean, Central and South America, Europe, and the Middle East."

AVERAGE NUMBER OF APPLICATIONS PER YEAR

Peace Corps receives approximately 9,700 applications per year.

AVERAGE NUMBER HIRED OVER THE LAST TEN YEARS

Approximately 36,500 Peace Corps volunteers have served in the last ten years.

ENTRY-LEVEL POSITION(S) AVAILABLE

"Peace Corps assignments are tailored to each volunteer's primary skills sets, as volunteers are given the opportunity to use their classroom knowledge to develop real-world skills. Positions are available in a variety of areas including education, agriculture, community development, information technology, health education, HIV/AIDS education and awareness, environmental awareness, or businesses development."

PERCENTAGE OF ENTRY-LEVEL HIRES STILL WITH THE COMPANY AFTER THREE, FIVE, AND TEN YEARS

"Peace Corps volunteers serve for a twenty-seven-month term overseas, which includes a three-month training session. Many often extend their two-year terms or apply to serve in a new country."

AVERAGE STARTING SALARY

Volunteers receive "a living allowance that enables [them] to live in a manner similar to the local people in their community. Volunteers also receive $225 per month toward a 'readjustment allowance' that they receive upon completion of their two years of service."

BENEFITS OFFERED

Volunteers receive comprehensive medical and dental coverage, plus a health insurance plan for eighteen months following the completion of service. "In most cases [volunteers receive a] deferment of Stafford Loans, Perkins Loans, Federal Consolidation Loans, or Direct Loans [and] a 15 percent cancellation of their outstanding [student loan] balance for each year of their two years of service. Deferment does not happen automatically; the volunteer must apply for the deferment."

CONTACT INFORMATION

Talk to a Peace Corps recruiter at 800-424-8580, or visit www.peacecorps.gov.

GETTING HIRED

The application process is "pretty long," according to one volunteer. "I applied in December, had my interview in January, and then did not hear about my actual assignment until May." Volunteers suggest that you "take the interview seriously. Although it is a volunteer position, treat the job application process as you would any other job. It is competitive, and Peace Corps attracts a high caliber of people. My interview lasted over an hour, and they asked a lot of questions about past experiences and interests of mine." Add Peace Corps representatives, "Applicants may be surprised that a recruiter asks personal questions during the interview. But it's important to us that all prospective Peace Corps volunteers consider the impact that service will have on their professional and personal lives." After the interview comes medical and legal screening, a step that eliminates a surprising number of potential members. "It's the most frustrating step for many because the exams are so thorough," is how one successful applicant describes it. Finally, people who are accepted are matched with an area needing their skills; orientation commences pretty soon thereafter.

MONEY AND PERKS

The word "volunteer" figures prominently in the position you'll be seeking, and for good reason; as the recruiters explain, "Peace Corps volunteers are not employees of the federal government and therefore do not receive a salary. However, Peace Corps provides volunteers with a living allowance and a 'readjustment allowance' that they receive upon completion of their two years of service. It is often used for a rent deposit, groceries, and other living expenses when the volunteer returns to the United States" Volunteers join for the experience, not for the money, and the experiences they have, they say, are the big perks. "The best fringe benefit was getting to live in a village in Africa for two years," writes a typical volunteer. "There is no other entry-level job that will give you such an amazing and life-changing experience."

THE ROPES

There are two phases of Peace Corps training: a brief, pre-departure orientation called "staging" and a three-month in-country immersion training in the language and culture of the host town or village. During staging, "Applicants meet their fellow trainees and begin to identify personal and cultural adjustments that will help them to promote their successful service." They fill out forms, get vaccinated, and learn Peace Corps policies and procedures, study risk identification and management, and adjust to life on a Peace Corps post. Immediately following staging, volunteers depart on their assignments for in-country training. Here's how one volunteer describes the experience: "Your first three months in-country are taken up by training. During this time you are taught the local language, and local culture, safety and security, and medical training. Training is extremely overwhelming. During the first three months you also live with a host family, which adds another dimension [to] your experience."

DAY IN THE LIFE

There is no typical day in the life for a Peace Corps volunteer. As one volunteer puts it, "I never knew what was going to happen that day when I woke up in the morning. Sometimes school would be closed, or there would be a big celebration. I loved that! Basically, I ran in the mornings, spent all day at school teaching, planning lessons, working with other teachers, and socializing with teachers. Then I would come home and help my host mother with dinner for a couple hours, eat for a couple more hours, drink tea for a couple more hours, and then read and lesson plan. Even though I was only actually working for six hours, I felt like it was a twenty-four-hour job because you always had to be 'on' and teaching and learning, even while [washing] the dishes." Adds another volunteer, "You cannot go into your village with a set idea of what *you* think needs to be accomplished. You need to spend time getting to know people and the realities on the ground and then work with people to do projects. For me, tasks in Peace Corps were much more long range. There were things I wanted to accomplish each month, but on any given day, I did not have definite things to do. It is such a different pace of life—without 'to do' lists, PDAs, cell phones, and endless meetings. You are really on your own schedule and [create] your work."

PEERS

"There is a huge sense of camaraderie among the Peace Corps volunteers I served with," enthuses one volunteer. "One of the greatest things about Peace Corps is the people you meet." They see each other "at big gatherings, go to each other's villages to work on projects together, [and sometimes] travel to the capital city and meet other volunteers for a movie, dinner, etc." Not all volunteers seek out fellow Peace Corps members, however. Some "want to focus on building relationships with the local people and do not want to socialize with other Americans. In general, Peace Corps can be very social, or you could totally immerse yourself into your own community."

MOVING ON

Some Peace Corps volunteers continue with the organization after their two-year term is up; several of our survey respondents, in fact, now work as Peace Corps recruiters. Others parlay their experiences in the Corps into springboards to graduate school or interesting job offers. Writes one former volunteer, "I now work for a consulting firm that does international development work. The fact that I had Peace

Corps experience was a big reason why I was hired. This company values the skills and experience you learn in Peace Corps." As organization representatives put it, "The Peace Corps experience enhances long-term career prospects, whether a volunteer wants to work for a corporation, a nonprofit organization, or a government agency. The Peace Corps can even open doors to graduate school."

ATTRITION

"You have to go into Peace Corps for the right reasons or else you will be disappointed," explains one volunteer. Those who are disappointed are often those who are "upset about the lack of direction Peace Corps gives you with what you're supposed to do in your projects." As one volunteer puts it, "If you are a person who likes to have exact direction and guidance to what you're supposed to be doing and when it needs to be done, Peace Corps may not be a good job decision for you."

PRICEWATERHOUSECOOPERS
Associate

THE BIG PICTURE

Whether PricewaterhouseCoopers (PwC) really is "the best of the big four accounting firms," as one first jobber tells us, is open to debate. What is certain is that this is a great place to start a career in the high-powered fields of assurance, tax preparation, and financial services.

STATS

LOCATION(S) WHERE ENTRY-LEVEL EMPLOYEES WORK

The company has offices in 150 countries.

ENTRY-LEVEL POSITION(S) AVAILABLE

New hires work as associates.

AVERAGE HOURS WORKED PER WEEK

New hires work from forty to sixty hours per week.

BENEFITS OFFERED

The company offers a choice of health plans, prescription plans, hearing/vision/dental coverage, and flexible spending accounts. Additional benefits include paid holidays; vacation; sick days; disability, life and accident insurance; mortgage program; retirement; and adoption assistance.

CONTACT INFORMATION

Apply for a job on our website at www.pwc.com/gx/eng/careers/main/index.html.

GETTING HIRED

The company "has an extensive campus-recruiting program across the nation and visits several schools with accredited accounting programs to staff their offices around the country." Undergraduates may also apply for associate positions online at the PwC website. Explains one associate, "The big four are actively recruiting. Once you choose the accounting major, there's only one goal, and that is to get an internship or associate position with a big four firm." PwC seeks candidates who "demonstrate the ability to work in a team, be organized, be [good at multitasking], work under pressure and be willing to learn. A person's resume should not be longer than one page and should be concise, detailing [his or her] education, past work experience, and extra-curricular activities. Although it is definitely helpful to have an accounting background, it is not mandatory, and, if qualified in other areas, PwC may still hire someone without the requisite accounting skills." A successful candidate advises that "it helps to follow up with someone in recruiting to make sure that [your] resume/cover letter [are] received and to establish a rapport with the recruiter. Because the firm receives so many resumes for positions every year, having a quick conversation with the recruiter and demonstrating your interest could make a difference in getting an interview." People who secure interviews tell us that the recruiters "ask a lot about working in teams [and] how you react in difficult situations. They want to find out what type of person you are." First jobbers also note that "a lot of juniors in college do the internship. The majority of hires are through the summer internship program."

MONEY AND PERKS

Although "salary isn't really negotiable—the current market situation determines your starting salary"—other aspects of the PwC job offer are. Associates tell us that "rather than give you one start date, PwC gives new hires certain date options of when they can start. Most new hires either start at the beginning or end of September or the beginning of January. The start dates usually coincide with the orientation/training programs PwC offers." They also report that "because PwC has offices around the world, location is negotiable, depending on the needs of that office location." PwC offers a generous benefits package. Other perks include "exposure to other companies. If somebody ever wants to leave public accounting field, you've worked with fifteen to twenty different clients, the contacts that you make definitely come in handy in the future." Associates also love the Spot Bonus Program, which "gives partners and managers the opportunity to recognize hard work or exemplary performance by members of their team by giving them bonuses in their paychecks at random points throughout the year. As an associate, it's a great feeling to know that your hard work did not go unnoticed."

THE ROPES

First jobbers at PwC tell us that "depending on what industry group a new hire starts in, the orientation program varies." Writes one associate, "It's a two-week program. Depending on what line of service you're in, they send you somewhere in the country—New York, Boston—[for] regional training. Mostly they go over the basics of when you start a new job, exactly what you're doing, how you'll be doing it, and they show you how to use the technology." Subsequently "you do a lot of icebreakers. Also, once you come to the office, they send you a lot of emails about online courses, try to get you familiar with things before you get into it. Basically everyone that works here is very friendly. They emphasize not to be afraid to ask questions when you have them." No matter how good your undergraduate program was, you'll have to be prepared to learn most everything from scratch at PwC; advises one associate, "The thing about the undergraduate accounting programs is that they expose you to financial statements and policies and techniques, but they don't teach you auditing. You really don't know what you're really doing until you show up and actually do it for a while. Even [during] the first two weeks of training, I didn't know exactly what the process was. Until you actually do it, there's only so much you can know."

DAY IN THE LIFE

"Typically what you do as a first-year associate is a lot of auditing of [easier] accounts," explains one PwC first jobber. "I do cash, fixed assets, accounts payable, [and] accounts receivable. They start you out with something you can succeed in." Young associates "travel out to the client site; the majority of work is there, not in the PwC office. You get there and might have two or three meetings a day to get information, ask questions, and get a feel of the account you'll be auditing. Then you go back to the audit room, evaluate the information you have, compare what you have with what they have, and then when you're finished, the senior will review your work. At the end of each engagement, the manager and partner will review everything, bringing you in as well." It isn't long before new hires are taking on increased responsibility, accountants tell us; says one, "One of the great parts about working at PwC is the amount of responsibility a new or experienced associate can have. Over time, associates are given more responsibility, have the opportunity to take control over more complex areas, and play an integral role in completing each audit." Notes another, "It is a rapid succession, a pretty quick learning curve. Most individuals make senior within two to three years."

PEERS

"At PwC, we work hard, but we like to play hard, too," first jobbers report, and "with everybody being the same age, and everybody being in Boston, New York, etc., it fosters an atmosphere of going out every night." It all starts in training. Writes one associate, "I was able to develop friendships with other new hires at training, and I still talk to several of them regularly. Because we all are at client sites on a regular basis, we rely on other social activities to see each other. The firm organizes several events for employees to mingle, network, and socialize including monthly 'hangouts' at the office, industry group social events (such as bowling), or happy hours. Teams also have their own happy hours, dinners, and events on a regular basis." First jobbers are "very impressed with how 'smart' and 'cool' PwC employees are. As a stereotype, accountants are supposedly quiet, nerdy, and unsocial. The people I work with are definitely a fun group of people who don't fit the stereotype. Everyone is here to challenge themselves, learn, work hard, and make the best of their experiences."

MOVING ON

First-jobbers come to PwC with the goal of building a career at a big four accounting firm. Still, "PwC gives you the opportunity to develop and hone skills that you can apply at many other jobs. Your skills are highly sought after by all companies who have accounting, finance, and risk-management departments and you can easily move to a job in any industry that interests you."

ATTRITION

The most common reason folks don't last at the company is "the incredible volume of work." The hours are long—too long for some. "It's a pretty constant fifty-hour workweek," writes one associate. Adds another, "People who are going through rough times often attribute it to having too much to do and working long hours. Working for PwC is not a nine-to-five job and you have to be willing to put in some days with long hours to succeed."

THE PRINCETON REVIEW
Various Positions

THE BIG PICTURE

It's the best company ever! But seriously, folks, for many, The Princeton Review (TPR) offers the ideal entry-level job, one that offers diverse work experience, unusual amounts of responsibility, and plenty of chances for advancement. The work force is unusually young, so the company's offices support an active, fun social scene that will probably remind you at least a little of your college days.

STATS

LOCATION(S) WHERE ENTRY-LEVEL EMPLOYEES WORK

TPR has nearly sixty offices across the country.

AVERAGE NUMBER OF APPLICATIONS EACH YEAR

The company receives 2,500 applications every year.

AVERAGE NUMBER HIRED OVER THE LAST TEN YEARS

The company hires 150 people per year.

ENTRY-LEVEL POSITION(S) AVAILABLE

New hires work as assistant marketing managers, research assistants, call center representatives, help desk assistants, production editors, and department coordinators.

AVERAGE HOURS WORKED PER WEEK

New hires work forty-five hours per week.

PERCENTAGE OF ENTRY-LEVEL HIRES STILL WITH THE COMPANY AFTER THREE, FIVE, AND TEN YEARS

After three years, 15 percent of entry-level hires remain with the company.

AVERAGE STARTING SALARY

New hires earn $28,000 per year.

BENEFITS OFFERED

The company offers a full medical coverage package. There is also an optional dental plan, 401(k) plan with company match (after one year of employment), tuition reimbursement of up to $1,000 per six-month period ($2,000 per year) after six months of service, pre-tax flexible spending accounts for transportation, and dependent and non-reimbursed medical costs. As a full-time employee, you can also take any of TPR's test prep courses free.

Visit the website at www.PrincetonReview.com.

GETTING HIRED

There are several ways to land full-time employment at TPR. The company posts positions on its website and on www.monster.com. Many start with the company as part-time teachers for its test preparation courses, then apply for office positions as they become available. The company reviews all candidates for "excellent academic background and internship experience. Soft skills we look for include high energy, excellent communication skills, enthusiasm, excitement about the product, [and] passion to learn." Consistent with the company's approach, the interview process is serious but informal. As one recent hire explains, "I was familiar with TPR's casual approach to business and decided that the tone of my email should be light, yet professional. I wanted to distinguish myself from other candidates, and my previous job in a similar field certainly helped land me the interview. I was interviewed by my current boss, who insisted that I come to chat wearing jeans. The interview was incredibly laid-back; I felt right at home and very comfortable. I remember on my second interview being asked by my boss' boss if I had $100 dollars, how I'd spend it. It was a great little ice-breaker, and it helped me open up some more. I knew that if I were hired, these were the two people I'd be working with closely, day in, day out, and no one else in such near proximity."

MONEY AND PERKS

Those who bring valuable prior experience to their jobs find that their salaries are negotiable; others will find less flexibility. Most people here "aren't in it for the money. I was more interested in landing a position with a company where I'd always wanted to work—a company that best represented my outlook on life— a casual approach and a young, energetic, palpable vibe that ran throughout." Others tell us that "the fact that the company is based in the academic world was also a big draw." What are the best perks here? "It's a tie between all the social events TPR sponsors and the tuition reimbursement," agree many. "Getting the company to help pay for the next stage in my education will be of immense benefit to me," writes one first jobber.

THE ROPES

The Princeton Review offers a brief orientation to new hires ("[where they] go over the company history, benefits, and our intranet. They also meet senior members of the company."), then sets them to work immediately. Writes one first jobber, "It was on-the-job training. The first kick I took was from the moment I stepped into the office. It was a Monday, it was summer, and there were forty sets of student materials that had to go out. I was processing enrollments within my first three hours, and I probably handled my first phone call by day number two. Training was ongoing; I'd learn how things were done and then develop my own system based on what I'd learned." Adds another, "As I have encountered situations for which I don't have the experience or am not familiar with procedure, I have been able to ask other members of the office staff for help. Everyone has been great about helping to get me oriented and functional."

Day in the Life

TPR offers a variety of positions to entry-level workers, so "there is no such thing as a typical day." Many people start out as assistant directors of an office; here's how one person describes the position: "From day one, I was doing it all, helping run a small business. You want stress, you've got it. Everything falls into your hands—phone calls, emails, enrollments, ordering supplies, getting office machines fixed. This isn't a cushy job; I had no idea I'd be getting my hands dirty, lifting packages and such. Here, from the moment I walked in the door, they sat me down at my desk, gave me a training schedule, and forced me to be their assistant director. We work hard, we drive for results, and we want the customer to recommend us." There's a lot of leeway in how you get your job done, as long as it gets done on time. Notes one employee in computer support, "As someone with a vested interest in the Internet, I felt this job would be a perfect match for me. It combined both my love of education and the Web, along with a casual work atmosphere. Where else can I grow a beard, wear shorts, surf the net, and get paid for it?"

Peers

There's always been a youngish vibe in The Princeton Review offices; notes one employee, "We're an office with a mean age of about twenty-three, so it's nice to be around so many people my age." Nearly everyone agrees that "there is much camaraderie at the office. Although I am the only first jobber in my division, we're all really close, and sometimes it seems as though we work in a sit-com. We interact twenty-four hours a day, seven days a week. I'm serious. There's no getting away from these people." Fortunately, "these people" are "a very cool group."

Moving on

For some people, jobs at The Princeton Review become careers, and they move on only if better career opportunities present themselves. For many others, TPR is like the old television show *Taxi;* people work at the company, but their *real* gigs are acting, music, writing, art, and other such creative ventures. A number of these folks have moved on to successful careers in their chosen fields. Others remain with the mother ship, waiting for their shuttle rides to fame and glory.

Attrition

People who leave the happy fold cite "overwork, with too many expectations being put on one person for the time allotted." One employee says it is not uncommon to hear "complaints about unrealistic expectations being put on us, particularly from national marketing. However, with that said, what I mostly hear [are] positive comments. People are happy to be working for a company that allows them to be who they are without laboring under massive corporate structures. Also, there is pride in serving students well and delivering a quality educational product."

P & G

Various Positions

THE BIG PICTURE

Proctor and Gamble (P & G) is one of the nation's corporate giants products that makes for personal care, beauty, health, house cleaning, and baby care. The company offers entry-level positions in just about every area essential to its business.

STATS

LOCATION(S) WHERE ENTRY-LEVEL EMPLOYEES WORK

"P & G is a promote-from-within company, which means that we hire almost exclusively from college campuses for both commercial and technical functions. Depending on the year, we will hire between 1,000 to 3,000 [entry-level employees] globally, of which about 50 percent are located in the United States. Of the people hired in the United States, about half are based in the greater Cincinnati area and half in subsidiary company, plant, or field sales locations throughout the country."

AVERAGE NUMBER OF APPLICATIONS EACH YEAR

"We typically receive over 100,000 applications each year, all of which are electronically processed via our online application system."

AVERAGE NUMBER HIRED OVER THE LAST TEN YEARS

"P & G has averaged 725 management hires per year over the last ten years with a high of 1,100 and a low of 450."

ENTRY-LEVEL POSITION(S) AVAILABLE

"Entry-level positions typically exist across all functional areas, including marketing, finance, accounting, tax, legal, marketing research, sales, engineering, purchases, PhD scientists, human resources, etc. In addition, we have a large number of nonmanagement positions in the administrative and technical area, most of which require college-level education. For example, we hire a significant number of research associates who are four-year degreed people with majors in the natural science areas."

AVERAGE HOURS WORKED PER WEEK

"Average workweek varies by function within [the] business unit. The company uses flextime and other flexible work arrangements to help people to maintain balance in their lives. Managers typically work about fifty hours a week with variation to meet important deadlines."

Percentage of Entry-level Hires Still with the Company after Three, Five, and Ten Years

"P & G hires for the long term. Our entry requirements are very high and we use a rigorous assessment process to select the best people we can find. Once in the company, many people choose to stay for their entire career, often working in different locations (domestic and international), different business units, or [different] functions. Early turnover is relatively low across all functions. Overall turnover is about 8 percent per year [of which] 3 percent are people who are retiring, so the three, five, and ten year turnover figures are roughly the same and stay in the 3 to 5 percent range."

Average Starting Salary

"We know from survey comparisons that our starting salaries are highly competitive versus a very strong competitor group of companies."

Benefits Offered

"Employees have a choice of medical plans designed to meet individual needs and preferences. Overall cost-sharing is about 75 percent company, 25 percent individual. The plans are designed to provide broad coverage and have reasonable co-pays, out of pocket maximums, and premiums. Coverage is available for individuals and families including domestic partners or legal dependents." Additional benefits include profit sharing, retiree health insurance, flex comp, pre-tax credits for various services and insurance, and paid holidays.

Contact Information

Mr. Bob Pike

Director College Relations

513-983-3788

Getting Hired

P & G takes the scientific approach to hiring; company representatives say, "The criteria we use for hiring is directly linked to our competency model that was developed by interviewing our top management, a sample of 1,600 employees from every region of the world in which we operate, [and] a sample of our alumni, customers, and investors. This effort is sponsored and led by our Global Talent Supply organization." The model calls for candidates who have "integrity, brainpower, and demonstrated leadership. They should be collaborators [and] embrace change. They must communicate persuasively and clearly. They must have an appetite for results and a flare for innovation. We expect mastery of their learned discipline." Applications are fielded online on the corporate website and supplemented by recruiting trips to thirty-five campuses; top applicants "are invited to [visit] with the company [for a day]," during which they "tour the city, tour the facility, and have the opportunity to meet with new hires (one to three years) during lunch and in one-on-one situations." During the visit, applicants also "have a behaviorally anchored interview by a panel of three people, and go through some form of cognitive assessment." Cautions one first jobber, "The tone of the interview was intense and serious. They wanted specific examples of how I was successful in previous roles that I have been in. It seemed as if no answer was a good answer because it would lead to a more probing question!"

Money and Perks

P & G offers solid starting salaries; reports one first jobber, "Their offer was much higher than the other offers I had." The same first jobber especially appreciated the company's flexibility; "At the time I was brought in, the business unit recruiting me was looking to fill several positions in engineering. My initial offer was for a position in a field that did not interest me. I made my hiring department aware of my preferences, and they were able to place me in one of the departments that appealed [more] to me." Other perks (that vary widely by department and function) include flex time, travel opportunities, and discounts.

The Ropes

The company has "an extensive [orientation] process that starts upon acceptance of our offer, utilizing a new hire pre-start website. Once a new hire is in the company, the join-up period lasts for one year and is centered around three major training events that give people exposure to each other, top management, functions, business units, company history and principles, and more. The events are fun, interactive, and thorough." Training sessions range from "one-day to one-week programs on such topics as company policy, inclusion training, women in engineering, or technology-related training." Subsequent training "is both formal and informal, offered by outside vendors, agencies, and upper management. All focus [is] on building business understanding early to help make an impact."

Day in the Life

First jobbers at P & G often find themselves waist-deep in responsibility almost from the get-go. As company officials put it, "New hire roles vary according to function, but all have tremendous early responsibility built into their work." Our survey respondents confirm this assertion; writes one, "When I was first hired, I was given three different projects to work on, each on a different product. This allowed me to know three different product lines very quickly. I was given clear direction and full reigns, and was responsible for all results. My manager wrote a work plan with me that described my responsibilities. This work plan included a list of key contacts, in my own and other functions, for each project that he suggested I meet with for join-ups. These contacts became an integral part of the project team and their collaboration helped to make me succeed. Essentially, I was given the tools and the contacts to get the work done and the rest I was responsible for."

Peers

For most first jobbers at P & G, there's "tons of interaction with new hires, including training and social events (informal and formal) on a weekly basis." Reports one, "About once a month there would be a happy hour or other event that allowed us to interact with others in their first year. There is also a sense of camaraderie within my group. I enjoy working with the others in my group and occasionally we meet up outside of work." In the larger offices, "it is difficult not to run into others and have a quick chat in the halls because of the cubicle environment," while engineers in the field tell us that "during plant visits, experiments comprise long days and sometimes long weeks, so [people] get to know each other very well while traveling. During these trips [people] eat all meals together and often have long commutes to and from work."

MOVING ON

Although "many stay for a career" at P & G, occasionally workers do move on. The Cincinnati location of the company's central office is occasionally an issue. "It's a conservative, family-oriented city with employment opportunities [that] are less robust than [those in] Chicago or New York. This is sometimes an issue," company representatives inform us.

ATTRITION

Less than 1 percent of first jobbers leave P & G within twelve months of being hired, according to company officials.

BEST AND WORST

"All of our CEOs started as first jobbers," P & G representatives tell us. "We have had many great leaders. We believe our current CEO, Mr. A. G. Lafley, is an example of the kind of leader we produce and [that he] will be one of the very best we have ever had." The worst first jobbers were "the people who joined P & G with skills, capabilities, and values that were not consistent with the culture of the company."

QUALCOMM
Various Positions

THE BIG PICTURE

You may know them as the company "that pioneered Code Division Multiple Access (CDMA) technology, which is now used in wireless networks and handsets all over the world." You may know them as the purveyors of your email software (Eudora) or as major players in the world of digital imagery. However you know them, know that they are major players in today's e-world, and they just may have a position for you.

STATS

LOCATION(S) WHERE ENTRY-LEVEL EMPLOYEES WORK

Qualcomm employees work in offices located around the world, but the majority of positions are at company headquarters in San Diego, CA.

ENTRY-LEVEL POSITION(S) AVAILABLE

Various positions are available to new hires, including financial analyst and marketing coordinator.

PERCENTAGE OF ENTRY-LEVEL HIRES STILL WITH THE COMPANY AFTER THREE, FIVE, AND TEN YEARS

"Qualcomm has been ranked for six consecutive years as one of the best places to work in the United States, so we have a very low turnover rate."

BENEFITS OFFERED

The company offers medical, dental, and vision PPO for employees and their spouses or partners. Additional benefits include a 401(k) plan, stock options, three weeks of vacation per year, on-site fitness center, income protection, survivor protection, and tuition reimbursement.

CONTACT INFORMATION

Visit the website at http://jobs.qualcomm.com.

GETTING HIRED

Many first jobbers begin their tenure at Qualcomm in the summer, either through the company's summer internship program or as new hires. The company posts open positions on its website, and they are open to all applicants. The advantage of interning, obviously, is that it allows people to establish connections with others within the company, which in turn makes the interviewing process flow much smoother. It also allows young job seekers to explore the company to determine the area that is best suited to their goals and talents. Most of our survey respondents describe their interviews as relaxed and very

California style; writes one new hire, "It was more like a conversation than an 'ask/answer' session. My interviewer was interested in what I had to ask and say as well, and although there were also technical questions, my interviewer helped ease the stress I was feeling so that I could better answer the questions. It seemed as if my interviewer remembered what it is like to interview and empathized with the nervousness and occasional 'blank mind' that occurs during a technical interview." Even so, interviews at Qualcomm sometimes resemble final exams. Writes one hardware design engineer, "Each of my interviewers had his own style. One interview included worksheets of binary logic, circuit analysis, and C code. The interviewers were relaxed and friendly, but it was obvious they took the screening processes very seriously."

Money and Perks

Qualcomm hires first jobbers in a number of different areas, and the negotiability of the offer depends on where they work. Most of our respondents say that only the start date was negotiable. One engineer, however, reports that "the job offer was negotiable. Qualcomm was able to match and beat offers from other companies." All jobs come with "lots of fringe benefits," including "fitness centers, free dinners Monday through Thursday, the lack of a dress code, the employee stock purchase plan, and flexible hours—[employees] can pick [their] own hours and take time at any time during the day to take care of life. The only expectation is that you get your work done, and you allow others to do the same." And don't forget "the Qualcomm yearly party. What an event! Each department within Qualcomm holds some sort of celebration about once a year during the winter season. Qualcomm really goes 'all-out,' and it is a great excuse to dress up, be elegant, and have a blast!" Money-wise, Qualcomm representatives say that "employees are eligible for two merit increases each year. Performances are evaluated and depending on how well they met their goals, [they] may receive a salary increase, a bonus, and stock options." Also, "some employees may be eligible for relocation assisitance, and we have a generous tuition-reimbursement program and on-site professional-development curriculum."

The Ropes

Qualcomm orientation is "very welcoming and informative. Employees learn about the policies, culture, and computer programs that are used at Qualcomm." Writes one first jobber, "At orientation, we got a packet of information that included two tickets for free lunch at the company café. It lasted an entire morning. I met my boss after the orientation, and we went to lunch [with the lunch tickets]." For many employees, subsequent training occurs on the job, mostly from coworkers and managers, and with occasional formal training sessions. The company offers engineers "a wide range of technical and management courses to get you up to speed with the technology."

DAY IN THE LIFE

Our respondents at Qualcomm included engineers, financial analysts, and designers. The majority of positions available are for engineers who begin their tenures by "following other engineers and learning from them what they were working on. If they needed help, they would show me how, why, what to do, and I would go ahead and work on the assignment. As I grew more familiar with the process, they would then assign more challenging tasks, without going into every detail of the task." Engineers tell us that you can't just sit around waiting for an assignment; writes one, "If I don't ask around and talk with my fellow engineers, I might not find out about key things that are going on. I have to make sure I move around every now and then so I can find out about any projects going on that I might have fun participating in, or that will give me added valuable knowledge and experience. People don't chase you around here, so you have to be motivated to keep yourself in the loop."

PEERS

Qualcomm is a big company, and the amount of peer networking first jobbers enjoy varies from area to area. Some tell us that "there is a pretty decent social scene here. There are a lot of young people at this company who are very active and various clubs and teams seem to form each year. For example, I am on a softball team now that is mostly Q-Commers." Others report that there's "not a big after-hours social scene, but every now and then on weekends, Super Bowl, etc., people have parties or even just hang out and play basketball or soccer." Most employees agree that "Qualcomm attracts great people who are all well-rounded and fun. They have open personalities and are very friendly."

MOVING ON

First jobbers are part of no formal training program with beginning and end dates; they are at the company for a while or until something better comes along. Most have a hard time imagining a better work situation, telling us that they love "the trust management puts into its employees. My manager trusts that when I am at work, I am working and on top of things. It is this absence of 'micromanagement' that motivates me to put 200 percent into my work, and overtime if I need to." One employee says, "When I talk to people outside of Qualcomm, I realized just how good we have it."

RANDOM HOUSE
Various Positions

THE BIG PICTURE

Find, develop, edit, print, and market books just like the one you're holding now! Entry-level positions in all facets of the publishing industry await you at Random House, a bellwether of the world of book publishing.

STATS

LOCATION(S) WHERE ENTRY-LEVEL EMPLOYEES WORK

Primarily New York, NY; the company also hires for individual publishing imprints in Colorado Springs, CO and Roseville and Santa Ana, CA. "Additionally, we have operations centers in Westminster, MD, and Crawfordsville, IN, that handle distribution and other critical support services. Entry-level employees are hired at all of these locations," company officials report, adding that "as the world's largest trade book publisher, Random House also operates in Canada, the United Kingdom, Germany, Spain, South Africa, Australia, New Zealand, Mexico, Argentina, Chile, Venezuela, and Japan."

AVERAGE NUMBER OF APPLICATIONS EACH YEAR

Random House receives 25,000 to 30,000 applications in the United States per year.

AVERAGE NUMBER HIRED OVER THE LAST TEN YEARS

The company hires 200 to 250 people per year in the United States.

ENTRY-LEVEL POSITION(S) AVAILABLE

The company tells us that, "For college grads interested in a career in book publishing, Random House offers an enormous range of opportunities. Entry-level employees usually start out at the level of 'assistant' and not only work in traditional publishing areas such as editorial, marketing, and publicity, but also in production, sales, information technology, finance, human resources, subsidiary rights, new media, and other areas." A one-year associate program "for entry-level hires who are uncertain as to which area they want to join but are committed to publishing" is also available.

AVERAGE HOURS WORKED PER WEEK

Entry-level hires work thirty-five hours per week.

AVERAGE STARTING SALARY

Starting salaries are competitive by publishing industry standards.

Benefits Offered

Regarding health coverage, PPOs and HMOs are offered; employees must contribute "but the company pays the majority of the cost." There are also options to participate in dental, disability, life insurance, spending accounts, the 401(k) program, pension program, tuition reimbursement, and profit sharing. Additional benefits include a *very* generous vacation benefit (four weeks per year after your first year!), paid parental leave, child care benefits, physical fitness reimbursement, flexible spending account for transportation expenses, and work/life assistance program.

Contact Information

To apply for a job go to www.randomhouse.com/careers/cg_entry.html.

Getting Hired

Random House says, "Most obviously, we look for employees in our publishing and sales divisions who are passionate about books. Beyond that, we also look for individuals who take initiative, possess strong communication skills, and work effectively with others." The company recruits on campus at certain colleges and also accepts applications via its website. The vetting process includes a two-stage interview. Recalls one employee, "My first interview was with human resources. The tone of the interview was very positive and friendly. I was asked about my educational background as well as my work experiences. I was then invited for further interviewing. I interviewed with several people, one from editorial and others from sales and marketing. All of these meetings were very informative and confirmed the positive impression of the company that had been established earlier." After that, it's a waiting game. According to one newbie who cleared the interview stage, "When a position became available that would allow me to utilize my major, I was asked if I'd be interested, and I was. I was hired about six months after my initial contact."

Money and Perks

Random House offers starting salaries that are "the most competitive in the industry," according to one employee. Still, this is publishing, so don't expect the megabucks. "Publishing is by no means a gold mine," jokes one worker. Avid readers and others will enjoy the many perks of working for Random House. They include "getting to read interesting books months before they come out. It's entirely energizing to stay ahead of trends and get a glimpse at innovative writing as authors are creating it and as it winds its way into the mainstream. Getting to go to book events and movie premieres and meeting literary greats is also wonderful." Random House employees also enjoy "incredible" medical coverage and a liberal policy toward vacation days, sick days, and holidays. Company representatives also think you should know that "many entry-level employees benefit from Random House's highly decentralized organizational structure. This enables each of its publishing divisions to maintain the ambience and creative and entrepreneurial autonomy of a small company while enjoying all the resources and operational support of a market leader."

The Ropes

Orientation at Random House is a relatively brief affair. Explains one employee, "The orientation process was quick—just one morning, [for] about three hours. We watched videos about the company and learned about benefits. But come lunchtime, I was already in my office, reading manuscripts and answering the telephone and communicating with authors. Publishing moves so fast these days and jobs are filled so quickly that it is necessary to hit the ground running and learn as you go." One new hire says, "Training is made available on a continuous basis. Also, my boss has [always] made sure that I had plenty of information about the organization, the structure, the various imprints, and key contacts." Occasionally workers "are invited to attend Random House's Luncheon Seminar series, which occurs regularly throughout the year. Here various executives share information about their areas of expertise, their career paths, and their workgroups. The series typically concludes annually with a talk by Peter Olson, chairman and chief executive officer."

Day in the Life

Random House offers entry-level jobs in editorial, production, publicity, marketing, customer service, and warehouse operations, so the daily experiences of new hires vary greatly. Those who enter through the associates program rotate among various jobs within a particular division. This path has its plusses and minuses; explains one employee who took this route, "As an associate, I was placed in an entry-level position for a period, after which I would move to a new position. At the end of the one-year program, I was expected to select a permanent position. The program's goal is to give a new employee a better understanding of the different work environments within a single publishing house. I liked this. It allowed me to take my time in deciding where I wanted to end up working, and what I wanted to do." Unfortunately, "being at the mercy of an open position—the very thing upon which the associates program relies—backfired for me. I had been hired, but I had no job. I sat for days, begging people for something to do. Most often the only bones I was tossed were tasks the other assistants simply didn't want to do themselves. I did many mailings, loads of filing, and days of permissions work. It was menial and taxing, but at least it gave me something to do all day." The program offers one undeniable benefit, though; as one associate explains, "I was able to grab a permanent position when it opened up. I was already hired; I just had to sit in limbo until I was needed. It was definitely a great advantage to already be sitting on the bench versus still trying to get into the stadium."

Peers

"There is tremendous camaraderie among first jobbers at the company," writes one newbie. "From the minute I walked to my new desk, people came to introduce themselves and offer help in my settling in." Many laud their "amazing peers, who are very diverse in their backgrounds and yet similar when it comes to career goals and aspirations." For some people, "there is a big after-hours social scene, mostly going out for dinner or drinks. Because publishing is such a social environment, I was able to see my friends for a good part of the day." Others tell a different story: "When the time came to go home, that's what people did. There were nearly no get-togethers after work. And when people did gather after work, no one talked about anything except work. I found it rather disheartening, but that's the price you pay for working in a place where everyone is so motivated and Ivy-Leagued," explains one worker.

MOVING ON

Entry-level jobs at Random House are designed to lead to better positions within the company. Many young workers stay to pursue their careers in publishing. "A major reason for voluntary departures is often to attend graduate school," note company officials, who also cite "relocation, career change, and personal reasons" as reasons why some employees leave the company.

ATTRITION

Personal relationships are important in publishing, and many who leave do so because they don't enjoy working for their superiors. "Enjoyment of one's entry-level job is directly proportional to how much one enjoys one's supervisor, professionally and personally," points out one successful entry-level employee. Other people leave because they are "not satisfied with the level of responsibility allocated to them. While grunt work is a part of every job, some felt that the *only* work given to them was grunt work." This feeling was especially prevalent among those participating in the associates program.

RAYTHEON COMPANY
Engineer

The Big Picture

In today's dangerous world, you can't really ask for a bigger potential growth industry than defense. Raytheon is one of the world's biggest defense and aerospace systems suppliers in the world, and its vastness allows engineers to work in virtually any area that interests them. In the process, they also get to, in the words of one engineer, "provide good countries, like the United States, with products that help maintain peace."

Stats

Location(s) Where Entry-level Employees Work

"Nationwide. Our forty-five locations that hire co-ops/interns and full-time entry-level employees include the following metropolitan areas: Boston, MA; Falls Church, VA; Los Angeles, CA; Southern California; Dallas, TX; Tucson, AZ; Denver, CO; St. Petersburg, FL; Ft. Wayne, IN; and Indianapolis, IN."

Average Number of Applications Each Year

"Our new electronic resume process logged 10,000 domestic United States entry-level candidates in Spring 2003. We expect to attract over 20,000 candidates in Fall 2003 [and] Spring/Summer 2004."

Average Number Hired over the Last Ten Years

"Raytheon grew to its current state through mergers and acquisitions in the late 1990s. The average number of entry-level hires for recent college graduates has been over 1,000 per year since then."

Entry-level Position(s) Available

"[There are from] 700 to 1,000 new positions for full-time, entry-level openings. Predominately, openings are for engineering positions in hardware, software, and systems designs of large, complex defense and commercial electronic systems. Raytheon fills the greatest number of openings with candidates who majored in electrical engineering, computer engineering, and computer science. [They] also hire graduates with the following majors for technical positions: mechanical engineering, math, aeronautical/aerospace engineering, physics, [and] material science. Raytheon recruits graduate engineering degree candidates from select universities to participate in a rotational engineering leadership development program. Finally, [they] hire candidates with majors in human resources, marketing, and finance/accounting/business for leadership development programs in support [and] functional organizations such as contracts, finance, human resources, information technology, and supply chain management."

Average Hours Worked Per Week

"Most recent college graduates are salaried positions. Hours worked vary according to individual program and the phase (proposal through detailed design and production). Employees average forty to fifty hours per week, but the greater focus is doing what is required to get the job done. Many employees enjoy a flexible work arrangement and are on a 9/80-workweek (nine-hour days for eight days and one eight-hour day in a two week period with every other Friday off)."

Percentage of Entry-level Hires Still with the Company after Three, Five, and Ten Years

After three years, 95 percent of all entry-level hires are still with the company.

Average Starting Salary

"Raytheon offers competitive salaries for new college graduates based on a number of criteria, including work location, degree level and major, academic qualifications, and work experience. Recent salary offers were $53,000 to 59,900 for technical [bachelor of science] degrees and $42,900 to $53,000 for nontechnical [bachelor of science] degrees."

Benefits Offered

"At Raytheon, we understand the importance of rewarding our employees for all they bring to the table. For a general overview of the health care, income protection, investment/retirement, and work/life benefits as well as some of the extras available to eligible Raytheon employees worldwide, please refer to our recruitment website at www.rayjobs.com/campus." Additional benefits include income protection (disability coverage, basic life insurance, accidental death and dismemberment insurance, and business travel accident insurance), investment/retirement plans (pension, savings, and investment plans, and [a] stock program), work/life (flexible work schedule, paid time off, holidays, dependent care reimbursement account, adoption assistance, employee assistance program, and business casual attire), and extras (educational assistance, internal job transfer system, relocation assistance, home and auto insurance, matching gifts, Raytheon Scholars Program, same-sex domestic partner benefits, and discounts).

Contact Information

Visit the website at www.rayjobs.com/campus.

Getting Hired

Raytheon recruits most aggressively at "twenty-six universities, nationwide; these 'strategic schools' are valued for our hiring history, potential to produce numbers of targeted graduates, and potential to produce females and minorities in our targeted degree majors. They also have research capabilities in technologies of interest to our businesses. We also actively recruit on campus at approximately 150 schools. All candidates are referred to our campus recruitment website where they can search for opportunities, complete a profile, and attach their profile to the jobs of greatest interest and match for them. This would include any candidates from schools where we may not actively recruit."

One engineer who landed a job explains how he did it: "I submitted a resume at the job fair and then was contacted by Raytheon for an on-campus interview. The on-campus interview was done with one interviewer, and it lasted about twenty minutes. It was a scenario-based interview; the interviewer would ask 'what would you do?' questions based on scenarios. Also, there were questions about my greatest accomplishments in college and what specifically useful classes/projects I had in college. After the on-campus interview, which consisted of thirty-two people from every department from the school, Raytheon invited four of us to a second round of interviews at Raytheon. In addition, there was a 'get acquainted' dinner the night before, a plant tour, and an information session before the interviews [where] we were given an overview of Raytheon, and the initial work for our security clearances was begun. After the plant tour and lunch, a second interview was held. There were two interviewers in this session, but the questions were basically the same as the on-campus interview. The interview was longer, approximately forty-five minutes, and more time was set aside to allow me to ask any questions that I had. About three weeks later, I received a job offer from Raytheon. My later understanding was that the second interview was more of a formality, and that the real cut point for getting a job offer was made during the on-campus interviews."

MONEY AND PERKS

Raytheon offers competitive salaries, so the first jobbers we surveyed saw no need to negotiate pay; they also tell us that start time and location are sometimes negotiable. Writes one, "I was given a six-month time window for when I wanted to start. The salary was not negotiable. However, the salary I was offered was $5,000 higher than any other offer I received, so there was no incentive for me to try to negotiate a higher salary. I felt the offer I was getting was more than fair." Company officials note that "salary increases are an integral part of an annual performance evaluation process. Increases are based on individual performance and company factors." Top perks include relocation allowances and the flexible work schedule. One engineer explains, "Two scenarios are possible within Raytheon: 80/9, eighty hours, four nine-hour days, taking every other Friday (or day of choice) off or 40/4, forty hours for four days. Basically, work your time and be flexible for the project, and you can make your schedule."

THE ROPES

Raytheon newbies are introduced to their new workplace through a brief orientation, which lasts anywhere between half a day and two days, depending on their placement. Writes one entry-level employee, "The initial orientation when I started was horribly boring. It was an introduction to the company, company policies, security polices, and so on. Although it was necessary, it was no fun." Some engineers report subsequently taking formal classes, but most of them tell us that the majority of their training came from their bosses. Explains one engineer, "I didn't receive any streamlined training. I was assigned to work on a project with another engineer the afternoon of my first day at work. He told me what we were working on and what he thought the next steps should be, and I basically jumped right in. I had enough theoretical and practical experience that a few questions here were all I needed to be helpful. After a few days my boss and coworkers trusted that I knew what was going on, and they started to let me suggest ideas and initiate experiments." Agrees another engineer, "Aside from a few training classes, all of which took place months after I started working, all of my training has been informal, 'ask-my-mentor' type training."

Day in the Life

Raytheon hires engineers and support staff in a variety of areas. Company representatives tell us that "New technical hires work in a wide variety of assignments ranging from production support, design upgrades, full-scale program design and development, advanced developments for concept demonstration, and pure technology development. In all cases, new grads work with experienced lead engineers, and it is common to have an additional senior engineer designated as mentor." Engineers must also be prepared to work independently; as one tells us, "When I was first hired, I had to design a graphical user interface in Matlab. I had absolutely no idea how to do this, so first I had to gather as much info as I could from the Web and books. Not many people I asked had any experience with it, so I basically had to teach myself how to do it, but that was probably a good first experience because I learned that I could do something on my own with minimal help from others." Company representatives point out that engineers have responsibilities that people might not normally anticipate, such as "the requirement to present and defend designs at a design review, develop documentation, work with tenured technicians, source parts and deal with vendors, workout at one of our 'on-site' athletic facilities, participate in a community affairs/outreach event at a local school, etc. The ability of new grads to perform well in these additional tasks is what separates successful engineers from those who become disenchanted with their role and/or Raytheon in general."

Peers

Most of the new engineers we spoke with tell us that there were "very few entry-level engineers" in their particular area, making it hard to develop a peer network. One first jobber found a solution: "A small unit of young engineers had posted emails and established a company-sponsored social group, which did help me get acquainted with other new hires. This enabled me to increase social interaction after-hours." Those who do have contact with other newbies enjoy the experience; writes one, "All of us play sports and drink together. I still have lunch every week with some of the other new guys at the other two facilities."

Moving On

Raytheon at one time lost a substantial number of first jobbers, but that has changed in recent years. Company representatives explain, "Early this decade, Raytheon lost many recent hires to the lures of very large salary increases and stock option hiring bonuses from now-defunct high tech companies. Attrition has since retreated to levels that defy statistically significant analysis." These days, most Raytheon workers are in it for the long haul. Writes one veteran, "Next year, I will have been here twenty-five years. While that sounds like a long time, it would place my tenure at fourth of five people in a small row of offices in the staffing systems and university programs office in Dallas. I've had the opportunity to do many different things during my career, from marine data collection on a seismic survey vessel in the North Sea, to technical writing, training and development, and staffing. This becomes one of the greatest strengths of a corporation the size of Raytheon: the ability of its employees to use internal job mobility to change assignments and even locations to facilitate personal career vitality. For many years, I have listened to experienced line workers, who we have assembled to share meals with new hire candidates, remark that once they had decided what they really wanted to do, all they had to do was ask."

ATTRITION

Less than 0.5 percent of first jobbers quit within a year of accepting a job at Raytheon, company representatives report.

BEST AND WORST

The best first jobber, Raytheon tells us, was "a guy hired from California Polytechnic University—San Luis Obispo with a bachelor of science degree in industrial engineering, named William Swanson. Why? He is now Raytheon chairman and chief executive officer."

REPUBLICAN NATIONAL COMMITTEE
Various Positions

THE BIG PICTURE

As an employee of the Republican National Committee (RNC), you will help solicit political donations, coordinate "get out the vote" drives, formulate the Republican platform, produce issue advertising, and devise election strategies. It's kind of like working for the Democratic National Committee, except your positions on the issues are different.

STATS

LOCATION(S) WHERE ENTRY-LEVEL EMPLOYEES WORK

Washington, DC

ENTRY-LEVEL POSITION(S) AVAILABLE

Various support staff positions are available to entry-level hires.

AVERAGE HOURS WORKED PER WEEK

New hires work forty or more hours per week.

PERCENTAGE OF ENTRY-LEVEL HIRES STILL WITH THE COMPANY AFTER THREE, FIVE, AND TEN YEARS

First jobbers typically stay for one election cycle, then use contacts made during their tenure to find other party/political jobs.

CONTACT INFORMATION

Contact your local Republican party office, via www.gop.com/contactus.

GETTING HIRED

You've got to hang around the grapevine to get a job at the RNC; at the time this book went to press, the organization didn't even have a jobs link on its website. All but one of the employees we spoke with told us that they learned about their jobs through personal contacts (the remaining first jobber, who works at GOP TV, was recruited). If you're active in the College Republican National Committee or with your state party organization, you're connected enough to find out about job opportunities at the RNC. Writes one newbie, "I found out through the Wisconsin state party. It was the perfect job for me—I wanted to move to DC to work in press and for a Republican. It had all three. Initially I passed my resume to everyone I knew at the state and national party. It was more word of mouth that helped me to get the initial interview. The interviewer just asked my background, told me what the job entailed, and I told them how I could carry out the necessary tasks. I called two weeks later to follow up, and we scheduled another meeting two days later [during which] I was hired."

Money and Perks

New hires at the RNC have some flexibility in defining their roles in the organization but find little wiggle room in negotiating start time, location, or salary. Most don't care; writes one, "I didn't put up much of a fight about anything because the job was what I wanted." Perks include "getting to help with all of the political aspects in Washington: campaign, convention, and other events," and the "exposure and contacts" employees make.

The Ropes

"There is no specific orientation process" at the RNC; it varies from hire to hire. For one newcomer, it was "one afternoon during my first week, mostly 'company' policy and insurance issues." For another, it was "a couple of hours on the first day," mostly just meeting the other staffers and getting settled in. Subsequent training is similarly informal. "I was shown around and trained by my boss's assistant, and it was 'learn as you go,'" explains one first jobber. "A guy who had held the position a year ago was very helpful," offers another. Advises a third, "Learn quickly!" The reason for this apparent lack of structure? Opined one fresh hire, "Obviously everything moves very quickly right now, including hiring and placement. Jobs develop because there is a need for the function, not because a title is empty."

Day in the Life

Support staffers at the RNC often find their days filled with administrative duties; they "answer phones, make copies, put press releases up on newswire, and handle any additional administrative tasks people have in the office. I also help plan events and communication in the office." Those who make a solid impression quickly gain more responsibility and eventually move up the organization's hierarchy. While they "spend very little time with high-level executives personally," it's "not uncommon to see the chairman roaming around downstairs talking to my bosses." Our first jobber at GOP TV has a radically different itinerary; he "coordinates reporters and crews, daily news feeds, and live-shot requests, liaises with capitol and presidential administration officials to plan and set up interviews for news and special feature programming, creates pitches and coordinates outreach and pitching efforts on behalf of GOP TV with national and local media," and makes preparations for coverage of the 2004 convention.

Peers

RNC staffers tell us that "there are many opportunities to meet other coworkers. We do have happy hours, for example." Writes one entry-level employee, "There is a good social scene and overall respect and camaraderie. RNC staff members are wonderful people!" They don't distinguish between first jobbers and more senior staff, though; there's "nothing special because we are first jobbers."

Moving on

Just about every RNC staffer we spoke with said he or she plans to move on when the 2004 election cycle ends. All of them will try to move onto other jobs within the world of party politics.

RR DONNELLEY
Various Positions

THE BIG PICTURE

RR Donnelley got into the printing business 140 years ago, and while it remains one of the nation's largest printers of books, catalogs, magazines, dictionaries, and retail inserts. Today the company also delivers information in all manner of virtual formats. With more than 30,000 employees in over 200 locations, RR Donnelley offers a wide variety of entry-level positions in marketing, sales, engineering, manufacturing, finance, and human resources.

STATS

LOCATION(S) WHERE ENTRY-LEVEL EMPLOYEES WORK

The main office is in Chicago, IL. Numerous regional offices are located throughout the United States and around the world.

ENTRY-LEVEL POSITION(S) AVAILABLE

Various entry-level positions; College Reserve Training Program

BENEFITS OFFERED

Employees can choose their medical plan, dental benefit program, health care flex spending account, and dependent care plan. Additional benefits include life insurance, accident insurance, disability, 401(k), adoption assistance, and tuition reimbursement.

CONTACT INFORMATION

Visit the website at www.rrdonnelley.com.

GETTING HIRED

Most first jobbers we spoke with at RR Donnelley found their positions through the career services offices of their colleges. Others discovered their jobs while interning for the company. Interviewing is a multistage process; writes one newbie, "My first interview was on the college campus, where I interviewed with a person who held the position I was interviewing for. I could relate to her and her description of the training program; the position and the work environment made me even more interested. The second interview was at RR Donnelley headquarters in the department where I work now. I interviewed with three different managers and had a lunch with the vice president of the department and another analyst. Everybody I interviewed with was very friendly and open about the company and the position. I liked the diversity of people I met, and I felt like I would fit in with the rest of the department. A few days later I received a call to come in and have lunch with a manager and a supervisor—people I did not get to meet during my second interview. They just confirmed my strong feelings about this position and the company in general. The next week I received the offer letter and accepted the position."

MONEY AND PERKS

RR Donnelley offers excellent compensation and benefits, so negotiating terms of employment, as one typical first jobber tells us, "never really became an issue. I was eager to start working right when I was done with school. The date that was assigned as the first day fit well with my schedule, so no negotiation was needed. The location was great—downtown Chicago—and the pay was competitive." Employees also see the benefits of "working at the corporate location with such a large company; it allows me to observe senior management of a Fortune 500 company and also be exposed to many different facets of business (finance, accounting, marketing, legal, operations)." They also tout the company's stock purchase plan.

THE ROPES

The formal College Reserve Training Program, according to one participant from the credit department, "is great. It is a very structured twelve month schedule, at the end of which you 'graduate' and are promoted to analyst. On the first day, you are presented with a calendar that lists meetings and training sessions to learn all there is to know about the company and the department. After six months of learning basic functions and practices, your responsibilities escalate. You have the responsibilities of a normal credit analyst; however, you work closely with a colleague who oversees all of your work. Then after the full twelve months, you are on your own as an analyst." Not all first jobbers start in the program, however; some come aboard as conventional hires. For many of them "there is no official training." Reports one such employee, "I was shown and assigned work, and if I had any problems or questions, there were several people that could assist me." RR Donnelley orientation "takes only about one hour. You meet with your human resources representative and go through the employee fringe benefits. Other human resources policies are [on the] Web so you can look at them whenever you like."

DAY IN THE LIFE

"The really great thing about the [College Reserve] Training Program," one participant tells us, "is that the new hires are gradually introduced to the workload. As I became more comfortable with certain job functions and performed them well, something new was introduced. I had the opportunity to really understand what my responsibilities entail and how to provide knowledgeable decisions. I am now in the training phase where I have the responsibilities of an analyst, but I am working closely with colleagues." The program offers "a perfect balance. There is never a dull moment, but at the same time I rarely feel overwhelmed. If issues arise, I have someone to go to for answers." First jobbers outside the program describe an experience more typical of any new job; explains a tax analyst, "I started my new job right before the state returns procedure began. I was assigned several returns. I was able to complete them with a bit of assistance. It's challenging work because payments or returns have to be in on time, or penalties could be assigned to the corporation. If a requirement is not completed it can also affect future grants or audits from the state." Entry-level employees in all areas can participate in mentoring programs.

PEERS

"RR Donnelley is an older company; the average RR Donnelley experience in my department is over twenty years, with a couple approaching forty years," a typical first jobber tells us. As a result, there is not a huge community of young employees; there is, however, a strong sense of community within specific departments fostered by "planned outings with the department to enhance camaraderie, as well as unplanned events like going to a White Sox game with other members of the department. There is an upbeat feeling in our department. It seems like everyone gets along well."

ATTRITION

As is the case at other companies during a suffering economy, "there are always people concerned about job security" at RR Donnelley. Also, "being at the corporate location [Chicago] means the presence of senior management tends to stress some employees." These pressures occasionally drive employees to seek employment elsewhere.

SCHLUMBERGER

Field Engineer and Research, Development, and Manufacturing Engineer

THE BIG PICTURE

Are you an engineer seeking entry into the world of bubblin' crude? You know, black gold? Texas tea? If so, here's your invite. Join Schlumberger, "a recognized technology leader providing products, services, and solutions to the oil and gas exploration and production (E&P) industry."

STATS

LOCATION(S) WHERE ENTRY-LEVEL EMPLOYEES WORK

"We recruit where we work worldwide, in approximately 100 countries, virtually everywhere you find oil and gas. In the United States, approximately 30 percent of the field engineers hired will start employment in an international location. Most RDM hires work in one of the United States facilities."

AVERAGE NUMBER OF APPLICATIONS EACH YEAR

The company receives roughly 4,000 applications for the FE position and 1,500 for the RDM position (both in the United States).

AVERAGE NUMBER HIRED OVER THE LAST TEN YEARS

The company hires 200 FEs and 50 RDMs, yearly.

ENTRY-LEVEL POSITION(S) AVAILABLE

"Schlumberger mostly hires engineers and technical professionals. The two main types of positions are for field engineers (FE) and research, development, and manufacturing (RDM) engineers."

AVERAGE HOURS WORKED PER WEEK

"Field engineers do not work a typical eight-to-five office schedule; the jobs often have long shifts (more than twelve hours per day) and/or odd hours. Time off is not on the normal weekend cycle; there is either a planned schedule (something like nine days on, three days off) or a minimum amount of days off per month (four). Research, development, and manufacturing engineers have a more typical schedule, with longer hours during peak project times, an average of forty to sixty hours per week, with weekends off."

AVERAGE STARTING SALARY

FEs earn $52,000, plus operating bonuses. RDMs start at $50,000, and MS Design Engineers average $55,000.

For health care coverage, Schlumberger offers flexible spending options for medical, dental, and vision care. Additional benefits include 401(k), pension, retiree medical, discounted stock purchase plans, and annual vacation time.

CONTACT INFORMATION

Visit the website at www.slb.com/careers.

GETTING HIRED

Schlumberger recruits "on forty-nine United States campuses, including most of the top engineering schools. Students from other schools are open to apply through our online system and many come to us through the referrals of current employees." The company seeks a complement of skills in its new hires, including technical aptitude, problem-solving skills, self-motivation, and interpersonal skills. First interviews are conducted by phone or on campus; subsequent interviews are held at company offices. The company notes that "because the FE job especially is quite different than the average engineering job on offer, attendance at the pre-interview information session the night before is critical." A field engineer reports that her first interview was with a recruiter on campus: "Questions asked ranged from how I handle stress to what activities I was involved in. About a week after the initial interview, I was contacted [and told] that I was a candidate for a second interview. Two months later, I was given a list of interview dates, and asked to pick the most convenient ones for me. It was a two-day interview, including a tour of one of the training centers, an overview of the company and positions available, and all of it was done in a relaxed manner."

MONEY AND PERKS

Field engineers "are promoted two separate times [during the training program] before finally being promoted to general field engineer. Each time the base salary increases incrementally. Each service segment also has an operational bonus structure based on its service delivery model. It can be highly dependent on work location and operational activity, but in general there is extremely high growth potential in the second and third years as the engineer assumes higher levels of responsibility." Research, development, and manufacturing engineers receive "bonuses and promotions linked to performance." New recruits tell us that "the job offer is generally negotiable in terms of start date. However the actual location, salary, and position are set." Perks include a new laptop, extra allowances for engineers placed overseas, and bonus pay.

THE ROPES

Orientation at Schlumberger lasts for ten days. Here's how one engineer described the experience: "The orientation process began in Houston for initial training into the Schlumberger lifestyle. Beginning on a Tuesday, the new hires spent five days covering company history, IT issues and setup, introductions to available resources for seeking help in anything, an introduction to the oil field setup, and issued proper personal protective equipment and a drug test. The next five days were spent in driver training near Tulsa, Oklahoma." Other components of orientation include "health and hygiene training from a certified Schlumberger instructor and alcohol and drug awareness training from an outside contractor." Training is an ongoing process throughout an engineer's tenure with the company; offers one worker, "I have spent over nine months in Schlumberger Training schools since coming to work for the company."

DAY IN THE LIFE

Research, development, and manufacturing positions frequently require an advanced degree; most offer entry-level positions as "sustaining engineers, responsible for sustaining and improving a variety of projects," gradually earning more responsibility and gaining more independence over time. For field engineers, the position that is more often available to recent college grads, "there is not much of a typical day." One new hire says, "When I was first hired, I was assigned a supervisor to shadow and learn from, so I was on call with his schedule, which meant working about seventy hours a week. On any given day, I would be on call. When I was called in, I had an hour to report to the office and prepare for the job. Over time, I have been given an exponential amount of responsibility. In four months I've progressed from being an observer on the job to nearly running the entire job when on location." Adds another FE, "I had to get dirty (every day!) with the operators and work like an operator to learn and appreciate the equipment and the operators' job responsibilities before I could sit in the big seat and run a job (you don't get as dirty there)." Field engineers love "the early responsibility, in-depth training, and the ability to really put engineering theory into application. And over the longer term, the diversity of career opportunities is really the most attractive aspect. We call it 'borderless careers,' and it means people have the option to move fairly fluidly between businesses, functions, and locations."

PEERS

Contact with other field engineers is enforced by the isolation of their work environment. Writes one, "I work offshore, therefore I live, eat, sleep, and work two weeks at a time with the same people. They become family and great friends." Agrees another, "There is a good amount of contact with other first jobbers. There are two other people who fall into this category [where I work]. As far as after-hours social interaction, we get together when we can, but that time is limited. At work, we spend some time together depending on how the rotations work out." Off the rigs, peer-to-peer contact at Schlumberger "depends on the location. Some new hires spend a lot of time together at work and outside of work and some do not. I spend time with peers outside of work fairly seldom. We spend so much time together at work that I try to spend time with other friends or family [on] my off time."

MOVING ON

Those who leave Schlumberger early "will [most likely enter] completely different industries. Those who stay on and gain a bit more experience will often go to operators (oil and gas companies) and to a lesser extent our competitors and other oil field services companies." Most people view Schlumberger as a good place to build a career. As one field engineer tells us, "If I have the opportunity to leave the company for an interesting position [that] I feel I can do well in, then I will. However, I will not leave intentionally to work for another service company. I would like to continue my career here if the opportunities within the company allow me that opportunity."

ATTRITION

Attrition rates are relatively high for field engineers; about one in five can't handle the long hours, the stress, and the separation from family and friends. As one field engineer puts it, "The first few that come to mind are the hours, schedules, and locations. We work twenty-four hours a day, seven days a week, and we do not stop for holidays. You do *not* have a schedule to follow and almost all locations are remote. You don't see many oil rigs in tourist-type locations." Research, development, and manufacturing engineers, who work under more conventional conditions, are much less likely to quit.

BEST AND WORST

Good first jobbers "learn early on how to strike a good balance between their work lives and their personal lives. A candidate who thrives in the face of challenge and takes an objective view of the long-term prospects will generally do very well." Failures "tend to be those who are less prepared for the transition into full-time job independence."

SHERWIN-WILLIAMS COMPANY
Management Trainee Program

THE BIG PICTURE

Sherwin-Williams, one of the nation's leading names in paint, painting supplies, wallpaper, and chemical coatings, offers college grads a thorough training program that transforms them from eager greenhorns into store managers in one brief but intense year.

STATS

LOCATION(S) WHERE ENTRY-LEVEL EMPLOYEES WORK

Sherwin-Williams has 2,700 stores throughout North America.

AVERAGE NUMBER HIRED OVER LAST TEN YEARS

The company hires between 450 and 500 people per year.

ENTRY-LEVEL POSITION(S) AVAILABLE

New hires work as management trainees.

AVERAGE HOURS WORKED PER WEEK

New hires work forty-four hours per week.

AVERAGE STARTING SALARY

New hires earn a $30,000 base salary (higher in metro markets), plus quarterly bonus.

BENEFITS OFFERED

Sherwin-Williams offers various choices in company-paid health insurance (with small employee co-payments), dental, and eye care. Additional benefits include a stock savings plan [401(k)] with company match, company-paid pension plan, tuition aid, sickness and accident leave, paid holidays, and vacation.

CONTACT INFORMATION

Visit www.sherwin.com, click "Careers," and look for the map of the United States. Click on the part of the map that interests you, and the recruiter for that geography will be identified.

GETTING HIRED

With the job market as tight as it has been the past few years, candidates have been taking increasingly novel approaches to distinguishing themselves from their fellow candidates. One successful hire at Sherwin-Williams recalls, "I focused on my cover letter, knowing that whoever read it would continue to my resume if I conveyed intelligence, structure, and personality, which are vital in a sales position. I sent my resume to the headquarters, and it made its way to the human resources director, who was the first person to interview me. I sent a shoe wrapped nicely in a box with a note on top that read 'Thank you for letting me get my foot in the door.' Since the interview process can be nerve-wracking, the strong cover letter and the ice-breaking shoe helped me feel a little calmer and more confident." Once your foot is in the door, interviewing at Sherwin-Williams is a three-stage procedure. Explains one who survived all three stages, "During my first interview with human resources, I felt the tone to be very professional but not too rigid. I was impressed that the interviewer was selling the company to me as much as I wanted to sell myself. He asked me questions about how I had handled situations in the past concerning customers and about setting and achieving goals and multitasking. His questions were all positive and directed toward my past work and school experiences. He explained to me the path I would take both with the interview process, and upon being hired, how the MTP [Management Training Program] worked in order to receive proper training. Following this interview I met with the district manager of the area where I would start and finally with the vice president of sales of the same division. The second interview had the same tone but had more specific questions applicable to the job and the management training program. The third interview felt like more of a formality and a get-to-know the company interview. During this interview, I was officially offered the job."

MONEY AND PERKS

At Sherwin-Williams, "All employees receive annual merit increases, plus bonuses. At such time, a trainee is promoted to manager or representative (about one year after being hired), there is a substantial promotional increase, [and] bonus potential increases threefold." Start date and location can be negotiable, if the company has numerous openings at the time of hiring. Salary is not negotiable. Most first jobbers agree that the best perks are "the paid vacation time and the 401(k)."

THE ROPES

New management trainees spend their first six weeks on the job "in a training store learning the basics of the business. The trainee is provided with videos and literature to help familiarize them with benefits, policies, and procedures. The training store manager is specifically trained in training techniques and is compensated, in part, on the success of the trainees. It is the responsibility of the training store manager to orient the trainee, introduce them to employees and customers, and ensure that they are familiar with policies and procedures and are aware of the resources available to them as new employees. After six weeks in a training store, trainees participate in one week of classroom training at their division training center. The third phase of training entails being assigned to a store as an assistant manager." Writes one former trainee, "The entire orientation process lasted about six months. During this time I completed courses that helped with all aspects of the job, including product knowledge, quality control, financial reports, managing employees, and time management. I also worked in several different stores. This helped me not only get to know the people in my area but also the market. The START (Store Training and Reference Tool) courses and books, floating around and working in different stores with different managers, and a week of training at the headquarters helped me to develop during the orientation process. One of the greatest things about this job is that you learn something everyday. After six years I still draw upon things I learned during the first six months, and I continue to learn more every day."

DAY IN THE LIFE

A current management trainee tells us, "When I was first hired, my biggest responsibility was to focus on training, learning all I could about my own duties as an assistant manager as well as my employees. I needed to know where the stock went and how to put it away, how to order, how to delegate tasks, and what tasks needed to be done; doing everything from mopping the floor, to filling orders, to helping customers find what they need for their project was included in a typical day; understanding the paperwork and what needed to be done was important so that I could learn how to prioritize and manage my time on the job. Another great thing about this position is that there are not many 'typical' days. Every day is different with different tasks to complete and new things to learn." Notes one former trainee who has since moved onto a management position, "At first, product knowledge is the toughest part of the job. However, over time your knowledge in products grows, and you then have to start learning your customers. You learn that each customer is completely different from the next. In this industry, you may see a person once a year or twice a day. The goal is to know what each customer needs no matter how often you see them." As time progresses, trainees "take over the tasks of the assistant manager. These tasks include making collection calls, fulfilling orders, staffing the store, and managing accounts payable."

PEERS

One Sherwin-Williams management trainee says, "[We] make lifelong friends during the management training program week [at division headquarters]. They are from different parts of the country, and we still keep in touch. I see them all once a year during the National Sales Meeting in Nashville, Tennessee." Once back at their jobs, however, they don't see other trainees regularly; explains one, "Since I was the only MTP in my district, I had very little exposure to other people throughout the country in my position. However, other employees throughout the district were very welcoming to me. I have had many opportunities to interact with other employees on a social basis as well as business. The mix between the two has made my first six months very enjoyable." First jobbers tell us that Sherwin-Williams has a congenial work vibe; notes one, "Friends are easy to make at Sherwin-Williams. Each day it gets hectic and chaotic. By busting your butt and getting the job done, everyone is brought together as a team. My best friend works at Sherwin-Williams!"

MOVING ON

Sherwin-Williams carefully tracks former employees. Although employee turnover is low (in the single digits), company officials tell us that out of all who leave, three-quarters of people leave for other job offers, about one in eight leave for personal reasons, and about one in ten leave for other reasons." Company representatives say that the vast majority of people leave to "start their own business, take a sales job in another industry, become a painting contractor, or go back to school." Those who stay say they like the fact that many different opportunities are available within the company. Writes one, "Sherwin-Williams allows for its employees to wear many different hats. If I wanted to get into the marketing side, I could choose to go to marketing. If I wanted to go into corporate management, I could have that opportunity. The fact is, with Sherwin-Williams you have the opportunities to grow into the position that would best fit you."

ATTRITION

Some folks can't hack it in Sherwin-Williams' Management Trainee Program; says one who could, "I found, and still find, that those people who drop out of the program or are dissatisfied are not ready to work. Most people were expecting to put on a tie and sit behind a desk after college. I felt like my strong work ethic set me apart from them, and I enjoyed my success." The job is certainly demanding; as one trainee tells us, "I guess the most common complaint that I have heard is being frustrated about not being able to learn fast enough. What is interesting is that I have never heard anyone complain about the program itself, but only complain about their own ability or inability to learn the products."

BEST AND WORST

The most successful first jobber ever, Sherwin-Williams tells us, is "John Morikis, who entered the program in 1984, and is now president of our stores division, a more than $3 billion business."

STARWOOD HOTELS AND RESORTS
Various Management Training and other Entry-level Positions

THE BIG PICTURE

Starwood Hotels and Resorts Worldwide, Inc., "one of the leading hotel and leisure companies in the world," is the proprietor of such world-famous facilities as St. Regis, the Luxury Collection, Sheraton, and Westin. Although a relative newcomer to the field, Starwood is a major player, with entry-level positions available in a broad range of areas including the coveted and more competetive positions at corporate headquarters as well as on the front lines at Starwood's various hotels.

STATS

LOCATION(S) WHERE ENTRY-LEVEL EMPLOYEES WORK

Almost anywhere. Starwood has more than 700 properties worldwide.

AVERAGE NUMBER HIRED OVER THE LAST TEN YEARS

"While Starwood has a centralized college relations program through which approximately 30 college graduates enter, college recruiting is not the primary way people join Starwood. But many permanent entry-level positions exist for college graduates."

ENTRY-LEVEL POSITION(S) AVAILABLE

Line-level, supervisory, coordinator/administrative, assistant manager, and manager positions are available in the following departments: sales, accounting, guest services, catering/convention services, rooms, food and beverage, six sigma, and other corporate management positions in IT, legal, hotel management, real estate, and revenue management.

AVERAGE HOURS WORKED PER WEEK

People can work thirty-five, forty, and 47.5 hours per week, depending on title, corporate/property, and union status.

PERCENTAGE OF ENTRY-LEVEL HIRES STILL WITH THE COMPANY AFTER THREE, FIVE, AND TEN YEARS

"Starwood is only five years old, so long-term numbers are not available."

AVERAGE STARTING SALARY

"[Salary] starts at $10 [per hour] for interns and goes up from there. [The] typical entry-level management [salary] is [from] $32,000 to $36,000, depending on region and hotel. We have a very competitive compensation structure and continually compare our structure against our competitors and other industries."

BENEFITS OFFERED

Starwood offers all standard benefits, including medical, dental, and vision insurance. Additional benefits include paid vacation, discounted hotel rooms, tuition assistance, savings and retirement plans, business travel and accident insurance, employee stock-purchase plan, long- and short-term disability insurance, employee assistance program, adoption assistance, life insurance, and accidental death coverage.

CONTACT INFORMATION

Visit the website at www.starwoodcareer.com or email collegerelations@starwoodhotels.com.

GETTING HIRED

For those seeking corporate jobs with Starwood, "a big plus is an early, demonstrated interest in the hotel and hospitality business through a hotel-school education—summer internships in hotels, resorts, and other customer-focused businesses." Hospitality, Starwood representatives note, "is very much a hands-on business, and we look for business professionals who also know how to work with customers, have a guest-service ethic, and also know how to lead those who serve the guest." Because of the high demand for corporate jobs with Starwood, the company "only recruits for the small-management training and internship programs from a core group of ten hotel schools and, currently, two business schools. Students from other schools are encouraged to contact hotels local to their homes or schools to inquire about available internships [and entry-level positions] throughout the year." Reports one successful hire, "I was explicit in my cover letter and stated that this was the job I wanted, it was my top choice, and if given an offer, I'd accept on the spot. I think this really helped my application." The hiring process for property positions is less formal; one accounts-payable employee who works at a hotel learned of the position through a college professor, sent her cover letter and resume, and underwent a "very laid-back, care free" interview. No matter what position you're applying for, all respondents agree that your cover letter and resume are important.

MONEY AND PERKS

Starwood representatives advise, "The hospitality industry in general does not have the reputation for very high entry-level salaries but, with time, it is known for great bonuses, the opportunity to work in different locations in the country (or world) throughout one's career, and the opportunity to be associated with a very old, yet also very exciting industry." The best fringe benefit, first jobbers here agree, are "the Starwood HotRates!!! Cheap five-star hotel rooms. I'd never be able to travel like this right out of college, but I stay at the top hotels in the world for next to nothing."

THE ROPES

Participants in Starwood's corporate management training program go through a number of rotations, allowing them to learn all the different responsibilities within a certain area of the company. Explain company representatives, "The program is a 12-week rotational training through all departments of the hotel with a concentration in one of three areas: food and beverage, rooms, or sales. At the completion of the program, each participant is placed in a position of responsibility at the same hotel where the management training program was completed." The experience starts with "an informal orientation process. For me, it entailed one day of touring our hotels in New York, NY and a couple of days learning about how Starwood's systems work and what each group does within STARS [Starwood Technology and Revenue Systems, the program in which this employee was enrolled]." The newbies we spoke with agree that "most of the real learning comes on the job." For positions at Starwood's properties, the orientation and training process is less prescribed and is specific to the position. For example, one such employee took classes on how her hotel "stands out from other [Starwood] properties." Another respondent took "classes pertaining to customer service and guest satisfaction, computer programs, or property management systems as well as brand standards."

DAY IN THE LIFE

Corporate management trainees agree that "the learning curve is pretty steep. You start right away on projects. A typical day includes some meetings, preparation for an upcoming presentation, and a dialogue with my boss around the issues that have come up and how we need to tackle them." Contact with Starwood higher-ups is fairly frequent; explains one employee in strategy, "We are always invited to meetings where we have done work to support the conclusions. We are encouraged to speak at meetings." Employees at Starwood properties seem less overwhelmed by their day-to-day tasks; for one employee in accounting, it is "pretty straight forward. I work from nine to five." A Whatever/Whenever agent—an aptly named position—agrees: "With each passing day, my resposibilities increase."

PEERS

The first jobbers we spoke with describe a pretty subdued peer network at Starwood. One person working at a hotel tells us, "We have special cocktail time within our property once [a] month, which allows us to interact with people from other departments, and we spend time together, like one hour, including lunch break. It all depends what kind of event we go to, but generally three hours in a week." People at corporate headquarters tell us that "the groups here are pretty small. There's not really an after-work scene, since the main office is in White Plains and most of us live in the city. It becomes difficult to coordinate and motivate when we commute. But we get together for special events and whatnot."

MOVING ON

Starwood does not track data on former employees. People we spoke with still work at Starwood and plan to remain there. They tell us that those with complaints "sometimes have problems with their specific bosses" and "wish there would be a little more training at the beginning."

TARGET CORPORATION
Various Positions

THE BIG PICTURE

Although most of the country regards Target as "the new kid on the block"—especially in relation to its downscale rival, Wal-Mart—this giant discount department store chain has actually been in existence since 1962. The company traces its roots back even further, to the Dayton Dry Goods Company, founded in 1903. Throughout its history, Target and its affiliates have earned a solid reputation for both contributing to its host communities and creating a hospitable work environment for its army of employees.

STATS

LOCATION(S) WHERE ENTRY-LEVEL EMPLOYEES WORK

Corporate hires work in Minneapolis, MN; the company also owns Marshall Field's (Minneapolis, MN) and Mervyn's (Hayward, CA). All of these companies have stores in many cities.

AVERAGE NUMBER HIRED OVER THE LAST TEN YEARS

Altogether, Target and its affiliated retailers employ over 280,000 people in forty-seven states.

ENTRY-LEVEL POSITION(S) AVAILABLE

Target offers entry-level positions in asset protection/loss prevention, direct marketing/e-commerce, distribution and logistics, finance, food service management, grocery leadership, human resources, marketing, merchandising/buying/planning, pharmacy, property development, store leadership, Target financial services, Target technology services, and trend merchandising/product design.

BENEFITS OFFERED

"[Benefits include] dollar for dollar (up to 5 percent of your salary) matching of our 401(k); company discount at all stores; savings on prescriptions, even discounts on airfare, car rentals, and hotels; and flexible work schedules. Each of the Target Corporation operating companies has specific benefits programs, but they share a focus on flexibility, family, and financial security."

CONTACT INFORMATION

Apply online at target.com/target_group/careers/jobs_main.jhtml.

GETTING HIRED

Target employees caution that "Target considers only resumes that are submitted to www.target.com and www.monster.com online; there's a Team-Member Referral program, but anyone referred to the company through a current employee still has to apply online." An exception is made for people who are recruited at campus events; students must submit resumes directly to the campus career center; learn more about these events at the Target website. The interview process "is the same style used by many other employers. First, there is a phone interview [conducted] by a human resources recruiter, then a formal interview with the human resources recruiter; afterward applicants have an interview with two of the people who would be managing [them], followed by an informal meeting with the national head of [their] department. The tone of the interviews are serious but friendly." This particular applicant "was asked job-related questions such as: 'Describe your past job experience. Why do you think you are right for this position?' Other questions that were also asked were geared toward finding out about my personality." Notes one first jobber, "One thing about Target—the company places a very high value on education. No matter how well you do your job, if you don't have a college degree, you will only go so far in the company. Many people want to advance but can't because they didn't go to college. Although many entry-level jobs seem mundane to someone with a college degree, you have to start somewhere—and you'll move up if you stick it out, demonstrate a work ethic, and have a degree." Target seeks "a diverse workforce to reflect the communities we serve."

MONEY AND PERKS

Most of the terms of employment at Target are negotiable, first jobbers tell us; as in all such cases, the more you bring to the table—and the less competition there is for jobs (such as when the economy is strong)—the better chance you have of negotiating a higher starting salary. As employees move forward, "It's hard to get a pay increase at any time other than at annual reviews. We're reviewed twice a year—the annual is in March." Top fringe benefits include "store discounts," of course, as well as "a cell phone and free meals" for those who travel on business.

THE ROPES

All Target employees start their tenure with the company with a half-day orientation class. Writes one first jobber, "It told you a lot about Target, what is acceptable (protocol, etc). A lot was geared toward harassment, benefits of Target, what they're trying to do to improve Target, and its history." In many areas of the company, subsequent training is handled by fellow employees on a "need to know" basis. Explains one newbie, "My training was conducted by the three individuals [who] I work directly with. Since my position was open they all helped to train me on the procedures, day-to-day activities, [and] all of the technical equipment that I would be working with." Some formal classes in technical areas, such as computers, are required of new workers in certain areas; these classes constitute part of the employee's formal work day.

Day in the Life

First jobbers work in all areas of the giant Target world, which encompasses nearly 300,000 employees. We spoke with first jobbers in many different departments doing a wide variety of jobs. All of them say that they quickly assumed important responsibilities, and that they felt their managers and bosses offered them sufficient support to get their jobs done. According to company representatives, workers benefit from "a fun and challenging work environment," one that rewards "performance-driven risk-takers."

Peers

Of the entry-level employees in several different areas and functionalities at Target, all of them agree that at Target "people are really friendly. The company is full of young twenty-somethings." Writes one, "We do things outside of work. We're going bowling tonight, for example." Notes another, "All of us get along and do happy hours regularly. Target has several touch football teams in the fall and baseball teams in the summer." Many do volunteer work together as well; reports one newbie, "Target does a *ton* for the community. I volunteer once a week at a local school, just reading to kids. There are always ways to get involved in the community, and that's been a good way to meet Target people who aren't in my department (and to get out of the office for awhile to do something helpful and fun)."

Moving On

Target did not respond to our request for information about former employees, and the first jobbers we spoke with have no plans of leaving the company. Some tell us that a few of their peers leave to return to graduate school; others pursue what they consider more interesting opportunities with other companies.

TEACH FOR AMERICA
Corps Member/Teacher

THE BIG PICTURE

Teach for America (TFA) finds recent college graduates to teach in understaffed, overburdened public schools serving low income communities across the country. If you're looking for a challenge and can't see yourself as a Marine, TFA might be for you. As one TFA alum says, "I knew that this was going to be the toughest job I could imagine . . . but boy am I glad I did it. [It was the] best three years and best first job I could have hoped for."

STATS

LOCATION(S) WHERE ENTRY-LEVEL EMPLOYEES WORK

20 urban and rural areas where they are needed most: Atlanta, GA; Baltimore, MD; Bay Area, CA; Chicago, IL; Detroit, MI; Houston, TX; Los Angeles, CA; South Louisiana, Miami, FL; Mississippi Delta; New Jersey; New Mexico; Greater New Orleans, LA; New York City, NY; North Carolina; Philadelphia, PA; Phoenix, AZ; Rio Grande Valley, TX; St. Louis, MO; Washington, DC

AVERAGE NUMBER OF APPLICATIONS EACH YEAR

The organization received 16,000 applications for the 2004 school year, and officials report that "over the last few years, applications for Teach For America have increased dramatically."

AVERAGE NUMBER HIRED OVER THE LAST TEN YEARS

TFA has hired approximately 1,700 people in each of the last two years. The organization anticipates 2,000 placements for 2004.

ENTRY-LEVEL POSITION(S) AVAILABLE

New hires work as corps members/teachers (available to recent college graduates).

AVERAGE HOURS WORKED PER WEEK

"In addition to the [more than] forty hours a week [that] corps members spend [in the classroom], they spend extra hours on the weekend and at nighttime preparing lesson plans, tutoring students, and/or attending graduate school."

PERCENTAGE OF ENTRY-LEVEL HIRES STILL WITH THE ORGANIZATION AFTER THREE, FIVE, AND TEN YEARS

"Approximately 60 percent of our alumni remain in education beyond their two-year commitment."

AVERAGE STARTING SALARY

Salary depends on the school district for which the corps member works. "Average salaries range from $22,000 to $41,000, depending on the region."

BENEFITS OFFERED

Benefits also vary by region, "however, corps members generally receive the same health benefits and insurance as other beginning teachers." Additional benefits include stummer training institute room and board paid for by Teach For America and financial aid packages that range from $1,000 to $5,000, based on demonstrated need and the cost of living in an applicant's assigned region.

CONTACT INFORMATION

To request admissions information for the 2002 corps, email admissions@teachforamerica.org. For staff positions, contact Kristie Woll, human resources associate, at woll@teachforamerica.org.

GETTING HIRED

Teach for America accepts applications through its website, www.teachforamerica.org. Once the selection committee has reviewed the initial application, it "invites the most promising applicants to participate in a day-long interview, which includes a sample teaching lesson, a group discussion, and a personal interview." One corps member advises, "The interview process is intense and time consuming. Once you have been asked to interview with TFA, you are required to create a five-minute lesson [plan] that you must teach to fellow applicants; this lesson is subject to their questions and critiques. There are also many roundtable discussions during the day of your interview." The final interview is conducted one-on-one by a TFA staffer. Recounts one program participant, "I have heard horror stories about people being grilled; this wasn't, however, my experience. The staff is looking for people who will ultimately persevere in difficult situations, and they want to make sure that each applicant will before supporting his or her application."

MONEY AND PERKS

Teach for America corps members "are paid directly by the school districts for which they work, [so] salaries and salary increases vary by school district." Corps members tell us that salary and start time were "not really negotiable. Maybe subject area [was]. Most folks knew this going in and were up for it." As for placement, "You are able to suggest where you would like to be placed in the country. TFA does consider your preferences. However, they must also adhere to the needs of the various districts." Fringe benefits are mostly nonmaterial and include "sleeping well at night knowing that you're making life a little more bearable for your students" and "the smile that the students would give me every morning as they greeted me, the gleam of understanding in a student's eye when they 'get it,' the look of pride in parents' eyes when seeing their child's accomplishments, the energy and motivation in the classroom when all students are involved in their learning, the satisfaction of making difference in these children's lives, take your pick!"

THE ROPES

Training for TFA corps members is rigorous. Writes one teacher, "We go through what is called 'institute,' which is a five-week training. It is now held in three cities and is a very intense and overwhelming training to create teachers out of newly graduated college students. It was a wonderful way to realize that we were all integral parts of a national corps and also a way to get a great deal of training in a relatively short amount of time." According to organization representatives, "A typical day of our training institute is full of activities designed to help corps members progress quickly as teachers. In the morning and early afternoons of the institute, corps members teach in a summer school program. In the afternoons and evenings, they participate in a full schedule of discussions, workshops, and other professional development activities with a faculty of exceptional corps members, alumni, and other experienced educators." The final stage of training is called "induction," during which "corps members learn about local, historical, social and political dynamics that may impact their students' academic experience and their schools' culture." As one Louisiana corps member explains, it means immersion in "Zydeco music, food, schools, students, teachers, neighborhoods, and parents of students."

DAY IN THE LIFE

Teach for America corps members are teachers, and like most teachers, they work long, difficult hours. Their responsibilities and tasks vary according to grade, subject, and students' level of ability. One TFA corps member described a typical day this way: "I would get to school at 6:30 AM to start school at 7:08 AM. I would prepare my classroom during my off-hour first period for the day, organizing lesson materials and arranging the seats according to the activity. I would teach for the next five periods with a thirty-minute lunch hour in between (eating with a co-teacher and two faithful lunchtime students). During seventh hour I would reorganize my room from the day's events, take a ten-minute break, and begin to prepare for the next day. I got into the habit of not leaving my classroom until all work was completed; I could be there late into the evening on many occasions." The goal is "to attain significant academic gains for students," a challenge even under the best of circumstances and doubly tough in the schools that typically hire corps members.

PEERS

"There is a great deal of camaraderie among TFA-ers," participants in the program tell us. "The support received from the corps member down the hall who taught the same students I did, my roommate, and corps neighbors was critical to my success." Explains another, "I met some of the most intelligent, passionate, innovative, socially conscious, motivated, empathetic, and just amazing people while in TFA. It was refreshing to find people [who] can talk about the state of education in our country on a Friday night and not feel like dorks!"

Moving On

Teach for America representatives report, "Approximately 60 percent of our alumni remain in education beyond their two-year commitment, while 40 percent go on to other fields such as law, business, medicine, and politics." Said a typical graduate of the program, "I fulfilled my commitment and discovered that my future was with education. I found I had a passion for teaching mathematics and was appalled with the number of teachers and students that I found had deep-rooted 'math phobia.' Thus, I just completed my master's of science in mathematics education and have started a PhD program in the hopes of becoming a professor. My intention is that in being a professor [I will help] future elementary teachers to love to teach math."

Attrition

According to the organization, "Between 85 and 90 percent of TFA-ers complete their two-year commitment." The others leave, according to one corps member, because "teaching can be tough and isn't for everyone. People tend to sometimes feel isolated and overwhelmed and not take full advantage of the network available to them." Another corps member adds, "Some of the locations and schools that Teach for America places corps members in are really difficult schools. The reality of our educational systems is that there are some schools where classrooms may have [over] thirty-five students, small cramped spaces (sometimes former closets), not enough books to go around, no air conditioning, students who have fallen [so far] through the cracks that they no longer care about their learning, students who come to school hungry and tired because their home environment is lacking, and an administration [that] gets caught up in the politics and forgets about the students they are serving."

TGI FRIDAY'S
Manager and Assistant Manager

THE BIG PICTURE

TGI Friday's management training program rotates future managers through all the hourly wage positions in one of its restaurants to teach them the ropes. It's a whirlwind tour that lasts a scant fourteen weeks, culminating in the trainee's ascension to the captain's chair. Graduates say it's a great way to quickly learn the chain restaurant business as well as an excellent means of getting ahead in parent company Carlson Restaurants (that also own the Pickup Stix chain of Chinese eateries).

STATS

LOCATION(S) WHERE ENTRY-LEVEL EMPLOYEES WORK

"We operate in forty-eight states, primarily east of the Rockies."

AVERAGE NUMBER OF APPLICATIONS EACH YEAR

"We review and receive over 500 applications a year for entry-level jobs."

AVERAGE NUMBER HIRED OVER THE LAST TEN YEARS

TGI Friday's hires fourteen people per year.

ENTRY-LEVEL POSITION(S) AVAILABLE

New hires work as assistant managers and managers.

AVERAGE HOURS WORKED PER WEEK

New hires work fifty-five hours per week.

AVERAGE STARTING SALARY

New hires earn $38,000 per year.

BENEFITS OFFERED

"We offer several different medical, dental, and vision plans." Additional benefits include vacation, 401(k), purchased time off, long-term disability insurance, and a complimentary dining discount.

CONTACT INFORMATION

Laura Kornegay

972-662-5495

lkornegay@crww.com

GETTING HIRED

TGI Friday's "visits specific colleges each semester to participate in career fairs, on-campus interviewing, and classroom presentations. Students from other colleges can apply online at www.fridays.com or send a resume to the college recruiter." The next step in the process is a personality-profile assessment; "If the result of the assessment fits our profile, then the candidate interviews with a general manager and spends time observing in a restaurant," company representatives tell us. "Finally, the candidate would interview with a director of operations. An applicant can be discontinued at any point during the interview process." Sound daunting? A successful applicant makes the experience sound a little less so. He writes, "I did not do anything specific to help me get an interview, but I did have some good experience. I was interviewed by the college recruiters over the phone and given personality tests. I was then interviewed by a few of the general managers from the local stores. After that I was interviewed by the regional manager. The interviews were all good; they asked me what I had done in the past, where I thought I would go with Friday's, what types of things I was looking to accomplish, and a lot of questions about my critical thinking skills. A few days later I was offered a position. From start to finish, the process took roughly two weeks."

MONEY AND PERKS

According to the trainees we spoke with, "start date, location, and salary are all negotiable" at TGI Friday's. Notes one, "Everything that was explained to me during the interview process is how it happened. I was told once I completed the internship and made the move to management [that] all I would have to do was talk salary and location; no additional training would be necessary. I also did research at school into similar jobs and what students were offered in terms of jobs and salaries, and the offer seemed pretty high." Regarding raises, "each manager's compensation is assessed yearly through a performance evaluation compared with a salary range. Average raises are 4 percent." Asked which fringe benefits they most enjoyed, trainees said, "Free meals during shift[s], being able to make [our] own schedule, and bonuses. If we hit pace dollars or pace percent, or if we hit our sales goal, we get a certain percentage of money in return. It's done quarterly, and it's a great incentive to manage responsibly and to pay attention to what is going on around you at all times."

THE ROPES

The management training program at Friday's is a fourteen-week period during which a future manager "spends time in each hourly level position learning those specific jobs as well as shadowing a manager and ultimately performing management level tasks." Explains one graduate of the program, "I was trained on every hourly position, both 'front of the house' and 'back of the house,' and then learned all management functions and procedures. I learned about food cost, beverage cost, and the different parts of the income estimate. When I learned the hourly stations, I was trained by hourly employees, and when I trained on the management functions, the general manager as well as the rest of the management staff trained me." Besides familiarizing the manager with each worker's role in the restaurant, the training regimen yields another valuable benefit; explains one manager, "If the restaurant ever gets so busy that someone needs help, I am able to assist in any position we have!"

DAY IN THE LIFE

Once the training period is over, management trainees drop the trainee designation and start managing. Here's how one describes her responsibilities: "I was placed in a high volume store and given the bar as my department. Aside from the typical management duties of running a shift, I also have the responsibility of beverage cost. I have to ensure that we hit our budgeted weekly/monthly/yearly beverage cost percentages. I also have the ultimate responsibility for the bar staff—hiring, promoting, training, and developing their abilities to take care of the guests—and the overall cleanliness of the bar. On a typical day, I start out with a pre-shift meeting with my employees for the shift, letting them know our sales projections, sales contests, any additional expectations, and what I would like to see on our shift. I then spend a majority of my time out on the restaurant floor talking to guests and making rounds to ensure the shift is running clean and smooth. If necessary, I help out in the kitchen or at the door when needed, running sales reports on a frequent basis to help keep the staff positive and motivated. At the end of the shift, I am responsible for the collection of any monies and the closing of the daily computer reports and functions. I then check out the employees to ensure they closed everything down, and it all looks clean."

PEERS

Sitting atop the hierarchy (or food chain, if you will) of a restaurant can be a lonely job; as one manager explains, "I don't have interaction with any first jobbers. Sometimes I hang out with other managers, but that is like once a month." Accordingly, "there are no after-hours social scenes. However, I do interact with my management team every single day. We communicate on a daily basis about the day-to-day operations of our job. I spend a lot of quality time with them at work. I don't spend much time outside of work with them. I would much rather go home and spend time with my family and my dogs. The only time I communicate with others outside of work is through voicemail to keep lines of communication open amongst us."

MOVING ON

People leave Friday's for a variety of reasons; for some, it's "not what they expected," while for others the "work/life balance" doesn't suit their goals. Some people, according to company representatives, have "unrealistic expectations of life after college." Some head for other industries, while others seek work at restaurants that do not keep late hours (TGI Friday's stays open until 2:00 AM, which some trainees consider a drawback).

ATTRITION

Friday's representatives tell us that "due to the interview and recruiting process, less than 5 percent of [their] first jobbers leave within twelve months."

BEST AND WORST

A great management trainee "is able to network and use their resources to better understand the business and the company, while successfully adjusting to the pace of the business." The worst, "besides the employees who are no longer part of the organization due to bad business/professional decisions," are "those who were unable to keep up with the pace of our business."

TURNER BROADCASTING SYSTEM
Various Positions

THE BIG PICTURE

Turner, also known as TBS Inc., is a Time Warner media company whose networks include TBS, CNN, Cartoon Network, TNT, and Turner Classic Movies. The company is a magnet for college grads looking to break into broadcasting, especially those graduating from Atlanta-area colleges and universities.

STATS

LOCATION(S) WHERE ENTRY-LEVEL EMPLOYEES WORK

Primarily in Atlanta; positions are also available in Los Angeles, CA, Washington, DC, Chicago, IL, and New York, NY.

ENTRY-LEVEL POSITION(S) AVAILABLE

New hires work as production assistants and hold office support positions.

AVERAGE HOURS WORKED PER WEEK

New hires work over forty hours per week.

BENEFITS OFFERED

Turner offers a variety of medical, vision, and dental plans; life, accidental death, and dismemberment insurance; flex spending accounts for medical expenses, and dependent care; disability; and same-sex domestic partner medical benefits. Additional benefits include transportation reimbursement, 401(k), and on-site credit union; stock purchase plan; tuition reimbursement and professional development; leaves of absence; a day care center (Atlanta); and discounts on sporting events, theater, airfare, hotels, etc.

CONTACT INFORMATION

Visit the website at www.turner.com/jobs.

(The site for Turner Temps is www.turner.com/jobs/temps.html.)

GETTING HIRED

Many first jobbers at Turner get their foot in the door via Turner Temps, an "in-house temporary agency for all TBS divisions in Atlanta." Warns one employee, "Even getting a temp job is a feat at Turner. For me it required persistence. I sent the resume several times over a period of about six weeks. That was in 2000, right before the crash. Turner is a very popular company, especially in Atlanta and especially for college grads." Temping allows you to network throughout the company; it also keeps you at the center of the action, so you'll be among the first to know when a full-time job opens. Interviews at Turner, we're told, are "very casual. Generally they're looking to find out about your career path. They don't want somebody who will leave them quickly. People want you to commit at least a minimum of one year to their department. They weren't so interested in levels of experience as they were with general education and ability to pick up on things quickly."

MONEY AND PERKS

"[My starting date] was negotiable, and that was pretty much it," explains one Turner first jobber. "They have a base salary here. The only time I've heard it was different was when somebody moved from one entry-level position to another in the company. Other than that, what they offer is what you get." Perks are numerous, as they are at many entertainment companies, and include "going to movies in the middle of the day, free movies, sporting events, [and] discounts on a lot of vendors the company works with." There's also the more mundane—but extremely valuable—benefits such as the "401(k) that's one of the best there is, a company match nonprofit contribution program, and free MARTA (Atlanta public transportation) passes." A few people point out that "even with all the fringe benefits Turner offers, the best thing may be the environment with so many other young, creative types. [People meet] many who inspire [them]."

THE ROPES

"In television, it's very much on-the-job training," a production assistant at Turner tells us. "Most people get overeducated in school. Each company does things differently. And it's also a very welcoming environment—that lack of knowledge. For instance, a lot of what you have to learn is just jargon, and they don't expect anyone to know it coming in." Notes another production assistant, "I learned it by watching, asking lots of questions, and learning from mistakes. Coworkers would take me on edit sessions and through their daily schedule. I'd be shadowing them, and it worked well," largely because "the folks I shadowed were very helpful." Orientation here "takes most of the first day. It's an overview of the company: policies, human resources, benefits, that sort of thing. They were there to answer any questions we had."

DAY IN THE LIFE

First jobbers at Turner are generally assigned lots of grunt work, the type of jobs usually foisted off on the inexperienced (and temps, which is what many first jobbers at Turner start as). They "answer phones, write correspondence, type up calendars and schedules, answer mail and viewer phone calls, handle data entry, log library tapes, keep track of databases, run errands, check equipment orders, and get lunch for everyone." Employees who make a good impression on their bosses soon take on more responsibility; writes one production assistant, "Over time I grew into actually scheduling originals, writing storylines for them, answering even more viewer mail, and helping to input the schedule for the entire network. I was included in more meetings about operations, scheduling, ratings, closed-captioning and so forth, so I became more and more an important part of the day-to-day." The pace of work at Turner can be crazed or sluggish, depending on the time of year; explains one first jobber, "Television goes in cycles. If you're in reruns, you have downtown [Atlanta]."

PEERS

"There is a ton of contact and camaraderie with other first jobbers" at Turner. Writes one new hire, "It was like being on a college campus or something. I hung out with the other first jobbers not only at Turner South, but [also] at all the other networks in our building. I met a lot of people, and there was always time to chat and laugh or hunt down the cute boy you saw walking on the third floor. There were also happy hours and parties. I would joke that I couldn't go out in Atlanta without bumping into someone I knew from work." Sums up one production assistant, "I felt as though my peers were very much like myself, but different enough to make being friends with them interesting. I made most of my friends here."

MOVING ON

Just about everyone we spoke with at Turner moved up the corporate ladder by reversing the letters in their job description: They went from PAs (production assistants) to APs (associate producers). Another advanced to the level of programming coordinator. None of them have left, and none of them have any intention of leaving. While "some people complain that it's hard to advance and that they can't get what they want out of the job," our respondents felt that plenty of opportunities were available to go-getters. Those who leave the company often go to other broadcast networks.

VH1

Various Positions

The Big Picture

"The wonderful thing about VH1 and a lot of cable networks is that they give young people a real hands-on chance to make television that wouldn't be afforded to them at a network," explains one first jobber, adding, "They also, by nature, don't pay as well, but the work environment and experience you'll accrue there is worth it." There you have it; at VH1, you'll have the opportunity to learn—learn how to select, produce, and market programming to adult music fans—and learn how to live on a tight budget. (Fortunately, you'll probably earn enough to watch it at home since VH1 is on basic cable.)

Stats

Location(s) Where Entry-level Employees Work

New York, NY

Entry-level Position(s) Available

There are various positions available to entry-level hires.

Average Hours Worked Per Week

New hires work over forty hours per week.

Contact Information

Surf to https://jobhuntweb.viacom.com/jobhunt/main/jobhome.asp, hit the "Job Search" link, then highlight VH1 in the "Channels" column. There is also a "Jobs" link at the bottom of www.vh1.com.

Getting Hired

Persistence is key to success in broadcasting, our VH1 entry-level employee correspondents tell us. Writes one, "In the film business, it's always said, 'It's all who you know.' Bull pucky! It's all who you extend your friendship, your support, and your best effort [who notice you] and [this helps] you [to get] jobs. I can't think of another profession where they don't care if you have two heads, dark green complexion, and no eyes. If you can do your job, they don't care about anything else. Where one went to school? No concern. Whom one is married to, it may get you a few doors opened, but if one isn't passionate and successful, out the door they go. It's all about the moment. Not yesterday or tomorrow, but what can you do *now*. I love that philosophy. Only *now* matters." Or maybe it *is* who you know; writes another of our correspondents, "I sent in my resume; my brother, who worked at VH1, passed it on; the interview was casual and comfortable. The head of www.VH1.com interviewed me, and he asked my familiarity with certain software." The company posts openings at the Viacom website; jobs at other Viacom broadcast companies can be browsed at the same location.

MONEY AND PERKS

"Nothing seemed too negotiable" in VH1's job offer to our first timers, which makes sense; as one employee puts it, "Since there's no shortage of people who want to work in television, the moment you've put in your time at a place like VH1 and start applying for more lucrative network television jobs, there's dozens of hungry young kids ready to take your place. To this end, some might say that cable networks serve as kind of a bush league to the free-access networks." Adds another newbie, "In the beginning there was no negotiation for pay or when and where one worked. One had nothing to barter with, but after having experience one could negotiate all of the above." The best perks of working at VH1 are "the casual atmosphere" and "the parties. At the end of a show's season there's always a party, and one gets to get crazy and hang with the creative pulse of the entertainment industry."

THE ROPES

Orientation at VH1 "lasts about half a day. It mostly covers benefits information." After that, first jobbers often find themselves "being thrown into the frying pan to learn it all" on their own. "It's the only way to learn," writes one assistant editor at the network. "I love being in over my head, and any chance I get I try to chew off way too much." To get up to speed, the editor "learned as much before and after work as I could. I asked coworkers for help when I couldn't figure [a] problem out. I learned if one constantly asks for help people tend to not give it, but if one attempts to go at it by oneself, people will come out of the wood work to help out."

DAY IN THE LIFE

First jobbers are scattered throughout VH1, performing all the various support jobs necessary to run a television channel. Those we spoke with logged and digitized video, edited rough cuts of programs, performed clerical duties, conducted research, and assisted the development of programming. All told us that those who asked for more responsibility were given it and that they were recognized and rewarded if they succeeded. Writes one, "I would recommend that any recent college graduate get their start at MTV Networks [VH1's parent company]. You'll probably have as much responsibility at your level as you want, and as they often promote from within, you'll rise through the ranks with other people you'll see again later down the road. It's a great place to start in television production, especially for fans of pop culture, and a splendid work ecology to make contacts and to try on a lot of different hats to see which one fits or inspires your career."

Peers

First jobbers at VH1 share the same ambitions and many of the same interests, so it's no surprise that many "make most of [their] friends at work. All of [them] are heading in the same direction: up." As one first jobber tells us, "There's definitely a strong bond between people working in show business. It comes from following dreams, and everybody understands you're going after the big prize because they're doing the same thing. And putting yourself out there like that brings everyone together." The company holds "after-hours parties for special occasions" and other similar events to "encourage camaraderie."

Moving On

VH1 first jobbers usually either move up the corporate ladder at Viacom, or they move on to other jobs in television.

WASHINGTON MUTUAL
PACE Program

THE BIG PICTURE

Through its rotational PACE management training program, Washington Mutual exposes entry-level employees to the various sales, management, and technical concepts required of a manager at one of the bank's financial centers. Call it a year-long financial boot camp, if you like; those who survive will find their future prospects considerably brighter than entry-level employees who haven't been through the wars that they have. Think of it as the difference between a West Point grad and an Army enlistee.

STATS

LOCATION(S) WHERE ENTRY-LEVEL EMPLOYEES WORK

Arizona, California, Florida, Georgia, Idaho, New Jersey, Nevada, New York, Oregon, Texas, Utah, Washington, DC.

AVERAGE NUMBER OF APPLICATIONS EACH YEAR

Washington Mutual receives approximately 600 applications each year.

AVERAGE NUMBER HIRED OVER THE LAST TEN YEARS

As a result of a change in the system used to track the PACE Program, this information is not available. Since 1986, approximately 400 trainees have graduated from the program.

ENTRY-LEVEL POSITION(S) AVAILABLE

Approximately 150 positions per year are available in the PACE program.

AVERAGE HOURS WORKED PER WEEK

New hires work forty hours per week.

AVERAGE STARTING SALARY

New hires earn from $2,000 to $2,600 per month in the Northwest, Florida, and Texas; they earn from $2,250 to $2,925 per month in California, New York, and New Jersey.

BENEFITS OFFERED

Trainees may be eligible to choose from three kinds of coverage options under the medical plan: no coverage, Preferred Provider Organization (PPO) options (known as the Washington Mutual plan), or Health Maintenance Organization (HMO) options in some areas. Additional benefits include dental coverage, supplemental life insurance, 401(k), pension plan, employee stock purchase plan, wellness center, transit subsidy, employee discounts, and flexible spending accounts.

Matt Biedermann

206-461-2076 or matthew.biedermann@wamu.net.

Offers Matt, "I will be happy to connect them with the appropriate manager for their area."

GETTING HIRED

Trainees find the PACE program through a variety of channels. Some candidates are recruited, and others are referred by friends or relatives currently working for the company; some are even company employees themselves looking for advancement opportunities. Washington Mutual vets applicants through a multiple interview process; company officials explain, "There are typically three stages of interviews. The first interview is with a recruiter, the second is with the PACE manager, and the third is with the PACE manager and PACE graduates." Trainees tell us that interviewers "ask scenario questions that require open-ended answers. The interviewers were polite, smiled, and took notes (but asked to take notes beforehand, so I would not become nervous when I saw them writing)." Why such a rigorous interview regimen? "Since Washington Mutual is a sales and service culture, we focus on sales and customer service abilities," explains the company. Interviewing is the best way to gauge these skills. In addition to completing the interviews, PACE applicants must also submit a "descriptive paper of a real situation in which they used their leadership or sales abilities, explaining the situation and the outcome of their actions. The paper must be typed, double-spaced, and no longer than one page." They must also complete an employment application and provide references from previous employers.

MONEY AND PERKS

The PACE program offers "a base salary range around $2,200 to $2,600 a month (depending on prior experience), with no commission or bonus," writes one trainee. Notes another, "[Trainees] have to tighten their belts for the year of the PACE program. All of us look forward to the income potential that we have *after* graduation." Perks include "free financial advice, free accounts," and an invite to a "national meeting of all management trainees within the Banking and Financial Services Division, [where trainees] have the opportunity to hear from top Washington Mutual leaders, learn key professional development strategies to prepare them for leadership roles at Washington Mutual, and meet and share experiences with other management trainees from across the country."

THE ROPES

The PACE Program begins with "a two-day welcoming orientation [that] gives [new hires] all the details of the program and the expectations they [have] of all of [them]." Writes one PACE trainee, "We were provided with well-organized materials that gave us all we needed to get started: contact numbers, how-to sheets, answers to frequently asked questions, and introductions to the current PACERS (six months ahead of us in the program) who were assigned to us as mentors. The orientation also included a lunch with regional and back office managers. It was a fantastic opportunity for us to begin building our network and 'getting our names out,' as well as get a great feeling for the culture and leadership at Washington Mutual."

Day in the Life

According to trainees, the primary goal of the PACE program "is to familiarize you with all aspects of the financial center. There is a set curriculum with time spent as a teller, a new-accounts representative, consumer and residential lending [agent], and an internship phase where you act as an assistant manager. Each phase has a number of required training courses." As such, "over the course of the year, PACE trainees spend approximately sixty days in classes. The training is provided by an excellent internal training staff and covers everything from operational training for job functions to leadership development and strategic planning." Classwork is "scheduled to correspond with the phase of the program [new hires are] in, allowing [them] each step of the way to combine 'book learning' and experience in the field." At every stage "trainers are always available and willing to help and follow up, whether it be after class, by email, or coming to the financial center to help you one-on-one. Because PACERS end up wearing so many hats, there is no typical day; a trainee's schedule depends on the phase of the program he or she is in." Because of the variety of trainings, writes one trainee, "After only one year, I have been fully trained in teller operations, accounts, lending, insurance and annuity sales, and in the operation and management of a financial center. That is amazing to me!" Another employee says, "Trainees never feel overwhelmed but almost always feel like we're in over our heads—but in a good way. Every day is an exciting new challenge."

Peers

PACERS, as trainees call themselves, form "great networks and great friendships." Explains one, "It seems as though we are a family. We depend on each other and use each other for support." However, "There is not a big after-hours social scene. If we gather after-hours, it is for volunteer projects, grabbing lunch together after a class, or having a dinner party or holiday celebration at someone's house. We enjoy each other's company, but most of us have families to get home to."

Moving On

All the trainees we spoke with hoped to remain with Washington Mutual when their program ended. "I'll stay as long as they'll have me!" writes a typical PACER. Company officials say, "Typically, trainees move into the role of assistant financial center manager and become eligible for incentive and a base salary." Some PACE graduates "have moved into numerous financial center manager positions, several regional manager positions, and even a group manager position." No wonder one trainee tells us that there's "lots of opportunity for promotion" at Washington Mutual.

WELLS FARGO
Management Trainee Programs

THE BIG PICTURE

There are over 140,000 jobs at Wells Fargo; this profile focuses on the approximately 100 positions available each year in the bank's professional development programs for recent college graduates. These programs offer rotational training to provide wide exposure to different aspects of Wells Fargo's business, allowing first jobbers to select the career best suited to their tastes and talents.

STATS

LOCATION(S) WHERE ENTRY-LEVEL EMPLOYEES WORK

"There are over 300 potential locations available, though most positions are clustered around our primary cities of employment: San Francisco, CA; Minneapolis, MN; Phoenix, AZ; and major cities in Texas."

AVERAGE NUMBER HIRED OVER THE LAST TEN YEARS

Wells Fargo has hired ninety-seven people per year for the last three years.

ENTRY-LEVEL POSITION(S) AVAILABLE

Professional development programs include audit (auditor rotational development program, business banking services), business banking associate, corporate/wholesale banking (relationship manager development program, finance), finance associate development program, internet services (information technology associate, technology and operations), leadership development training program, and wholesale finance (financial analyst training program).

AVERAGE HOURS WORKED PER WEEK

New hires work about forty to fifty hours per week, with the chance of having to work longer hours during a large project.

PERCENTAGE OF ENTRY-LEVEL HIRES STILL WITH THE COMPANY AFTER THREE, FIVE, AND TEN YEARS

After three, five, and ten years, the percentage of people who remain with the company are 99, 94, and 73, respectively.

AVERAGE STARTING SALARY

"[Starting salaries] vary by position, but [they] also [vary by] program depending on geographic location, prior work experience, market reference point for the function, etc. Overall, our programs ranged from $41,000 to $65,000, plus bonus and benefits, in 2002."

BENEFITS OFFERED

In terms of health care coverage, "this varies by state. But Wells Fargo offers comprehensive medical, dental, mental health, and vision plans. There are also a number of medical cash balance plans, etc., to help offset the cost of treatments. Benefits are available to all team members, spouses, and dependents." Additional benefits include "up to twenty-five days of paid time off per year, [and] discounts on services and goods at nationwide vendors, etc. Paid time off, matched 401(k) plan, tuition reimbursement, commuter benefits, financial product discounts, flexible spending accounts, [a] stock purchase plan, [and] disability/life insurance" are all also available. It's worth noting that "Wells Fargo is also recognized for its flexible work arrangements, making it one of *Working Mother* magazine's Top 50 Places to Work."

CONTACT INFORMATION

Students interested in applying should visit www.wellsfargo.com/jobs and select "Find a Job" or "Undergraduates."

GETTING HIRED

Wells Fargo interviews on nine campuses each year and "reviews applications from hundreds of campuses nationwide. Wells Fargo hired students into these programs from approximately forty campuses this year." Applications are accepted online at www.wellsfargo.com/jobs. Interviews are conducted in two stages; the first is handled by a recruiter, [and] the second by one or more managers. The bank advises that "candidates who research the company are always the strongest. We make it easy by providing much of the information a candidate needs to know on our website at www.wellsfargo.com/jobs. We also encourage candidates to call up alumni from their campus that are current Wells Fargo team members to inquire about their experiences. These resources can offer tremendous insight." A few entry-level employees we spoke with noted that "some of the interviewing questions were pretty difficult; they were trying to get a feel how you handled yourself under pressure."

MONEY AND PERKS

Raises "vary dramatically based on team-member performance, potential relocations, etc." According to people we spoke with, location and start date are negotiable for some positions, while starting salary may be, but is not always, open to discussion. And although Wells Fargo offers generous benefits, most newbies focus on the intangible perks. "The best fringe benefit has been working with all of the great people in my group. They have made the work fun and exciting while also an educational experience," says one. "I've enjoyed becoming very involved in the community by attending numerous sporting events, shows, luncheons, etc. That's been the best perk," notes another. An especially pragmatic employee appreciated the availability of paid time off.

THE ROPES

Every professional development hire next year will participate in Wells Fargo's Class of 2004 program, "a year-long corporate-level program focused on broadening their understanding of Wells Fargo—its businesses, values and strategy—and helping them build their professional network at the peer and executive level. The highlight of the year is a three-day forum in San Francisco, where participants are introduced to our chief executive officer and leadership team." Professional development programs also involve rotational training, supplemental classroom training "to build in-demand skill sets," and mentoring. Writes one participant in the business banking services program, "I have received extensive training from many different avenues, including, but not limited to, my boss, classes, online tutorials, and my mentor. The training was on accounting, office applications, credit underwriting, treasury management, sales, and personal growth."

DAY IN THE LIFE

Wells Fargo offers seven different professional development training programs; profiles detailing a typical day in the life for most appear at the company's website, www.wellsfargo.com/jobs, under "Undergraduates." Nearly all the profiles involve numerous rotations, which newbies see as "a good opportunity to try different job functions and see what would be a good fit." One explains that "we're sent out to all rotations to learn, to network, to seek out projects; it's a very developmental program. On the microlevel, I'm in charge of my own development [so I can] do the best job I can do while learning. With programs like this, it's less about productivity and more about development." Still, they warn that "some rotations will not be as exciting as others; this will vary on personal interests as well as assigned hosting managers. Many times the assignments can be overwhelming; they expect a lot from the students." And if you're not feeling overwhelmed, just ask; someone will happily find something else for you to do or learn. As one trainee tells us, "There is such an incredible breadth of learning resources, such as online training, that there was no time to be bored. With the amount of work that is being done, if an individual has any initiative whatsoever, the management team is quick to respond, and you can often receive incredible opportunities merely by asking."

PEERS

Entry-level employees' peer network and social scene at Wells Fargo "is dependent on work location and rotation group." Most people work with only a few other newbies, so there isn't much of an after-hours scene. As one first jobber tells us, "Being straight out of college, I still enjoy all of the things that college kids do. Most of my coworkers are older and live a more domestic lifestyle than I do. But they are wonderful people, and I truly enjoy spending my days with them and spending nights and weekends with my friends." Trainees stay in touch through "numerous networking events" and "constant telephone contact."

Moving On

Wells Fargo tracks information about where its trainees wind up if they leave the bank, but informs us that, "this information is gathered during exit interviews, which are confidential. Sorry!" None of the employees we spoke with offer any further insight on this subject. But as the numbers above attest, most people stick around for at least three years, and with the depth and breadth of experience in finance that they are likely to receive during their tenure, many will be well positioned for other jobs in the industry.

Attrition

Wells Fargo tells us that "there are usually no more than two program participants who drop out of a program in any given year. Generally, a dropout that early on has to do with an unusual or unexpected personal situation. We find that it's rarely a reflection on the program." Employees agree; one tells us, "Everyone that I have spoken with seems extremely satisfied with the job. All of us appreciate the amount of responsibility that we are given and have been able to maintain a good balance between our work and outside lives."

Best and Worst

"One of our recently retired executive vice presidents started with Wells Fargo as a proof operator, a person that visually verifies that cashed checks have accurate information, before being referred into one of our programs. At retirement he oversaw a business line that was responsible for approximately 30 percent of Wells Fargo's earnings and reported directly to our chief executive officer."

WILLIAM MORRIS AGENCY
Assistant and Trainee

THE BIG PICTURE

In operation for more than a century, William Morris Agency is the oldest and largest talent and literary agency in the world, and industry insiders consider it to be one of Hollywood's two most powerful agencies today. Its agents represent all "above the line" talent, including actors, writers, directors, producers, musicians, comedians, hosts, and a variety of companies (many entertainment entities and others seemingly unrelated to Hollywood) that have interests that can be furthered using the Agency's extensive experience and connections in the industry. The three main departments that assistants work in are television, motion picture, and music (there's also a noteworthy consulting department in Beverly Hills and a significant theater department in the New York office). Even though the pay is lousy and the hours for assistants are ridiculous, "it's known as one of the best places to start, whether you want be an agent, producer, filmmaker, whatever. It's the graduate program in entertainment." Expect to work hard, earn little, get yelled at a lot . . . and love it.

STATS

LOCATION(S) WHERE ENTRY-LEVEL EMPLOYEES WORK

Beverly Hills, CA; New York, NY; Nashville, TN; Miami, FL; London, England. The vast majority of entry-level employees start in Beverly Hills or New York.

ENTRY-LEVEL POSITION(S) AVAILABLE

New hires work as assistants or trainees.

AVERAGE HOURS WORKED PER WEEK

First jobbers work from forty to sixty hours per week.

PERCENTAGE OF ENTRY-LEVEL HIRES STILL WITH THE COMPANY AFTER THREE, FIVE, AND TEN YEARS

We had access to no official figures, but from anecdotal evidence, attrition among trainees and assistants is high.

AVERAGE STARTING SALARY

According to our respondents, the starting salary is not much. One new hire goes so far as to call it unlivable, but another says that if you can handle a humble lifestyle for a little while, you can even manage to save a little dough.

BENEFITS OFFERED

Writes one first jobber, "I received a basic HMO-type medical plan, for which I had to pay a small monthly fee. I had the option of paying more for a far superior PPO plan, but the additional cost did not justify the benefits for most healthy twenty-somethings." Additional benefits include two weeks' vacation and paid sick leave.

CONTACT INFORMATION

www.wma.com/0/careers/wmacareers/

Beverly Hills	New York City	Nashville
Human Resources	Human Resources	Human Resources
William Morris Agency, Inc.	William Morris Agency, Inc.	William Morris Agency, Inc.
One William Morris Place	1325 Avenue of the Americas	2100 West End Ave. #1000
Beverly Hills, CA 90212	New York, NY 10019	Nashville, TN 37203
FAX (310) 859-4205		

(The Beverly Hills office is the only one that accepts fax submissions.)

GETTING HIRED

Competition is fierce. Notes one first jobber, "There are two application processes—one for those who have industry connections, and one for those who do not. The former almost always are offered interviews; the latter almost never are. I originally sent my resume directly to the human resources department, and I was fortunate to be offered an interview. (Incidentally, I was offered an interview only after I followed up with a phone call after faxing my resume, and I highly recommend that everybody do this.) I met with two people from the human resources department, and they seemed to have two primary concerns. First, they wanted to make sure I knew what I was getting myself into (low pay and high stress in a fast-paced environment). Second, they wanted to make it clear that I would have virtually no contact with celebrities. While I was waiting for them to get back to me with a job offer, I did my homework and found an alumna from my college who worked there. I faxed her my resume, and the next thing I knew, I had an interview with an agent she knew. That agent offered me a job, but he also introduced me to the gentleman who eventually became my boss."

MONEY AND PERKS

Like most highly desirable gateway jobs, entry-level offers at William Morris are essentially a take-it-or-leave-it affair. Writes one assistant, "Most things were not negotiable. I had the option of starting the week after I was given the offer or the week after that. The salary was set, and I was expected to do what my boss told me to do." The pay would be decent if you lived in central Mississippi; it's not so good for folks living in big, expensive cities, though. Assistants start at about $500 per week and can earn overtime; trainees earn about $400 per week and don't earn overtime pay, "although they surely work overtime hours." The perks are good; reports one first jobber, "Although people often work on the weekends, the work is often semi-enjoyable (reading scripts, attending social events, etc.) and does not require people to come into the office." Another plus: "You can get into any party in Hollywood. You have access to anybody in entertainment." One trainee sums it up this way: The perks are fun. The in-office desk is pretty tedious and can oftentimes be awful, but you will always have better stories than your friends. 'Yeah, I was hanging out with Martin Sheen. Yeah, I was hanging out in the skybox with DiCaprio.' It becomes a way of life. The glam wears off eventually, though, and it becomes a job. If you want to be an agent, you stay focused and stay at the Agency."

THE ROPES

For assistants, "the orientation process is about a week long. Along with the other people starting that Monday, you attend computer training sessions and a variety of meetings with people from human resources. When you're not in formal training, you're working alongside an experienced assistant on your new boss' desk." Training is "mostly trial and error, although sometimes your predecessor will spend few days training you." Explains one assistant, "Once I earned my boss' trust, he would often take me aside and give me mini-tutorials on different aspects of his job. Almost daily, we would have informal discussions about things I read in the trade papers, questions I had about the business, interests I had in my boss' phone conversations, etc. This was unusual, though; most agents don't make the time to become a formal mentor to their assistants." Trainees often start in the mailroom. Writes one, "They threw you in there right away. Orientation and training comes in bits and pieces. You did an afternoon of computer training for two hours, then were back in the mailroom. Then a day or two later you'd do phones for forty-five minutes, then back. It lasted over a few weeks, but each specific session was very brief." A trainee adds, "You learn by doing, [by] getting in people's faces, and [by] asking if you can help them. The benefit of starting in the mailroom is that you get a chance to decide what area of the department you want to work in. Television, new media—you get a chance to decide, and you go and jockey for position, trying to get out of the mailroom and get a desk when it opens up. That's when you really start your formal training on how to become an agent. The mailroom is basically boot camp."

DAY IN THE LIFE

Assistants serve as agents' gophers. "I was little more than a glorified secretary when I began my job," writes one. Trainees do all the other grunt work at the Agency, and in terms of sheer quantity, it usually well outweighs the assistants' responsibilities. Trainees traditionally have the inside track on opportunities to advance within the Agency. Explains one assistant, "More is often expected from trainees, but more is offered to them (in terms of future possibilities) as well. I think trainees have a slightly better chance of being promoted to agents—after all, they were handpicked from the start. It's a bit like honors classes in high school—it's not impossible to get into an Ivy League school without being in all the honors classes, but if you're playing the odds, you're going to bet on the kids in the honors classes." One trainee disagrees; he says, "It used to be that the only people that'd get promoted were the trainees. My class and those after me have found that you're no more likely to get promoted [as a trainee] than as an assistant. The only value is that you're able to pick your path. As an assistant, you have to go where the opportunity is." Regardless of their point of entry, successful first jobbers soon find themselves with growing responsibilities. Writes one, "By the end of my first year, I was my boss' right-hand man. If he was unavailable, I might be asked to listen in on a phone call in his place. Experienced assistants will tell you that they do pretty much everything that their agents take credit for. Admittedly, this is an exaggeration, but only slightly so."

PEERS

"There is a great deal of contact and camaraderie" among William Morris Agency's first jobbers, "but there is also a bit of competition, especially among trainees." Agrees one trainee, "Some peers become your best friends, [and] some become your enemies. There's more competition in a mailroom between the trainees than any other job in Hollywood. You can't trust anyone. The desk will be opening up, and it won't be on the board. So oftentimes there'll be a couple people there, and you'll get screwed out of it if you're not on top of your game." The after-hours scene "is fairly large." Many people view after-hours socializing as part of the job. Writes one trainee, "It's not a job where you punch in, punch out, and go home. I would get home on average at 11:00 PM [or] 11:30 PM, and I'd be out till 4:00 AM sometimes. You should always have dinner or drinks to schmooze."

MOVING ON

Is there life after William Morris Agency? You bet there is. "People who leave the Agency find success at studios, production companies, management companies, publicity houses, other agencies, and as personal assistants to the stars. The list of possibilities is virtually endless." As one assistant puts it, "for every career in Hollywood, it's *the* best place to start and to learn quickly. They run Hollywood; they have all the information."

ATTRITION

Many of those who leave WMA do so because they grow disillusioned with the industry while others decide that they would rather work in a different facet of the industry. Producing is a popular aspiration among people who leave these days, for example, and many who leave pursue creative executive positions at studios. Some "point out that the place is not especially friendly toward women and minorities (almost all top agents and executives are white men, and the Agency does not seem to prefer women or minorities in promotions in the interest of fostering a more diverse work environment). People displeased with the Agency also argue that, due to the very low salaries for trainees, only applicants from wealthy backgrounds are able to remain on the trainee track long enough (usually four-plus years) to have a shot at being promoted to agent. And even then, your chances are quite slim." It's important to note, however, that in regard to these issues the William Morris Agency is not unique among talent agencies. The most powerful executives in the most powerful entertainment companies continue to be mostly white males these days. Also, WMA does seem to make an effort to hire significant numbers of women and minorities into entry-level positions; it's just that most of them tend to leave the Agency before they are promoted to agent.

YMCA

Various Positions

THE BIG PICTURE

Working at the YMCA is a great way to get involved in a local community. Y's across the country offer child care, education, athletic training, youth counseling, and a host of other services, all in pursuit of a single goal: to "help people develop values and behavior that are consistent with Christian principles." The YMCA needs young, enthusiastic employees to fulfill its mission.

STATS

LOCATION(S) WHERE ENTRY-LEVEL EMPLOYEES WORK

"There are over 900 independent YMCAs in communities throughout the United States. Many of these independent not-for-profit corporations have multiple locations in the same city or region. All totaled, there are over 2,400 YMCA locations in the United States. In addition, there are YMCAs in more than 120 countries around the world."

AVERAGE NUMBER OF APPLICATIONS EACH YEAR

"Given the highly decentralized nature of the YMCA organization, this information is not available."

ENTRY-LEVEL POSITION(S) AVAILABLE

"The number of entry-level positions changes frequently, often on a day-to-day basis. Most professional level employment opportunities are posted on the YMCA National Vacancy List, [which you can find] at www.ymca.net." Click on "Employment" at the top of the page, then click on "Job Opportunities" in the left-hand column of the next page. Scroll to the bottom, and click on "National Vacancy Listing."

AVERAGE HOURS WORKED PER WEEK

"Employment conditions for salaried staff are defined by the local YMCA."

PERCENTAGE OF ENTRY-LEVEL HIRES STILL WITH THE COMPANY AFTER THREE, FIVE, AND TEN YEARS

After three, five, and ten years, the percentage of people still with the company are 74, 33, and 18, respectively.

AVERAGE STARTING SALARY

"For [fiscal year] 2004, the YMCA of the USA recommends that local YMCAs hire entry-level staff at a minimum salary range of $25,000 to $28,000, taking into consideration cost of living, cost of labor, and specific responsibilities of the position. Each local YMCA establishes compensation based on local market conditions and its own salary administration plan."

BENEFITS OFFERED

"Each local YMCA establishes a benefits package to meet the needs of its employees. The National Y Employee Benefits Trust provides consultation and offers a menu of benefits for YMCAs to choose from." Additional benefits include "the YMCA Retirement Fund, Inc., [which] is a retirement plan created to meet the specific needs of YMCA staff. Most YMCAs in the United States participate in the YMCA Retirement Plan."

CONTACT INFORMATION

People who are interested "should contact the leadership development department at YMCA of the USA and request to speak with a leadership development consultant or a human resources consultant (800-872-9622)." Also, check the YMCA national vacancy list at www.ymca.net.

GETTING HIRED

Local YMCAs are encouraged to post all available full-time salaried positions on the website; many hires we spoke with, however, tell us that they learned about their prospective jobs through word of mouth. "A college friend introduced me to the staff, [with whom] I immediately bonded. In conversation, the available position was mentioned," writes one. Adds another, "A relative told me about it, and I needed a job." The Y seeks candidates with "a passion for positively influencing the lives of others, a commitment to the mission of the YMCA, the ability to thrive in a fast-paced environment, a strong sense of customer service, a commitment to applying ethics and values in the workplace, and technical skills in a specific program area of not-for-profit administrative application." Many who work at the YMCA have extensive prior experience with the Y, most often as members but sometimes also as interns and volunteers. Here's how one successful hire (to a teen programming position) describes the process by which he got his job: "My resume reflected my previous part-time employment, including certification I earned through the YMCA of the USA. I was interviewed by the senior program director and the executive director of the YMCA branch. For much of the interview we discussed my previous work with the YMCA and my involvement with teen leadership programming as a teen participant. We also discussed my vision and philosophy of teen programming. Upon my request, I sat in on a teen leadership club meeting. A week later, I was offered the job. We negotiated for about one week prior to my acceptance."

MONEY AND PERKS

The YMCA informs us that "entry-level candidates typically spend two to three years in their first YMCA positions (especially in situations related to program and membership services). Salary increases are usually merit-based, based upon individual accomplishment of agreed-upon goals. As the skills and competencies of that job are mastered, higher-level jobs, with increased responsibility and increased remuneration are developed." Salaries are determined by "guidelines established on a national basis, which are then applied by local YMCAs taking into account local market conditions, cost of living, and cost of labor." Fringe benefits offered at one local YMCA include "being given three hours a week [of paid time] to enjoy the outdoors, exercise facilities, beaches, etc." The Y also provides "an extensive leadership development program of certification courses offered throughout the country." "[And] most local YMCAs participate in the YMCA Retirement Fund."

THE ROPES

The YMCA is not a highly centralized organization, and local Y's have wide latitude in determining services, hiring, etc. The YMCA of the USA tells us that "each local association establishes its own orientation process," but also notes that "many utilize the YMCA of the USA's 'New Employee Orientation Tool,' a computer-based training module designed to provide new staff insight into the history and scope of the YMCA movement. Additional orientation to the local Y structure and specific job are generally part of the orientation process." Local Y employees have access to the national organization's "team of leadership development consultants, who are dispersed throughout the country and who have the responsibility for counseling and mentoring Y staff regarding career development issues." Most first jobbers we spoke with tell us that the Y offers training relevant to their job descriptions, often in relatively short training programs conducted in a classroom environment.

DAY IN THE LIFE

"The YMCA hires a workforce that has considerable diversity in job focus," the YMCA of the USA tells us. It also notes that "many new entrants are focused in program and membership positions. Others may be employed in administrative or business functions required to effectively operate a nonprofit organization." New hires usually benefit from mentors, as "supervisors typically work closely with new entrants to assist them in fully understanding their goals and responsibilities. Performance management systems are frequently utilized to create measurable goals and objectives."

PEERS

Entry-level employees are spread among the YMCA's 2,400 local centers, and they are often among a small number of similarly experienced peers. Writes one, "It has been a year and a half since I started, and I am still the newest staff member. The other people who are first jobbers at this YMCA are older than I am." Even so, most "still spend time with a lot of the staff even though there is an age difference," and "the social scene is active. We gather once a week to go bowling, have game nights weekly, and get together to watch movies from time to time." They regard their coworkers as "some of the greatest people [they've] met so far in [their lives]."

MOVING ON

The YMCA's national office informs us that "there is no comprehensive data on the reasons that entry-level staff leaves YMCA employment for other pursuits. The conventional wisdom is that there is no significant difference between the for-profit and not-for-profit sectors on this issue." Some of the workers we spoke with said they would consider leaving the Y if opportunities for advancement did not present themselves. Education and community service are sectors accommodating to former Y workers. It should be noted that many here are clearly satisfied with their jobs; about one in four YMCA employees has been with the organization for at least fifteen years. Apparently, it really is fun to stay at the YMCA.

ATTRITION

Low wages, long hours, and the frustration of trying to run projects on an ever-shrinking budget are the chief complaints of Y employees and the main reasons that they leave the Y to pursue other career opportunities.

BEST AND WORST

"[The best] are hundreds of senior-level staff at YMCAs ... [who] moved into positions of increasing responsibility over time, including chief executive officers and senior leaders of YMCAs in communities in almost every state in the United States. It is not unusual to have staff members with more than twenty years of professional experience in the YMCA movement." The worst are "first-time employees who are hired without full appreciation of the organization. The work of the Y is demanding, requiring a desire to build strong kids, families, and communities. Those without a true passion for helping others may find the work unrewarding."

JOBS WITHOUT ORGANIZATIONS

CONGRESSIONAL STAFFER

THE BIG PICTURE

First jobbers hired to congressional staffs rarely get to do glamorous work; for the most part, they answer phones, respond to letters from constituents, and do all the other tasks their superiors are too busy to perform. However, they do get to enjoy a front row seat to America's legislative process. Opportunities for advancement abound for go-getters, a term that describes most people who land these jobs.

STATS

LOCATION(S) WHERE CONGRESSIONAL STAFFERS WORK

Entry-level employees work in Washington, DC, and the "home offices" of members of Congress.

ENTRY-LEVEL POSITION(S) AVAILABLE

Congressional staffers work as staff assistants, correspondence assistants, and legislative assistants.

AVERAGE HOURS WORKED PER WEEK

Congressional staffers work forty hours per week.

AVERAGE STARTING SALARY

Employees earn from $25,000 to $40,000 per year.

BENEFITS OFFERED

Federal employees receive excellent medical benefits. They also receive a handsome array of additional benefits. Learn more about them at www.usajobs.opm.gov/EI61.asp.

CONTACT INFORMATION

You can find available assistant jobs in both houses of Congress and for both major parties at www.hillzoo.com/jobs.htm.

GETTING HIRED

Congressional staff positions are determined by individual members of Congress, and each follows a different hiring process. In all cases, however, the same basic rules apply. First, submit your resume with a letter demonstrating your passion for politics and your commitment to the congressperson's agenda. Second, be persistent; make a follow up call, and, if no positions are available at the time you apply, continue calling every so often to see whether a position has opened up. Explains one staffer, "I followed up regularly after submitting my resume and after my first interview. After that, I had second- and third-round interviews with several members of the staff. The interviews were all fairly casual, and we primarily talked about my political interests and academic focus. After three interviews for a legislative assistant position, I was told (and was well aware) that I didn't have enough Hill experience to be a legislative assistant; they offered me a staff assistant position instead. I was very pleased with this, as I had no expectations to get the legislative assistant job given that I had never worked or even interned on the Hill before. The staff assistant position was a perfect entry into the field." Many successful hires present a resume "with lots of political internships."

MONEY AND PERKS

Congressional staffers don't make a whole lot of money. In fact, most employees would agree that "Hill staffers, with the exception of committee directors and chiefs of staff, make abysmal salaries that are incredibly difficult to live on in Washington, DC." According to one staffer, the allure of this job lies not in the financial rewards but rather in the "exposure to a variety of issues that I knew little or nothing about before I started; the relationships with other offices and outside groups; and the education in lawmaking and the political process from the inside out." As another staffer explains, "When I took this job, I cared about only one thing—getting onto the Hill—so salary never mattered. Also, I had always counted on my talents to move me out of an entry-level position as fast as I could negotiate it, so I figured that if I didn't like my work, I could change things."

THE ROPES

For most congressional staffers, orientation is a brief meet-and-greet around the office; training occurs on the job. "There was no formal orientation process," cautions one staffer, "but I suppose the first month was probably an ongoing orientation for me." In many cases, first jobbers replace a staffer who is moving up to a more responsible position in the same office, and that person provides all the necessary training. Recalls one staff assistant, "I was trained by the legislative correspondent, who held the staff assistant position before me. I was also trained by the office manager because she and I would be doing administrative work together. I was trained on the phones, the mail system, the coding system, and the office computer programs." Those who have previously interned on the Hill explain that they already know most of what is required of them, since their jobs are "extremely similar to [their] internships."

DAY IN THE LIFE

Most entry-level positions are for staff assistants who "do mostly grunt work, albeit work that needs to be done so the office runs smoothly and others can get more important work done." On a typical day, a staff assistant "answers phones, sorts the congressperson's public email account, does the daily news clips, sorts and codes the mail twice a day, gives tours of the Capitol, and assists the legislative staff whenever they ask." Some work on the staffs of individual members of Congress; others serve all the party members on a particular committee. For most staffers, the next step up is to the position of legislative assistant, where they "work on various issue areas for a congressperson or committee, write letters, review legislation, and attend meetings throughout the day."

PEERS

A common passion for politics and access to the thriving and legendary nightlife of Capitol Hill make for "a great after-hours social scene." Because "most staffers have families and children at home," the social scene generally includes only the youngest staffers. Writes one staffer, "There is a lot of camaraderie among the younger staff in the office and with other offices, and we are constantly interacting at work and often outside of work as well."

MOVING ON

Entry-level staff jobs pay poorly and involve a lot of grunt work, so first jobbers try to move on to staff jobs with better salaries and more responsibilities as quickly as possible. Some people use the contacts they've made through work to find other positions in the government, while others return to school or use the experience to launch a career in elective politics (see "Best and Worst" below).

ATTRITION

Low pay is the chief complaint among congressional staffers. As one explains, "There are certainly those who are much less fortunate than us young Hill staffers, but for the amount of work that we do, the responsibility that we carry, and the education that we all have under our belts, the pay should be an embarrassment to the federal government. My friends make at least $10,000 [a year] more than [I do], even those working in nonprofits. But the best part about it—and this is why we all put up with the terrible pay—is that it looks good on any political resume. People know the sacrifice that's involved with these positions, even if they don't work in DC."

BEST AND WORST

The best workers include many former congressional staffers who currently serve in Congress (such as John Breaux, Hillary Rodham Clinton, Tom Daschle, Mitch McConnell, and Trent Lott). The crown unquestionably belongs to Lyndon B. Johnson, who went to Washington as a legislative assistant in 1932 and eventually served as a United States representative, senator, vice president, and finally president in 1963. Johnson passed more legislation through a single Congress than any president before or since.

LEGAL ASSISTANT (AKA PARALEGAL)

THE BIG PICTURE

The job of a legal assistant "is definitely not an exciting one;" its challenges usually result from the amount of work required rather than the ability level necessary to do the work. It is, however, a great way "to experience law before you actually decide to go to law school. Most assistants work for a year or two and then decide that either they want to be lawyers and go to law school or switch careers." It's also an important gateway job; many law schools expect prospective students to have put in time at a law firm typing, photocopying, proofreading, and getting yelled at for things that aren't their fault.

STATS

LOCATION(S) WHERE LEGAL ASSISTANTS WORK

Anywhere that law is practiced (most often available in large firms).

AVERAGE HOURS WORKED PER WEEK

Legal assistants work from forty to eighty hours per week.

AVERAGE STARTING SALARY

In 2000, the median salary for paralegals nationwide was about $35,000 per year.

BENEFITS OFFERED

Benefits vary according to the firm.

CONTACT INFORMATION

Send a resume and cover letter to every law firm in your area; follow up on each with a phone call, unless specifically instructed not to by the firm's website.

GETTING HIRED

Some paralegals find their jobs by mass mailing their resumes; others use contacts: either friends who are already at firms, professors, or mentors, who can help influence the hiring process. Interning at a law firm while still in college can be very helpful in leading to a paralegal job after graduation, many of our respondents tell us. They say that when crafting an application, "the secret is to talk to people to find out what the job is like—its responsibilities, the personality traits that fit it best—and then tailor your resume and cover letter accordingly." Pay careful attention to the type of law practiced by the firms to which you apply, as "most firms hire certain types of personalities and skill sets for litigation paralegals and corporate paralegals; litigation paralegals tend to be more outgoing and less business-oriented. Corporate paralegals are often economics, finance, and accounting majors, who often go to law school, but are considering business school as well." In all instances, remember that "law firms always want to hear that you're good at multitasking, have no objection to working overtime—a lot if it, can function within a hierarchical environment, and can shoulder your share of less than glamorous tasks. So a successful applicant would describe in a cover letter how his or her previous job experience and activities in college helped develop these skills."

MONEY AND PERKS

Paralegal salaries are "normally nonnegotiable because the prestigious firms have someone just as qualified lined up right behind you who would be more than happy not to give them problems by trying to negotiate the salary. The base salary should be between $31,000 and $35,000, with most firms leaning toward $35,000." Many paralegals earn substantially more in overtime pay; explains one, "Most of these places give you enough work that if you want to earn twice your salary in overtime, you can." Among the perks most paralegals enjoy are "car rides home and the free meals. That said, after about the first month, you don't really view it [as] a benefit anymore. Most firms allow you to bill dinner and a cab ride home if you're working past 8:00 PM. And, when you work seventy-hour weeks, you pretty much think you're entitled to these things. And you are."

THE ROPES

Every law firm is different, of course, and each firm handles orientation and training its own way. In general, larger firms have formal orientation and training programs; smaller firms "wing it," since the number of new paralegals they see each year can be as few as none. For most paralegals, training covers "the basics of litigation and procedure, basics of document productions, basics of preparing for a trial, services within the firm, and firm policies," as well as "learning the different software programs and how to do legal research on Lexis-Nexis and Westlaw." A typical legal assistant at a smaller firm reports, "They sort of threw me right into it, which made me learn everything very quickly. I loved it, though. I like constantly being challenged, and in order to help me learn about law and civil procedure, the two partners let me participate in everything they did, from client conferences to drafting, to billing, everything. I had a lot of responsibility and also a lot of support from them to make sure I did things correctly."

DAY IN THE LIFE

"The work I do is definitely grunt work, but someone has to do it. I'm sure that I could be fired today and replaced with someone tomorrow, and there would be no effect on the company," writes one paralegal, neatly summing up what all of them tell us. Notes another, "I am always bored, always. There are some scraps of interesting work that get thrown my way, but 99 percent of the time, I'm performing tasks that a third grader could do: making sure copies match the originals, making copies, assembling binders, indexing documents." The job does offer some real rewards, legal assistants concede; explains one, "It's not that you don't learn anything as a paralegal at a large firm. But you reach a plateau within two or three months and then there's not much else to learn. You can always learn more if you want to take the initiative—read the briefs and filings of the cases you're on, ask the attorneys questions. And it's not that most legal assistants don't want to do that. It's just that there's no time, and it's not what you're there to do." And the job can even be interesting, occasionally, as when you're "doing a lot of legal research, tracking down records and documents from a million different places (which is fun—almost like detective work), putting together files for individual clients, and drafting and filing documents with the court or other agency, if applicable." Even so, paralegal work isn't for everyone. "The hours can be very long, and the work can be very boring and tedious. I truly hope that people know what they're getting themselves into. I had one friend who started as a paralegal at a law firm and quit after three days because he hated the hours. This job's really for those interested in pursuing a legal career. And, if you can tolerate the long hours, the overtime pay is great."

PEERS

At large firms, the peer network among legal assistants is typically strong. That's a good thing because these folks spend plenty of time with each other. According one legal assistant, "Hands down, the best part about my job is my relationship with other legal assistants [who] I work with. All of us are between twenty-one and twenty-five years old, we spend a lot if time with each other having to survive the same tedious work, and all of us become really good friends as a result. We go out after work for drinks often (maybe one night during the week) and often on the weekends and for special occasions. Some of the best friends I've ever made have been at the firm, and I couldn't think of a more ideal segue from college into the corporate world than getting to work with fifty twenty-somethings." At the smaller firms, "There are only a few legal assistants who are the same age as [your typical legal assistant]. Some of the first-year associates are also friendly. Everyone seems to get along, but we tend not to spend time together outside of work." Writes one paralegal at a small firm, "There were no other first jobbers, nor was there an after-hours scene. There were five people working there, and I was about thirty years younger than the next person closest to my age."

MOVING ON

It's rare to find a legal assistant who isn't gunning for law school one or two years down the line. Working as an attorney's lackey is a means to that goal, which means few drop out, despite the negative aspects of the job. Many of those people who quit do so when they realize that a life in law is not for them; they either return to school to seek an unrelated degree or move on to unrelated careers.

ATTRITION

Legal assistants are largely aspiring lawyers, and they are driven by that goal. Few quit, although fewer enjoy the job; most will also tell you, however, that "there's more to this job than its negative aspects. It does teach you to learn how to work with difficult people, and the work forces you to be extremely focused. This type of position also looks great on a resume for law school or graduate school."

BEST AND WORST

Most lawyers have at one time worked as legal assistants, meaning that the best and worst to emerge from their ranks can be found among today's political leaders, judges, attorneys, and a host of others in a myriad of professions.

MODEL

The Big Picture

Modeling can be "really fun, but it can also very challenging." It can be pretty lucrative as well, but it can also be incredibly frustrating; as one model tells us, "It's very hit-or-miss. Clients definitely know exactly what they are looking for, so if you aren't that, it isn't your fault. Just keep going on to the next casting until someone wants you." If you've got the temperament to deal with the ups and downs of freelance work and " [a] very superficial [industry that] requires a strong-minded person who is naturally very thin," you might want to consider a career in the world of runways and photo shoots.

Stats

Location(s) Where Models Work

Major cities, especially New York, Los Angeles, Chicago, Miami, Dallas, Atlanta, and Seattle

Average Starting Salary

Because of the freelance nature of this job, models can earn anywhere from minimum wage to a fortune.

Benefits Offered

Typically, models do not receive benefits because they are independent contractors responsible for their own insurance. If you're successful, though, the benefits include travel opportunities, lavish parties, and socializing with the rich and famous. If you're not successful, there are no benefits.

Contact Information

There is no contact information, but you should have photographs taken of you, send them to every modeling agency, follow up with phone calls, and attend open calls.

Getting Hired

You don't need to be stunningly gorgeous to get a job as a model. "I've seen girls who don't look particularly amazing without makeup; it's all about being transformed into something different," writes one model. But it certainly can't hurt in an industry that's "completely based on looks. It's sad, but you have to realize it is all an image. You aren't being rejected because you aren't nice or smart, it's just on what people want to look at, at that time." There are many different ways of getting into the business; as one model puts it, "The modeling industry, at entry-level, only requires one to be confident enough to pursue the position." Some people take modeling classes, which are "pointless, but they brought me to a place where I knew about the business of it and how it worked," explains one model. Other new models circulate photographs to modeling agencies, attend open calls, and enter contests. Some models are even discovered while minding their own business, just like in the movies.

MONEY AND PERKS

In modeling, "There is no guarantee of work or pay. Payment fluctuates from job to job, though there are certain understandings—lingerie shots pay more than regular clothing [shots], longer jobs are paid by the day and not the hour, etc. Notice of auditions or work is often last minute—a day or an hour in advance—and can interfere with other work." In many markets, rates are good when you work, running from $100 an hour for catalog shoots to four figures a day working a runway. Be forewarned, though, that even working models consider themselves lucky "to work once or twice a month—but there's a lot of small, local work out there." Models enjoy "the many opportunities to travel and make significant [money] with little work involved," as well as "meeting interesting people, learning fashion and makeup tricks, and occasionally getting gifts or clothes. And the after-parties are great."

THE ROPES

"The orientation process is basically the same as the application process" for models; it's "a thirty-minute meeting and a 'we'll call you.'" An agent can help you learn about the business; explains one model, "I met a lot of agents and development people from [my agency's] New York office. They taught us how to work the runway. A man actually did; a man in high heels. He was huge, and I wish I remembered his name. I owe him a lot." Models can also "learn things from stylists, makeup artists, hair stylists, other models, designers, photographers, and people running fashion shows. You pick it up as you go along." One model explains that ultimately, "you really have to figure it out for yourself. It's all experience. You can tell when girls have worked before, and I always try [to] help out the new girls. I don't know as much as some, but there are a few basic things that you have to know or you will get completely lost."

DAY IN THE LIFE

One model we spoke with says, "There is no 'typical day' in modeling. You may do nothing. You may have castings and fittings, then a shoot, and then have to run to your agency to meet with someone. It can get pretty hectic. I am supposed to stay good looking, though; that's my real job. I have to be nice to clients and be prompt and quiet and really pay attention to what people are telling me to do. And I have to stand up straight. That part's hard. I'm too tall to stand up straight." At first, the unpredictability of the work schedule, the frantic pace during busy periods, and the unrelenting pressure to stay thin can be extremely wearing, but "over time, you get more used to it and better able to meet expectations as expediently as possible. You get used to chatting blithely with makeup artists and walking around half-naked in slippers and then going back to the real world." People who deal best with modeling are those who don't take themselves too seriously; as one model puts it, "Looking pretty isn't important. Selling clothes and shoes and makeup is important to the people who profit from it, but my job isn't to look pretty and run a business or save the planet or cure cancer. It's such a silly business and so much money goes into and comes out of it, it's unbelievable. I enjoy doing it and fashion is important in some ways, and someone has to do it, so I may as well." The job certainly has its own rewards, and not just monetarily. Sums up one of our respondents, "Being a model has a lot of negative connotations, but the confidence gained through your career can put you in a place, mentally, that you wouldn't have been in if you hadn't explored that opportunity, thus giving you the opportunity to explore other career possibilities that you may not have ever considered."

PEERS

Because models are often in competition with one another for jobs, modeling is not a profession that typically breeds deep, long-lasting peer relationships. As one model explains, "My peers are often smart, cool, well-read, well-traveled, and very fashion savvy. They're usually liberal and good at chit-chat. That said, they're also often shallow and competitive. I haven't made many friends, but I've enjoyed hanging out during assignments—you're thrown together with these people you have little in common with [except for] a certain look, and you make do." Adds another, "Most models think about their appearance too much, and all they talk about is modeling, which is annoying. Work is work, and fun is fun."

MOVING ON

All the models we spoke with knew exactly when it would be time for them to move on; says one, "If I leave, it will be because I am old and overweight and not so cute anymore, or if I had another job that I liked more. It's not really up to me. When I stop getting work I guess my modeling career is over." Agrees another, "If and when I have a child or my body changes, I will no longer be as marketable. I'm not terribly concerned with doing this for the long-term. It's a fun experience while it lasts, and I'm open to doing it for as long as I can find work without much sacrifice."

ATTRITION

Modeling is not for everyone. You have to have thick—but also smooth and beautiful—skin to deal with "the rejection involved when trying to get a job, the criticism of your weight," and "the pressures— to have whiter teeth, to take more inches off your hips, to refrain from playing sports that might bulk up your thighs, to avoid pasta, all the stereotypes—which are ridiculous." Those who can't cut it eventually give up, as do many who are chronically underemployed.

BEST AND WORST

The worst model ever was a fictional character; his name was Chris Peterson (professional name "Sparkles"), played by Chris Elliott in the short-lived television series *Get a Life*.

PERSONAL ASSISTANT TO SOMEONE FAMOUS

THE BIG PICTURE

Celebrities write books, direct movies, star on television shows, and run giant corporations, so they are left with very little time to make dinner reservations, shop for birthday gifts, pick up the dry cleaning, and answer the telephone. That's where a personal assistant comes in. It's a great job for people who want a glimpse at how the truly fabulous live. It's also a great way to break into glamour professions because of the many of the contacts you make—not the dry cleaner, necessarily, but many of the others—will be invaluable.

STATS

LOCATION(S) WHERE PERSONAL ASSISTANTS WORK

New York, NY; Los Angeles, CA; Vail, CO. Basically, wherever the rich, beautiful, and famous people dwell.

AVERAGE HOURS WORKED PER WEEK

Personal assistants work from forty to eighty hours per week.

CONTACT INFORMATION

Although some agencies may find places for personal assistants to work at, people usually find these jobs through word of mouth.

GETTING HIRED

One personal assistant describes the hiring process: "A friend of mine told me that the celebrity was in need of an assistant and thought I'd be the perfect candidate for the job. I figured 'Why not? It could be fun." What follows may be the most nerve-wracking interview in the job world, since it almost invariably involves meeting with the celebrity. Explains one assistant to a pop singer, "I was first interviewed by the vice president in X's production company, then by X. The vice president asked general questions to make sure I was not an aspiring singer/actress who would try to compete against X. X asked questions about home and personal management. Her old assistant sat behind her, waving at me—'Not to worry' about any of her questions [because] I would be hired. X loved that I was a writer because she liked creative people on board." It's an odd business from beginning to end, so it should come as no surprise that there's no conventional way to learn you've gotten the job. Writes one assistant, "I figured that I didn't get the job, and then out of the blue X's business manager called me and invited me to a lunch at a corner deli, just an average place, and it was there that I met X for the first time—over a very casual and fun lunch. It was a couple [of] days later that the business manager called me and began to have me do things—make some calls, pick up laundry, etc., and I realized that I had been hired."

MONEY AND PERKS

Most assistants are drawn to the job by the glamour of celebrity, not by the promise of cash. As one explains, "I was too naïve at that point to know [that I should negotiate my starting salary]. It could've been negotiable, but it was so exciting to be offered the job that I didn't ask." Asked to name the fringe benefits of their job, assistants list "free travel and life experience" and "the opportunity to know an American legend on a personal basis." For a personal assistant to a major fashion designer, the major perk was "the clothes, hands down. We had the best wardrobes in town. I hate shopping now. It was definitely the best."

THE ROPES

"The orientation of the job was 'Hi, I'm X.' *GO*," is the way one assistant describes how her job started. This is typical of nearly all the assistants we spoke with. The fortunate assistants get to learn from their predecessors; writes one assistant to a movie star, "The old assistant and her house sitter filled me in on a thing or two: her likes and dislikes, shopping lists, petty cash, info about her family, her charity work, clothing/costume donations." The learning curve is steep and can include such subjects as "the type of dry cleaning that had to be done, the airline tickets, or the fact that X had no clue how to handle money and that I had to give him only certain amounts at a time because he would just go through it like it was water." The best experience for the job, most assistants would agree, is to have worked in jobs commonly associated to teenagers who work for spare cash: "I had worked in the entertainment industry most of my adult life, and I knew about the 'babysitting' that usually goes on, so I wasn't surprised that this is in fact what I was called on to do," explains one assistant. Asked what they wish they'd known going into the job, assistants answered, "I didn't realize how much of my life I'd have to give up. They told me I'd be in from 8:30 to 5. It didn't happen like that at all. I wish I'd spoken to other celebrity assistants."

DAY IN THE LIFE

For a personal assistant, "No two days are ever the same." There are the standard chores—"setting up X's calendar, getting his clothes and bags ready, getting him food, responding to fan mail, getting him personal things to fulfill his habits, and anything that would make his life more comfortable"—and then there are the unexpected extras. Writes one assistant, "Often I would have to get in a cab and run after X if he lost his cell phone (which happened nearly every week) or forgot where he was going. In addition, I had to handle all calls from his manager, lawyer, ex-wives, college-age children, etc. Just a managing of his life." For some, this winds up being "too much info. This job is perfect for someone who wants to be on the 'inside' of a celebrity's personal life because you will know *everything*. I saw my boss naked, saw her break down in tears, watched her fight with her husband . . . it was all too much for me." For others, however, getting up close and personal with a celebrity is a revelation: "I have met celebrities, and I learned that they are just like you and me—they have a normal side to them in addition to this larger-than-life cachet," writes an actor's assistant. Most people concede that much of what they do is grunt work, but they consider it *important* grunt work. "I felt that in helping him, I was letting the world know of his talent, and the joy that he has brought to the world is immeasurable," explains one assistant.

PEERS

Some famous people have more than one assistant working at a time, and assistants to such celebrities do enjoy a certain amount of camaraderie with their peers. "The assistants were together twenty-four hours a day, in-office and socially. One is still my best friend. She'd only been there four months, but we hit it off," reports one assistant. Most, however, work solo; offers one, "I had absolutely no contact with any other assistants working with other celebrities—I had contact with the celebrity's manager and lawyer, etc., but that was just business, nothing social." Some assistants do manage to become pretty close with the celebrities they work for; "X taught me about life and what people are really like. He was a good friend," writes an assistant to a comedian.

MOVING ON

Personal assistants—especially good ones—can make amazing contacts in their boss' industry, and these can often lead to better jobs. One assistant moved to a network position. Another used her experience in the fashion industry to establish herself as a fashion publicist. An assistant to a movie actress landed an agent and is currently writing screenplays in Hollywood.

ATTRITION

It's often difficult to be anyone's personal assistant, since the job typically requires a volatile combination of extreme intimacy and extreme subservience. "Everything when you work for a celeb is based on them. If they're in a good mood, you are. If they're in a bad mood, you are," explains one assistant. Add into the mix the general weirdness of a celebrity's life and the eccentric personality traits of most celebrities, and you know why some folks don't last long in this job. As one lucky assistant tells us, "I have heard and read folks say that many celebrities are just overgrown children and that they are selfish and difficult and outrageously impossible to work for. I was just blessed with working with a neat human being who also happens to be a household name."

INDEXES

ALPHABETICAL INDEX

Jobs Within Organizations

Jobs Without Organizations

INDEX BY INDUSTRY

Dot-com

Education/for-profit

Education/international

Education/nonprofit

Energy

Environmental Activism/nonprofit

Financial

Freelance

Health Care

Hotels and Leisure

International Service/nonprofit

Legal

Marketing

Media

Pharmaceuticals

Politics

Printing

Public Health

Publishing

Rental Services

Restaurant

Retail

Software

Talent Agency

Technology

Technology/defense

Theater

ABOUT THE AUTHORS

Ron Lieber is a consumer reporter for the Personal Journal section of the *Wall Street Journal*. In past jobs, he's written about career issues for *Fast Company* and contributed to the cover package for *Fortune Magazine's* first list of the 100 Best Companies to Work For. His first book, *Taking Time Off,* encourages students to take a year off before or during college. The book, coauthored with Colin Hall, was a *New York Times* bestseller in 1996 and is now available in an updated edition from The Princeton Review. His second book, *Upstart Start-Ups,* is about young entrepreneurs. He lives in Brooklyn with his wife, Jodi Kantor, who edits the Sunday Arts & Leisure section for the *New York Times*.

Tom Meltzer is a freelance writer who has taught and written materials for The Princeton Review for eighteen years. He is the author of eight books covering such diverse subjects as United States history, government and politics, mathematics, and the arts, and he is a contributing editor to both *The Best Colleges* and *The Best Business Schools* guidebooks series. Tom is also a professional musician and songwriter who performed for many years with the band 5 Chinese Brothers. He attended Columbia University, where he earned a bachelor's degree in English, and currently lives in Durham, North Carolina, with his wife, Lisa, and his two dogs, Daisy and Lebowski.

NOTES

BOOK STORE

WWW.PRINCETONREVIEW.COM/COLLEGE/BOOKSTORE.ASP

In addition to this book, we publish hundreds of other titles, including guidebooks that highlight life on campus, student opinion, and all the statistical data that you need to know about any school you are considering. Just a few of the titles that we offer are:

- The Best 85 Business Schools

- The Best 97 Law schools

- The Best 83 Medical Schools

- The Best 357 Colleges

- The Best 112 Graduate Programs: Arts and Humanities

- The K&W Guide to Colleges for Students with Learning Disabilities or Attention Deficit Disorder

- Paying for Graduate School Without Going Broke

For a complete listing of all of our titles, visit our **online book store**:

http://www.princetonreview.com/college/bookstore.asp

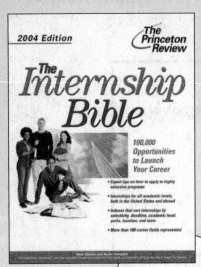